William Romaine

Twelve Discourses upon the Law and the Gospel

preached at St. Dunstan's Church, in the West, London

William Romaine

Twelve Discourses upon the Law and the Gospel
preached at St. Dunstan's Church, in the West, London

ISBN/EAN: 9783337285067

Printed in Europe, USA, Canada, Australia, Japan

Cover: Foto ©Lupo / pixelio.de

More available books at **www.hansebooks.com**

TWELVE DISCOURSES

UPON THE

LAW AND THE GOSPEL.

PREACHED AT

ST. DUNSTAN'S CHURCH, IN THE WEST,

LONDON,

By *W. ROMAINE*, M. A.

LECTURER OF THE SAID CHURCH.

THE FOURTH EDITION.

The Law was given by Moses, but Grace and Truth came by Jesus Christ.—John i. 17.

LONDON:

PRINTED AND SOLD BY M. TRAPP, NO. 1, PATER-NOSTER-ROW, NEAR CHEAPSIDE.

MDCCXCIII.

Entered at Stationers' Hall.

PREFACE.

MANY are the mistakes at present about religious matters; but none are more destructive than those which concern the law and the gospel. The generality of our people confound them, and put one in the place of the other. Some suppose they are to be accepted of God for their works, and that they can be justified by the law in the sight of God. Others make their keeping of the law the condition of their receiving the blessings of the gospel, as if these were to be the purchase and reward of their partial obedience. Some are persuaded they must do all they can, and keep the law with all their might, and wherein they come short of the perfect demands of the law, Christ will, out of his merits, atone for their failings. And others again think that Christ has abated the rigour of the law, and that the gospel is nothing more than a new law dispensation, in which the Lord has been pleased to declare that he will accept of sincere obedience instead of perfect. These and many more such like mistakes prevail in our times, and they are exceedingly dangerous, tending to the utter ruin both of body and soul. In the following discourses I have endeavoured to distinguish, and precisely to settle the difference between the law and the gospel. Some of the principles upon which I have proceeded are these:

1. The Lord God, the Almighty Creator of all things visible and invisible, has an unalienable right to make laws for the government of his creatures. This right

right *is founded in his absolute dominion and sovereignty over them They are his property, the work of his hands. He hath created and made them, and not they themselves. Their life, and all things belonging to it are his, coming from his gift, and continued by his bounty; and therefore he has a most indisputable claim to their obedience. What he requires they must perform: Because they are his creatures. The relation between the Creator and his creatures puts them under a necessity of obeying his law and will, or else of suffering whatever he shall threaten to inflict upon their disobedience.*

2. *The law of the Lord God the almighty Creator is unalterable. It changeth not: For it is the copy of God's most holy mind and will, in which there can be no variableness, neither shadow of turning. If the mind and will of God were to change, then God would be a changeable being, and whatever is changeable is imperfect; but God is perfect, therefore his mind and will change not. His word will he not break, nor alter the law that is gone out of his mouth. His infinite wisdom, and his almighty power, stand engaged to maintain its dignity, that it may be always an holy, just, and good law, which he will not break or alter.*

3. *The moral law, which the Lord God revealed to Adam in Paradise, required of him perfect uninterrupted obedience. The whole moral law is summed up in one word, namely, love; love to God for the blessings of creation and providence, and love to man for God's sake. This love was the indispensable homage due to the Creator. It could not be alienated from him, and given to any other object without idolatry: For which reason the moral law is unalterable. If a man withdraw his love in the least from God, he breaks that law which positively enjoins him to love the Lord his God*

God with all his heart, with all his soul, with all his mind, and with all his strength.

4. The law given to Adam being unalterable, all his descendants are bound to keep it: For they are all under the law, as God's creatures. His will is the indispensable rule of their obedience. He requires their love, and if they refuse to give it him, then their will is opposite to his, which is rebellion against their sovereign Lord, and which must bring upon them swift destruction.

5. All mankind have sinned and broken the moral law. The authority of God's word is positive and express. "We have before proved, says the apostle, "both Jews and Gentiles, that they are all under sin, "as it is written, there is none righteous, no not one. "There is none that understandeth, there is none that "seeketh after God. They are all gone out of the way, "they are altogether become unprofitable, there is none "that doeth good, no not one." Rom. iii. 9, 10. &c. And after the apostle has proved these truths from various arguments, he sums up the evidence thus, ' Now "we know, that what things soever the law saith, it "saith to them who are under the law; that every "mouth may be stopped, and that all the world may "become guilty before God: Therefore by the deeds of "the law, there shall no flesh be justified in his sight." Rom. iii. 19, 20. It is evident from these authorities, that all have sinned, and are transgressors of the law.

6. The law has made no provision for the pardon of the least transgression. It requires perfect unsinning obedience in thought, word, and deed. This is its just demand. And in case of the least failing, it immediately passes sentence and condemns. It will not accept of sorrow or tears, of repentance or amendment, as any satisfaction; but its language is "Do this, or "thou

"thou shalt die." There is not a word said about sorrowing for what was past, and reforming for the future, as if the style of the law was, "Be sorry for thy sin, and reform, and then thou shalt not die:" But it is positive and express, "Keep the law, and thou shalt live. Transgress it, and thou shalt die: for cursed is every one, who continueth not in all things, that are written in the book of the law to do them."

7. From those premises it follows, that the law being unalterable, and all men having broken it, and there being no provision made in the law for the pardon of the least transgression, but a punishment threatened to the least, they are therefore guilty before God. The law brings them in guilty, and condemns them, and divine justice is bound to inflict the deserved pains and penalties; so that there can be no possibility of justifying them by the law. By the works of the law shall no flesh be justified: for the law is expressly called by the apostle, the ministration of condemnation, and the ministration of death.

8. Since the law is thus unalterable, and punishment is threatened to the least breach of it, and since all men have broken it, and all the world is guilty before God, and condemned by the law to death and hell, and without strength to do any thing for their deliverance, it follows that there can be no salvation by the law.

From these particulars we may be able to state the true nature of the moral law. It is the revealed will of God discovering to his creatures what obedience he requires of them, namely, perfect unsinning obedience, an absolute conformity to the law in thought, word, and deed. It is an unalterable law, founded on God's unalterable will, and therefore it requires this perfect obedience of all men, and at all times. It has made no

provision

provision for partial obedience, or for sincere obedience, but insists upon man's continuing to do all things that are written in the book of the law, if he hope by the deeds of the law to be justified and saved.

If this be the true state of the case, how widely do these men mistake the nature and demands of the moral law, who expect to be made righteous before God, by their partial obedience. The law knows nothing of any righteousness, but what is perfect. If you put your trial at God's bar upon this issue, that you have kept the law in most instances, having failed only in some few; this is pleading guilty. It is owning your transgression, and confessing that you have not such a righteousness, as the law demands: For a part is not the whole. And the law insists upon the whole, and in case of failure, passes sentence, and condemns you · For it is written, —" Cursed is every one, who continueth not in " all things, &c."

But some may ask, Will not the law accept of sincere obedience? Nay. It will abate nothing of its demands. It will have absolutely perfect obedience, if by the works of it a man be justified before God. There is not one word in the law about sincerity; no, not a single hint, as if a man might be pardoned, who kept the law sincerely, although imperfectly. The law says—Do all things which God has commanded, and continue to do them with all thy heart, mind, soul, and strength, and then thou shalt be justified by thy works; but if thou offend in one instance, thou comest under the curse: For he that offendeth in one point is guilty of all, and consequently sincere obedience failing in one point leaves a man guilty, and under the curses of the broken law.

It highly concerns those persons to consider this matter well, who fancy that Christ came as a great lawgiver, to publish milder terms of acceptance than the moral law had required. They have a notion of Christ, as if he

were

were only the publisher of some new remedial law, which abated something of the demands, and mitigated some of the rigour of the moral law. Whereas he came not to publish any new law, but to save his people from their sins committed against the old law. He came to be a Saviour, and not a lawgiver. Indeed he preached the law, but it was to bring men to the knowledge of sin, and to see and to feel their want of his salvation. But he preached nothing new. He only enforced the law in its spiritual nature, and in its full extent, shewing the length and breadth, the depth and height of the commandment. He would not have his people so much as entertain a thought of his coming to make any change in the moral law. "Think not, says he, that I am come "to destroy the law, I am not come to destroy, but to "fulfil it:" And he did fulfil it; for he was born under the law, and was obedient to it even unto death. The law was unalterable. It could not change, unless God's most holy mind and will could change, which is impossible, and therefore the law being broken could not remit the deserved punishment, unless some infinitely perfect obedience should be paid, and some infinitely meritorious sufferings should be undergone in the sinner's stead, by which the law might be magnified and made honourable. And the Lord Christ undertook to do this. He vouchsafed to obey and to suffer for his people, to obey the precepts, and to suffer the pains and penalties of the law. The law had indicted them, and found them guilty of disobedience. Christ came to obey for them, as it is written, "By the obedience of one shall many be made "righteous." The law had put them under the curse, and he came to redeem them from the curse of the law. The law threatened to punish them, and he came to bear their sins, and the punishment due to them in his own body upon the tree. So that Christ came not to publish a new remedial law, but to glorify the moral law, and to demonstrate the unchangeable nature of it, since no obedience, and no sufferings, but his, which were absolutely perfect, divine, and infinite, could work out such a righteousness for any one sinner, as the law required, in order to his being justified in the sight of God.

As these arguments shew that the sinner cannot of himself attain the perfect righteousness which the law demands, so do they prove that he cannot by any means in his own power escape the punishment which the law threatens. The law requires unsinning obedience, and enforces it upon those sanctions, Do this, and thou shalt live: In the day that thou transgressest, dying thou shalt surely die. These sanctions of the law are as much the mind and will of God, as the rule of the law itself. And his will is unalterable, consequently upon transgression the sanction took place, and the transgressor became subject to the first, and to the second death, which justice was bound to see inflicted upon him. What could he do in this case to deliver himself? Could he offer any thing to divine justice to save himself from receiving the wages of sin? No. They are his due, and he must receive them. Say, he is sorry for his sin, and weeps and mourns bitterly. What does this avail? This is only an open confession of his guilt, and an acknowledgment that he deserves punishment. Suppose he amends and reforms his life. What atonement is this for his former bad life? The law will not be satisfied with such partial obedience. But he promises never to sin for the future: If he could keep his promise, it would not satisfy the law, for what becomes of his past disobedience? One single sin cuts him off for ever from being saved by the law; and since all have sinned, consequently by the works of the broken law can no man living be justified.

This is the true state of all men by nature. They are all sinners, and they cannot be saved by the moral law.

It

It can neither altogether, nor in part justify them, and therefore it shuts them up under guilt, and leaves them without remedy, and without hope. As soon as man was fallen into this state, it pleased God to reveal that rich plan of grace and mercy, which is contained in the Gospel, of which this is a short sketch.

1. The gospel is salvation from the law. It brings glad tidings for poor convinced sinners, discovering to them how their sins may be pardoned, and they may be redeemed from the curses of the broken law. It reveals to them what Christ has done and suffered to satisfy the law, and how he endured the pains and penalties of it; dying the death, to which the law had sentenced them. And the gospel calls upon them to receive the benefit of what he did and suffered as his free gift, proposing to them, without money and without price, all the graces and blessings which the Saviour purchased with his life and death.

2. The gospel sets forth to the convinced sinner salvation from guilt and punishment, by giving him freely as perfect a righteousness as the law demands. It invites him to receive the righteousness of Christ, against which the utmost rigour of the law can make no objection: Because it is the righteousness of God, a divine, infinite and absolutely perfect righteousness. When this righteousness is imputed to the sinner, he is pardoned, the law ceases to accuse, conscience no longer condemns, he has peace with God, and the love of God reigns in his heart.

3. In order to receive this righteousness the gospel requires no previous qualification. The sinner is not regarded, as fit and meet to receive Christ's righteousness by any thing he himself can do. Christ freely wrought it out, and he freely gives it. The works of the law have no merit to purchase it: For it is written, " We " are justified freely by his grace, through the redemp-
" tion

" tion that is in Christ Jesus." And if it be by grace, then it cannot be by any works or qualifications.

4. But how is Christ's righteousness received, and the sinner made righteous by it at God's bar? By faith, and not by works: "For to him that worketh not, but " believeth on him that justifieth the ungodly, his faith " is counted for righteousness. Where is boasting then? " It is excluded. By what law? of works? Nay, " but by the law of faith. Therefore we conclude, " that a man is justified by faith without the deeds of " the law."

5. With respect then to the sinner's acceptance and justification before God, the law and the gospel ought to be distinguished in these as well as in other respects.

According to the law salvation is by works, according to the gospel it is by grace.

The law says, Do this; but the gospel says, Believe this, and thou shalt be saved.

The law threatens to punish the sinner for the first offence, but the gospel offers him pardon for many offences.

The law leaves him under guilt and condemnation, the gospel invites him to receive pardon and salvation.

The law sentences him to death, the gospel offers him justification to life.

By the law he is a guilty sinner, by the gospel he may be made a glorious saint.

If he die under the guilt of the broken law, hell will be his everlasting portion; if he die a partaker of the grace of the gospel, heaven will be his eternal inheritance.

6. But if the law and the gospel are distinct in these and several other respects, some persons may think the law is totally repealed by the gospel: for they cannot see wherefore serveth the law, unless it be to justify a sinner. The law is unalterable. It cannot change any more than God can change. To this day it stands in full

full force, and not one tittle of it is repealed. It is still the revelation of God's most holy mind and will concerning the obedience which he requires of his creatures. And if they disobey, the law immediately passes sentence and condemns them to death. While they continue careless and secure in sin, they consider not the law as the ministration of death and condemnation; and none of them see it in this light, until the holy Spirit awaken them. It is by his preaching of the law to their consciences, that they are alarmed with fearful apprehensions of their guilt, and of their danger. He brings them to see the exceeding sinfulness of sinning against the holy, just, and good law of God, and convinces them that the broken law can never make them legally righteous. This puts them upon seeking such a righteousness as the law requires, and disposes them to receive gladly the righteousness of the Lord Christ: For he is now the end of the law for righteousness to every one that believeth.

7. Thus the Holy Spirit convinces sinners that the law is not repealed by the gospel, and when he gives them the righteousness which is of God by faith, and they have justification to life freely by grace, does he teach them to make void the law by faith? God forbid. Yea, they establish the law: For they consent unto it that it is good. They delight in the law of God after the inward man, and they keep it in their outward life and conversation. It is the rule of their holy walking. They are free from the law as to its condemning killing power, but they are under the law to Christ. They know, that if the law had not been unalterable, and of indispensable obligation, Christ had lived and died in vain. And he did not come to give his people liberty to break the unalterable law; that would be a contradiction in terms. But he came to establish the law, by restoring it to its honour and dignity, by his obedience to its precepts, and by his suffering its pains and penalties, and then by making it

honourable

honourable in the confession of convinced sinners, and in the lives of his redeemed people.

These are some of the principal points treated of in the following discourses. In which I have endeavoured to follow scripture closely. This has been my guide; and I have constantly desired his teaching who inspired it. And I now pray him to shine into the heart of every one who reads these discourses. May he always accompany the perusal of them with his divine grace and blessing; and if they be made useful to the church of Christ, may his be all the glory. Give it him, reader; for it is his due, and pray for thy hearty well-wisher,

W. R.

CONTENTS.

DISCOURSE I.
The Neceſſity of Divine Teaching.

JOHN vi. 45.

It is written in the prophets, And they ſhall be all taught of God. P. 17

DISCOURSE II.
Upon the Moral law.

ROM. vii. 12.

Wherefore the law is holy, and the commandment holy, juſt, and good. P. 51

DISCOURSE III.
Upon the Ceremonial Law.

SOLOMOM'S SONG iv. 6.

Until the day break, and the ſhadows flee away, I will get me to the mountain of myrrh, and to the hill of frankincenſe. P. 89

DISCOURSE. IV.
Upon the Law of Faith.

ROM. iii. 27.

Where is boaſting then? It is excluded. By what law? Of works? Nay, but by the law of faith. P. 123

CONTENTS.

DISCOURSE V.

Upon imputed Righteousness.

2. COR. v. 21.

He hath made him to be sin for us, who knew no sin, that we might be made the righteousness of God in him. P. 157

DISCOURSE VI.

Upon being Righteous over much.

ECCLES. vii. 16.

Be not righteous over much. P. 191

DISCOURSE VII.

Upon the right Knowledge of the Lord God.

MARK xii. 28, 29, 30, 31.

And one of the scribes came, and having heard them reasoning together, and perceiving that he had answered them well, asked him, which is the first commandment of all. And Jesus answered him, the first of all the commandments is, Hear, O Israel, the Lord our God is one Lord; and thou shalt love the Lord thy God with all thy heart, and with all thy soul, and with all thy mind, and with all thy strength: This is the first commandment. And the second is like, namely, this, Thou shalt love thy neighbour as thyself; there is none other commandment greater than these. P. 223

DISCOURSE VIII.

Upon the right Love of the Lord God.

MARK xii. 28, 29, 30, 31.

And one of the Scribes came, and having heard them reasoning together, &c.　　P. 255

DISCOURSE IX.

Upon the right Love of our Neighbour.

MARK xii. 28, 29, 30, 31.

And one of the Scribes came, and having heard them reasoning together, &c.　　P. 297

DISCOURSE X.

Upon the cleansing Virtue of Christ's Blood.

ZECHARIAH xiii. 1.

In that day there shall be a fountain opened to the house of David, *and to the inhabitants of* Jerusalem, *for sin and for uncleanness.*　　P. 337

DISCOURSE XI.

The balm of *Gilead.*

JER. viii. 22.

Is there no balm in Gilead? *Is there no physician there? Why then is not the health of the daughter of my people recovered?*　　P. 381

DISCOURSE XII.

Upon the Promises of God.

2 PETER i. 4.

Whereby are given unto us exceeding great and precious promises.　　P. 423

THE
NECESSITY
OF
DIVINE TEACHING.

DISCOURSE I.

John vi. 45.

It is written in the prophets, And they shall be all taught of God.

THIS is a sweet promise, full of comfort to the children of God. So soon as he has given them a desire to be taught, the Lord has spoken it by the mouth of his holy prophets, that they may come to him to receive instruction. He, the all-wife God, will be their teacher. He will open the eyes of their understandings clearly to discern spi-

ritual things, and will make them wife unto falvation. In the book of Pfalms we find frequent prayers for this divine teaching, and among the high and honourable titles of God, this is ufed to defcribe his goodnefs to the children of men—" He that teacheth man " knowledge :" and not man confidered merely as ignorant, but alfo as guilty. " Good " and upright is the Lord, therefore will he " teach finners in the way," Pfalm xxv. 8; which fhews the wonderful condefcenfion of our divine teacher. He vouchfafes to be the inftructor of finners, in order to bring them out of darknefs into light, and out of mifery into happinefs: " For bleffed is " the man," fays the Pfalmift (xciv. 12), " whom thou teacheft out of thy law." He is bleffed, becaufe he is taught of God, and taught by him out of the law, to know his guilt and mifery; and taught alfo to know the remedy provided for both. Bleffed furely is he, whom God thus teaches; and yet how few among us feek this bleffednefs? Even among thofe who profefs their belief of it, its importance is not fufficiently valued. The privilege is great, ineftimably great, but they are too apt to neglect it; while others proudly fancy they can teach
themfelves;

themselves; or they think it no honour to be taught of God; they disbelieve the reality, or they neglect the importance of divine teaching. Some of these reasons prevail with the generality of nominal Christians, and hinder them from being convinced of the truth of what is written in the prophets, " And they shall be all taught of God." But he that teacheth man knowledge can, and, glory be to his rich grace, he does, convince him of the necessity of being taught of God. He does enlighten the darkest, he does humble the proudest mind, and bring it earnestly to pray for instruction—" Lord " what I know not, that teach thou me." May this be the prayer of all your hearts, while I am explaining the nature of the promise in the text, and may God fulfil it to you at this time, that you may be convinced

    First, Of the necessity of being taught of God:

    Secondly, Of the manner in which God teaches his people:

    Thirdly, Of the proper disposition of mind

mind which he gives them, in order to their receiving and profiting from his divine teaching.

First. Divine teaching consists in opening the eyes of the understanding to perceive spiritual and divine objects, and to see their value and importance, in disposing the will to choose them, and the heart to love them. The divine teacher is the Holy Spirit. He prepares the mind to receive his instruction, and then fills it with the knowledge of his will in all wisdom and spiritual understanding. The necessity of his doing this is founded in the present state and circumstances of fallen men: for through sin all the faculties of the soul were lost, and the understanding, which is the eye of the soul, was left in the same condition as the bodily eyes would be if they had no light. Hence the Psalmist declares, that there is none who understandeth the things of God, and he represents God as looking down from heaven to see if there were any who did understand and seek after God; but he found none, no not one. They all had their understanding darkened, being alienated from the life of God through the ignorance

norance that is in them, becaufe of the blindnefs of their heart. The prophets give us the fame character, and fpeak of men as if they were all blind, and defcribe the Meffiah to be the fun of righteoufnefs, the light who was to arife to lighten the Gentiles, and was to be the glory of his people Ifrael. Thus Jehovah fays of his beloved Son, "I the Lord will give thee for a co-
" venant of the people, for a light of the
" Gentiles, to open the blind eyes." Ifa. xlii. 7. And again—" I will alfo give thee for
" a light to the Gentiles, that thou mayeft
" be my falvation unto the ends of the
" earth." Ifa. xlix. 6. How did our Lord fulfil thefe prophecies? He did not, while he was upon earth, open the bodily eyes of any blind perfons among the Gentiles, but he has fulfilled them, and, glory be to his great name, he is daily fulfilling them in the gentile world, by opening the blind eyes of our underftandings to fee and to difcern the things of God. In this fenfe the Pfalmift, fpeaking both of Jews and Gentiles, fays, Pfalm cxlvi. 8, " The Lord openeth the
" eyes of the blind," that is, the Lord Chrift: for we read, Ifa. xxxv. 4, 5, " Say
" unto them that are of a fearful heart, be
" ftrong,

"strong, fear not, your God will come and
"save you, then the eyes of the blind shall
"be opened: for in that day (Isa. xxix. 18)
"shall the deaf hear the words of the book,
"and the eyes of the blind shall see out of
"obscurity, and out of darkness." All these
scriptures had their happy accomplishment,
when God, who was to come and save us,
spake with his own mouth, and said, "I am
"come a light into the world, that whoso-
"ever believeth on me should not abide in
"darkness." John xii. 46.

From these authorities it is certain, that fallen man is in darkness, and cannot see the things of God. The eyes of his understanding are in the same condition as his bodily eyes would be without light. He cannot see any spiritual objects, and how then can he come to the knowledge of them, unless he be taught them of God? By what other way or means can he discern them? Has he any powers or faculties of his own, which can help to enlighten him? No, he has none: for, since the eyes of his understanding are in darkness, all his endeavours to enlighten them, without divine teaching, will be like those of a blind man, who only

makes

makes his blindnefs more manifeft the more he labours and ftrives to give an account of thofe objects, which he never faw nor felt.

But cannot the arts and fciences enlighten his blind eyes? No. They cannot help him to difcover one fingle fpiritual idea.—The arts and fciences treat of the objects of fenfe; to thefe they are confined, and cannot get beyond the bounds of nature: for it is a certain truth, and indeed it is at prefent a received opinion, that all our ideas come from fenfe. We are not able to form an idea of any thing, unlefs it fall under the obfervation of fome of our fenfes. If any one of the fenfes be deftroyed, the man is not able to form an idea of any object peculiar to that fenfe. A man born deaf has no idea of founds, nor a blind man of colours. Since then the arts and fciences treat entirely of the objects of fenfe, how can they give us any ideas of thofe things which are not objects of fenfe: for was it ever known that the ftream rofe higher than the fountain head?

From hence it appears, that if the underftanding be ever fo greatly refined and enlarged with the knowledge of arts and fciences,

ences, yet it stands in as much need of divine teaching, as the most ignorant peasant does; because the things of God are not discoverable by the arts and sciences. Let matter of fact speak to this point. Has there not been a total ignorance of divine things, whenever the light of revelation has been extinguished? Look into the learned ages of Greece, and you find the several sects of philosophers enquiring, What is the chief good of men; and none of them could discover what it was, and disputing about the origin of evil, and never coming near the truth. Look into the times when Rome was raised to its highest glory, and was as famous for its learning as for its conquests, and you will not find one learned Roman, who can tell you what God is. Tully has written a book upon the nature of the gods, and it is one of the most valuable of his writings; for therein he gives us the opinions of the philosophers upon this subject, and shews his own and their exceeding great ignorance of it. From these instances, not to mention others, it is evident that a man may have all the knowledge which arts and sciences can give him, and yet be totally ignorant of God, and of the things of God. This has appeared

appeared from undoubted matter of fact. We know from the experience of the Greeks and Romans, that arts and sciences never did lead them to the knowledge of any spiritual and divine objects; and we are assured from the testimony of God's word that they never can. Man, in his natural state, blinded by sin, and under the power of it, cannot attain to any such knowledge. The Apostle has decided this point for us. Speaking of the politest classical age of Rome, he says of her great philosophers, and celebrated authors, that they were without understanding, that they became vain in their imaginations, and their foolish heart was darkened. What! was Tully without understanding, was the imagination of Virgil vain, and the heart of Seneca foolish? Yes, in the things of God:
" for the natural man receiveth not the
" things of the Spirit of God, for they are
" foolishness unto him, neither can he know
" them, because they are spiritually dis-
" cerned." 1 Cor. ii. 14. While he remains a natural man, it is absolutely impossible that he should know them, " neither *can* he know them," because he has no spiritual discernment, by which alone spiritual objects can be discovered; and therefore

fore he muſt remain for ever ignorant of them, unleſs God ſhould open the eyes of his underſtanding, and bring him out of darkneſs into his marvellous light.

This is a very humbling, but it is a real view of human nature, and I need not to have gone to diſtant ages and countries for proof. We have it near enough at home, if men's pride would but let them ſee it; but their pride ariſes chiefly from their ignorance of it, and helps to keep them ignorant. If they had but a little humility they would diſcover how imperfect their knowledge is, even of the things about them, and they would therefore ſee the neceſſity of being taught of God in theſe things, which were out of the reach of their ſenſes: ſuch are all ſpiritual and divine things, and in theſe they want divine teaching, and the promiſe is, concerning theſe, " All thy " children ſhall be taught of God." Now God never acts in vain. Unleſs his children wanted teaching, he need not be their teacher: but in what belongs to the ſpiritual world they are entirely ignorant, and they have no means of diſcovering, unleſs they be taught of God, what ſtate they are in by nature,

nature, and if it be a state of guilt and misery, how they are to be delivered from it. God has revealed in his holy word the knowledge of what belongs to these two states; but sin has so blinded men's understandings, and depraved their judgments, that they will not assent to what is revealed, nor be determined by it, until the Holy Spirit convince them what they are by nature, and what they may be by grace. Accordingly the scripture declares, that the Holy Spirit is the inspirer of every good thought, and word, and work. He enlightens the children of God with saving truth, and subdues the opposition which was in their wills to it, and that enmity which was in their hearts. From the first moment he awakens them, and opens the eyes of their understanding; until he bring them safe to glory, he is their teacher. He teaches them to look upon sin, as it is in itself, exceeding sinful; he alarms the conscience, and makes it feel the guilt and danger of sin; he leads the humbled and convinced sinner to Christ for pardon; he gives him faith, and hope, and love; and, by grafting him, like a living branch, into the true vine, enables him to bear much fruit to the glory of God. And since every thing good in him comes from divine teaching, is it not absolutely necessary that he should be taught of God?

If you will consider all these authorities together, I hope they will convince you, my brethren, that there is a necessity for your being taught of God: for by nature you are ignorant of all spiritual and divine things; and you cannot, by any means in your own power, attain to the knowledge of them; the arts and sciences can give you no assistance. It is a matter of fact that they never did, and the scripture declares that they never can, help any man to discern the things of the Spirit of God. The natural man, while he remains such, be he ever so learned, *cannot* know them. And how then can he ever attain any ideas of them but by divine teaching? If this evidence has convinced you, you are prepared to follow me in my second enquiry, which relates to the manner in which God teaches his people.

His established method is by the word, and by the Spirit. In all divine teaching these

these two go together, the word, and the Spirit explaining and applying the word. The word is the whole will of God, which he revealed to be the means of bringing sinners from darkness to light, from sin to righteousness, and from the power of satan unto God, and unto the kingdom of his dear Son, here in grace, and hereafter in glory. These great things are spoken of the written word: for it is able, according to the Apostle, to make a man wise unto salvation; but then the quickening Spirit must accompany the hearing, or reading of it, or else you will never find in it this saving wisdom. It is only a dead letter, unless the living Spirit animate it: for the 'letter killeth, but the Spirit giveth life. The word is the means in the hand of the Spirit of beginning, carrying on, and perfecting, the life of God in the soul. When the Spirit works in it, and by it, he makes it effectual, through his mighty operation, to build up and to perfect the man of God. He works in the word; for the Spirit is received in it, as the Apostle shews, 2 Cor. iii. 8, where he calls the preaching of the gospel, " The ministration of the " Spirit," that by which the Spirit was administered and given, and he says to the

Galatians,

Galatians, that, by this hearing of faith (which hearing was of the word of God), they received the Spirit; Gal. iii. 2. And being received, he enlightened their minds and opened their underſtandings, that they might underſtand the ſcriptures, and thereby he wrought that faith in them, which cometh by hearing: for faith is his gift. It is called, Gal. v. 22, " the fruit of the Spirit;" one of the fruits produced in the heart by his grace, upon which account he is called " the " Spirit of faith," 2 Cor. iv. 13. And when he has thus wrought in the word, he then works by it, and helps the believer to act faith upon it. The Holy Spirit puts it into his heart to deſire the ſincere milk of the word, that he may grow thereby. And he does grow, and is nouriſhed up, as Timothy was, in the words of faith, when he is enabled by the ſame Spirit to act faith upon the word; for then the word preached profits him, when he can mix faith with it—when faith and the word, like two fluids of the ſame properties, readily mix together, and cloſely incorporate. Thus the word nouriſhes him in the inner man, and he grows thereby. The Spirit applies it and renders it effectual to the promoting of every gracious

cious purpose, for which it was revealed, and by its means he makes the man of God wise unto salvation, through faith, which is in Jesus Christ.

This is the usual and common way in which God fulfils the text. He teaches his children spiritual and divine things by his word, as explained and applied by his Spirit: which two cannot be put asunder. The word is the eye, and the Holy Spirit is the light shining upon it. Now a man cannot see without eyes, and having eyes he cannot see without light. So if you have the word without the Spirit, you have eyes without light; and if you have the Spirit without the word, you have light, but no eyes to see it: the word and the Spirit therefore must go together. To expect that the Spirit will teach you without the word, is rank enthusiasm, as great madness as to hope to see without eyes; and to expect that the word will teach you, without the Spirit, is as great an absurdity as to pretend to see without light; and if any man says, that the Spirit teaches him to believe, or to do what is contrary to the written word, he is a mad blasphemer. God has joined the word and the Spirit; and what God has joined together, let no man put afunder.

Convinced of thefe things, have you, my brethren, reduced them to practice? Do you go with humility to the word of God to be taught, and do you find that inftruction from it, of which you ftand in need? Perhaps you fay, you do read it, but you find it very difficult: it is fo hard to be underftood, that it is for the moft part to you a fealed book. This is a very general complaint; but what is the caufe of it? Certain it is, that this fcripture cannot be broken—" All thy children fhall be taught of God." The fault is not in God, nor yet in his word. Surely then it is in yourfelves. Either you have not been deeply convinced of your own blindnefs in fpiritual things, and therefore are not practically perfuaded of the neceffity of the word; or you have not looked up to the Holy Spirit for his divine teaching, praying him, in the prophet's words, " Lord, " open thou mine eyes, that I may fee " wondrous things out of thy law:" for until he opens your eyes and enlighten them, you cannot fee any of the wonders contained in the book of God. Confider thefe
points

points then, and examine them closely. Be faithful, my brethren, to your own souls, and be not afraid to discover the true ground of your complaint. Have you been led to read and to hear the word of God under a strong sense of your darkness and blindness without it? And do you always seek the grace of the Holy Spirit to explain and to apply it? The first of these is absolutely necessary; because you will not ask wisdom of God, until you be convinced you lack it. And you will ask it with more or less earnestness in proportion to the sense you have of your want of it; so that when you are made deeply sensible of your great ignorance, then you will become very humble and teachable. This is the proper disposition of mind which the Holy Spirit must work in you, both before and under divine teaching, and the consideration of which was the third particular I proposed to speak to.

Divine teaching is absolutely necessary for the learning of divine things, and God teaches his children by his word and by his Spirit. You may be convinced, my brethren, of these truths in speculation, but it is very difficult to bring them into practice. For such is the pride of the natural man, that he will not submit to be taught, no, not of God. He will exalt his own reasoning faculties above the wisdom of God's word, and above the teaching of God's Spirit. Although he has nothing to be proud of, being a creature made up of ignorance and sin, yet is he excessively proud: for pride is interwoven in his very frame and constitution. Our Lord says, pride proceeds from within, out of the heart, Mark vii. 21. It comes from a corrupt principle that is within us, in the heart; there it has taken deep root, and, grown luxuriant, bringing forth a vast crop of proud looks, words, and works. Nothing but the almighty grace of God can pull down the high opinion which this proud creature entertains of himself, and which he will continue to entertain, until he be well disciplined into the knowledge of himself. He must be brought to see his ignorance, and to feel his guilt and misery, before he will be humble enough to apply to God for instruction. And this is the work of the Holy Spirit. It is through his gracious operation that the proud, self-sufficient sinner is made thoroughly acquainted with his ignorance and his sinfulness. The Holy Spirit gives him a view of himself in the glass

of

of the law, and fhews him and makes him feel the entire corruption of his nature, the blindnefs of his underftanding, the depravity of his will, and the rebellion of his heart. The natural man is a bad fcholar at this humbling leffon. He learns it very flowly, and with great pain and difficulty. The practice of it is like plucking out a right eye, or cutting off a right hand: for his inbred fins are as dear to him as any member of his body. But the Holy Spirit fo alarms him with his guilt, and with his danger, that by degrees he is brought heartily to wifh for deliverance from his ignorance, and from his fins; and thus he is made teachable. He becomes fimple, and is willing to be taught of God. He is brought into a proper frame of mind to fit with Mary at the mafter's feet, hearing his word, in order to be enlightened with faving wifdom, and to be bleffed with the comforts of faving faith. To perfons of this humble, teachable temper, the fcripture has made many fweet promifes, both when they at firft go to the fchool of Chrift to learn his will, and alfo when they afterwards fit at his feet hearing his words, that they may do them. In general, it is faid, that God giveth grace to the

the humble, and particularly grace to learn his will, as Pſalm xxv. 9. "The meek will "he guide in judgment, and the meek will "he teach his way." The meek are they, who, with an humble and lowly ſpirit, receive the word of God, according to the Apoſtle James, i. 21. "Receive with meek- "neſs the ingrafted word, which is able to "ſave your ſouls." They ſhall be taught of God, whom he has diſpoſed to receive his word with meekneſs, he will engraft it inwardly in their hearts, and will enable them to bring forth the precious fruits of it in their lives, and thus he will teach them his way. And then they will be able to take up the words of Chriſt, gratefully acknowledging what God has done for them—"We thank thee, "O Father, Lord of heaven and earth, be- "cauſe thou haſt hid theſe things from the "wiſe and prudent, and haſt revealed them "unto babes." The things of God are ſtill hid from the wiſe and prudent, from the wiſe and prudent ones of this world, who ſeek the knowledge of them by mere human learning, which, without grace, only puffs them up, and hinders them from ſeeing their want of divine teaching; from all ſuch he hides the knowledge of ſpiritual things,

things, but he reveals them to thofe whom the Holy Spirit has made humble and teachable. When fuch perfons come with a meek temper to be taught of him, then he manifefts to them the fecrets of his kingdom: for he reveals them unto babes: unto them that bleffed promife of the New Teftament is fulfilled, " If any of you lack wifdom, and is " humbled under the fenfe of his want of it, " let him afk it of God, who giveth unto all " afkers liberally, and upbraideth not, and it " fhall be given him." James i. 5.

This then is the proper difpofition of mind with which the Holy Spirit prepares the children of God for divine teaching, and by which he helps them to profit under it. He makes them humble, meek, and lowly in their own eyes, and defirous of being taught of God. To fuch perfons he giveth grace to underftand the word, to apply it, and to be edified by it. To thofe whom he has humbled he giveth his grace, becaufe they will take no merit to themfelves; but will afcribe the glory of what they learn to their divine teacher, and ufe it to the praife of the glory of his grace. You are, I hope, convinced of thefe great truths, but perhaps fome of you

you do not see clearly how you are to attain this humble, teachable disposition. Are you convinced of your own want of it? If you are, this is the work of the Holy Spirit. He has begun to make you sensible of your ignorance; and he must prepare you to receive instruction, as well as give it you. The desire to be taught of God cometh from him, as well as the teaching itself. He must work in you both to will and to do: for it is written, Prov. xvi. 1, "The preparations of the "heart in man are from the Lord;" if there be any preparations in your heart to be taught of God, this is not from yourself, it is from the Lord, and is expressly ascribed to him, Gal. v. 23, where meekness is mentioned among the other fruits of the Spirit, that meekness whereby we receive the engrafted word is the fruit of his grace in the heart. Apply to him for it, and he will make you an humble, teachable scholar in the school of Christ; and when he has thus disposed you to give him all the glory of teaching you, then to you his promise shall be fulfilled, and you shall be taught of God.

From what has been now offered, the doctrine of the text is, I hope, made plain and

and clear: if scripture authority can convince, and if matter of fact can determine the point, they give in full evidence for the necessity of divine teaching, which is farther confirmed from the established method in which God teaches his children. He revealed his word for their instruction, and his Spirit still accompanies the hearing or reading of it, and renders it effectual to the purposes for which it was revealed. He still, by his grace, prepares the sinner's mind to receive it, by convincing him of his ignorance of the things of God, by bringing him with an humble, teachable temper to learn them from the word of God, and then he works faith in the sinner's heart by the word, and helps the believer to act faith upon the word of God's grace, which is able to build him up, and to give him an inheritance among all them which are sanctified. These particulars have been established upon express passages of Holy Scripture; and what effect, my brethren, has our present consideration of them had upon you? Has it been the means of shewing any of you how much you stood in need of divine teaching? Has it stirred up fervent desires in any of you for the teachings of God's Spirit? If

neither of thefe good effects followed, what is the caufe which hindered? If you believe the fcripture to be the word of God, you cannot deny the doctrine. No words can be plainer than thefe written in the prophets, " They fhall be ALL taught of God." If all are not to be taught of God, how do you underftand the words? Do you think they fpeak only of the apoftles and primitive Chriftians, to whom they were fulfilled, but we are not now to expect their accomplifhment? This is the opinion of many perfons, but it is quite unfcriptural. The 54th chapter of Ifaiah, as explained by an infallible interpreter in the New Teftament, treats of the Gentile church in the laft days, of which it is faid, verfe 13, " And all thy " children fhall be taught of the Lord," ALL without exception, all God's children among the Gentiles in every age fhall be taught of the Lord. To the fame purpofe the Prophet Jeremiah, ch. xxxi. fpeaks of the new covenant, which was to be eftablifhed in the laft days, declares from the mouth of God, ver. 34, " And they fhall teach " no more every man his neighbour, and " every man his brother, faying, Know the " Lord; for they fhall all know me from the
" leaft

" leaſt of them to the greateſt of them, ſaith
" the Lord." This promiſe belongs to the
new covenant, under which God himſelf
engages to teach his people, and they all,
from the leaſt to the greateſt, ſhall know the
Lord. And when our bleſſed Saviour in
the text referred to theſe and ſuch-like promiſes, which are written in the prophets, he
made no limitation, but ſaid, " they ſhall
" be all taught of God,"—*all* in every age
of the church, who are made ſenſible of
their want of divine teaching, and look up
to heaven for a divine teacher, ſhall be taught
of God. Certainly theſe paſſages cannot be
ſo far wreſted and tortured as to make them
ſpeak for divine teaching in one age of the
church only. How can you, with any appearance of truth, fix a limited ſenſe to theſe
univerſal propoſitions—ALL thy children
ſhall be taught of the Lord—they ſhall ALL
know me from the leaſt to the greateſt:
for they ſhall be ALL taught of God—All
were to be taught by him, all his children,
therefore his children now have the ſame
promiſe of divine teaching which the primitive Chriſtians had; for the promiſe is to
us, and to our children, and to all that are

afar

afar off, even as many as the Lord our God shall call.

Since then the scripture so clearly confutes this absurd and wicked opinion, do you, my brethren, give it up, and acknowledge the necessity of divine teaching? If not, what other objection have you against the doctrine? Have you been used to think, that it carried with it an air of enthusiasm? I know many persons look upon it in this light. If any of you do, pray tell us what you mean by enthusiasm? for it seems to us only a bad name given to the best thing. At this day the knowledge of vital and experimental religion is so far lost, that whenever the generality of our people hear it spoken of, they do not understand it; and what they do not understand, they reject under the odious name of enthusiasm; so that this name does not stand for any bad properties in the thing to which they apply it, but only signifies their dislike of it. And if they express their dislike by an hard name, what hurt can that do? Can it really turn the words of truth and soberness into enthusiasm? Can that be enthusiasm; which

believes

believes God to be a faithful promise-keeping God, and that his word cannot be broken? What! is it enthusiasm to desire to be taught of God, and to ask wisdom of him, after he has commanded his children to ask it, and has engaged to teach it to them? Surely, no. God's promises must be fulfilled, and they, who seek their accomplishment, cannot be disappointed. He hath spoken by the mouth of his holy prophets, that all his children shall be taught of God; and heaven and earth shall pass away, before one tittle of these words shall fail. Men and brethren, what do you think now of this objection, which wants to make God a liar, for promising to teach his children, and which treats them as enthusiasts who expect to be taught of him? Certainly you cannot defend such a blasphemous opinion. Well then, the way is farther cleared for a favourable reception of the doctrine; and do you indeed receive it? Perhaps you assent to it. But what sort of an assent do you give? Is it active and operative? If not, what will it avail? You will learn none of the things of God, by simply believing that God does teach them to his children. You must ask, if you would have: you must seek, if you

would

would find that wisdom which cometh from above. And you must ask with earnestness, and seek with diligence; not as if you could thereby merit, but to express your wants and your humility. The divine direction in this case is, Prov. ii. 3, 4, &c. " If thou criest " after knowledge, and liftest up thy voice " for understanding," not asking faintly, but crying aloud, and lifting up the voice through the fervency of the desire after wisdom. " And if thou seekest her as silver, and " searchest for her as hid treasures," seeking with as great pains, and searching with as constant application, as ever worldly man took to enrich himself: " Then shalt thou " understand the fear of the Lord, and find " the knowledge of God: for the Lord giv- " eth wisdom," he giveth it to every one who seeks with humble diligence.

These are words of comfort to you who desire to be taught of God, and who are seeking of him the knowledge of divine things. Seek, as he has directed you, and you shall find. He will teach you, because he has made you teachable. He has already taught you one lesson, which is perhaps the hardest you have to learn. He has convinced

vinced you of your entire ignorance of divine things. You no longer take up your rest in the fancied abilities of nature, but are consulting the word of God, and praying for the teachings of the Spirit of God. This is the appointed way to receive instruction. And if you wait in this way, he who directed you to the way will meet you and instruct you in it. Only remember, that his glory, being the motive and end of all his dealings with men, must be your motive and end in learning divine things. You must have a single eye to his glory in asking knowledge of him; and what he gives, you must use to his glory. His glory must be promoted by all that he teaches you: and therefore you must come to learn of him, *humble*, under a continual sense of your ignorance and unworthiness, and *meek*, disposed like a new-born babe to receive the sincere milk of the word, that you may grow thereby, and you must be *a diligent scholar*, you must read much, and pray more; yea, you must watch in prayer with all perseverance, and then the promise, which wisdom itself has made, shall be fulfilled to you. Prov. viii. 34, " Blessed is the man that heareth
" me, watching daily at my gates, waiting
" at

"at the pofts of my doors." He that watches and waits thus, is bleffed: for God, who commanded light to fhine out of darknefs, will fhine into his heart, to give the light of the knowledge of the glory of God in the face of Jefus Chrift.

What thanks can we render unto God for his exceeding grace, who ftill fhines into the hearts of his children? Glory be to his great name, there are many among us who have reafon to praife him for his divine teaching. They have found him faithful to fulfil his promifes: for he has opened their blind eyes, and has led them into the knowledge and belief of the truth. Daily are they magnifying the riches of his infinite love, which has brought them out of darknefs into his marvellous light, and has tranflated them out of the kingdom of fatan into the kingdom of his dear Son. Thefe perfons are witneffes for God, and can fet to their feal that he ftill teaches his children by his word and by his Spirit: for they have been illuminated with the true knowledge and underftanding of his word, and by their living they fet it forth and fhew it accordingly.

This

This is the happy state of so many of you as are real Christians. You have experience of the truth of the text, and know it to be an undoubted matter of fact. My Christian brethren, what return will you make to your divine teacher for the comfortable lessons which he has taught you? What less can you do, than praise him with your lives, as well as with your lips? Praise him for what you have already learnt, and continue humbly to wait on him for your growth in knowledge. Remember that the new man which you have put on is to be renewed in knowledge day by day. The spirit of wisdom is to help you to grow in grace, and in the knowledge of your Lord and Saviour Jesus Christ. This is your privilege; and it is your interest to make a constant use of it. The wisest of us know but little of what is to be known, therefore you should be diligent in your attendance upon the means appointed of God for your teaching. Read the word, and meditate in it day and night; and when the Holy Spirit explains and applies it, then it will be a lantern unto your feet, and a light unto your paths. Pray over the word. Prayer will digest it, and the prayer of faith mixed

with

with it, will make it nourishing and strengthening to the inner man. And thus you will grow in grace, and be renewed in knowledge—the understanding will be renewed with still clearer views of spiritual things, the heart, no longer prejudiced against them, will be renewed with a more determinate choice of them, and the affections will be renewed with a more hearty love, and a fuller enjoyment of them. Hereby your sanctification will be carried on, and you will be renewed day by day in true holiness after the image of him that created you.— Having therefore these privileges, dearly beloved brethren, having such a teacher, and such things to learn of him, having the Spirit of the Most High God to teach you all things, which belong to your present peace, and to your eternal glory. Oh what diligence should you use in attending upon the means, by which your divine teacher has promised to instruct you. In them be ye constantly found waiting, waiting with humble, teachable tempers, and praying for the blessing of God upon the use of his appointed means. And while you thus continue to wait upon God, he will continue to teach you. He has promised it to his children

dren, and he cannot lie. He will make you wife unto falvation.

Having thus exhorted you, my Chriftian brethren, to make a diligent ufe of the great privilege of the new covenant, I have nothing farther to offer, but my prayers. May he that heareth prayer, fend down his blefling upon what has been now fpoken. May the God of our Lord Jefus Chrift, the father of glory, give unto you the Spirit of wifdom and revelation in the knowledge of him, that the eyes of your underftanding being enlightened, ye may know what is the hope of his calling, and what the riches of the glory of his inheritance in the faints, and what is the exceeding greatnefs of his power to us ward who believe. Oh may our God manifeft thefe great truths to your underftandings, and give you the fweet experience of them in your hearts, that you may be filled with the knowledge of his will in all wifdom and fpiritual underftanding, and that ye may walk worthy of the Lord unto all pleafing, being fruitful in every good work, and increafing in the knowledge of God, until you fee him face to face; and then fhall you know, even as alfo you are known. To this perfect knowledge and ever-blessed fruition of God may the Lord Jesus bring you all by the ministry of his word, and by the teachings of his Spirit, that you may be for ever happy in giving thanks and praise to the three divine persons in one Jehovah, to whom the church in earth and heaven ascribes all glory in time and in eternity. Amen, and Amen.

UPON THE
MORAL LAW.

DISCOURSE II.

ROMANS vii. 12.

Wherefore the law is holy, and the commandment holy, just, and good.

THE great Creator and Possessor of heaven and earth hath an indisputable authority to make laws for the government of his creatures, and to require their obedience. Since every thing that they have is received from his hands, and held under him at his pleasure, it therefore behoves them to enquire upon what terms they hold it. And if God has given them any laws, it is their duty to study them, and their interest to obey them. If there be any sanctions to enforce these

these laws, any rewards or punishments, they should enquire, where these things are to be known, and by what means discovered, that they may obtain the reward and escape the punishment.

Whenever a serious unprejudiced person desires to be satisfied in these points which so nearly concern his present peace of conscience, and his future happiness, he will soon be convinced that God has made a gracious provision for his instruction. God has opened his mind and will in this matter. He has recorded his laws, and published them. The sacred volume of divine statutes is in our hands, and in our mother tongue. It is so very short that none can want time to peruse it, and it is so very plain and intelligible, as to the rule of duty, that none can plead ignorance. He that runs may read it, and the simple may understand it and learn knowledge: for upon a very cursory view of this divine treatise, it will appear, that there are three distinct bodies of law mentioned in it, namely, the moral law, the ceremonial law, and the law of faith. We are all highly concerned to enquire into the nature of these laws,

and

and therefore I purpose, through God's affistance, to enquire into the scope and design of each of them. At present I shall confine myself to the moral law, which alone is spoken of in my text. The apostle is treating of its usefulness to discover the sinfulness of sin: "I had not known sin," says he, "but by the law;" the law must first lay down a rule, before it can be known what sin is, which is the transgression of that rule: "For I had not known lust," and that the very first rising and motion of evil in the heart was a sin, "unless the law "had said, Thou shalt not covet." This is the law of the tenth commandment; from whence it is very evident that St. Paul is here treating of the moral law, which is of such perfect purity as to reach to the desires and covetings of the heart, and which, by restraining them, makes them appear more sinful and grow more outrageous. "But "sin taking occasion by the commandment, "wrought in me all manner of concupi- "scence: for without the law sin was dead," although it be in us, yet it is not perceived, until it be held before the holy spiritual law of God, and then it begins to stir and rage: for as it follows, "I was once "alive

" alive without the law," says the apostle, when I knew not the law I thought myself alive, my conscience never troubled me, nor did I apprehend the deadly nature of sin, " but when the commandment came," when I began to understand the commandment in its spiritual nature, and it came to my conscience, and was applied with a divine power to my heart, " then sin revived, and I died," I found myself dead in trespasses and sins: " for the same commandment which was " ordained unto life was found to be unto " me unto death: but sin took occasion by " the commandment," not through any fault in the commandment, but entirely through my own fault, " deceived me, and by it slew " me. What shall we say then? Is the " law and the commandment sin? God for- " bid. The law is holy," all the fault is in us, who abuse the law, " and the com- " mandment is holy and just and good." The occasion of the words and the context thus in part opened and explained may help us to determine,

First, What the moral law is.

Secondly, Whether it be still in force.
Thirdly,

Thirdly, Whether we have all kept it, and if not,

Fourthly, What is the penalty due to the breach of it; and then I shall draw some practical inferences from these particulars. And may the Spirit of the living God apply what shall be spoken. May he enlighten all your understandings with a clear view of the spiritual nature of the moral law, that by it you may be brought to the knowledge of sin, and to see and to feel your want of a Saviour. Under the teachings of this good Spirit let us consider,

First, What the moral law is. I define it to be the holy, just, and good will of God made known and promulged to his creatures in all these particulars, wherein he requires their perfect obedience, in order to their happiness. The law is the discovery of his will: for the almighty Creator and sovereign Lord of heaven and earth governs all his works and creatures according to the good pleasure of his own will. His will is the absolutely perfect law of the natural world. He hath given to the inanimate works of his hands

hands a law which shall not be broken. The active powers in nature shall work, and passive matter shall obey by an unalterable rule, until the heavens be folded up like a scroll, and the earth and all the works therein shall be burnt up. And his will is as absolute a law to his rational creatures, as to the natural agents: because he can enact no laws, but what partake of his own adorable perfections. His law is his will made known. It is a copy of his infinitely pure mind. It is a fair transcript of his holiness, justice, goodness, and of every other divine attribute: for by the law he discovers to his creatures what it is his will they should be and do, in order to preserve his favour. He would have them holy, just, and good, and the law makes known to them the rule of their obedience; by an exact conformity to which they are holy, just, and good. The will of God revealed in the law is holy, and conformity to it is holiness. Holiness, in the Old Testament language, signifies a separation from impurity, and when applied to the divine nature, it rather expresses what God is not, than what he is. It is a negative idea, denoting an entire separation from every thing which can defile. Holiness in God excludes
all

all poffibility of pollution. In him there neither is, nor can be, the leaft impurity. He is of purer eyes than to behold the leaft iniquity. He cannot even look upon any thing which is in the leaft unclean: for without holinefs no man fhall fee the Lord. Now the law is an exact copy of God's holinefs. It is the outward difcovery of his moft holy mind and will, informing his creatures how perfectly pure they muft preferve themfelves, if they would preferve his favour. The law difcovers to them what God is, and fhews how like him they ought to be in holinefs. And fince God cannot behold the leaft impurity, confequently his law cannot, becaufe it is his mind and will revealed concerning this matter. He will not fuffer any deviation from his law, no, not in thought: for the language of the law is pofitive and exprefs out of the mouth of the fupreme law-giver himfelf—" Be ye " holy, for I am holy." And are you, my brethren, thus holy? This fhould be a matter of clofe examination. Are you what the law requires you to be? Do you look upon the law as perfectly, infinitely holy in itfelf, even as holy as God is; and have you confidered fin as an offence againft the

holiness of God and of his law, even such an unpardonable offence, that you could never make the least satisfaction for it? It is very evident these things are not well understood, because the practice of mankind shews what low ideas they entertain of them. What makes sin appear light and little, and some offences small? Is it not because sinners are ignorant of the absolutely perfect holiness of the law? And after they have broken it, how mean an opinion have they of its holiness, when they think that a little sorrow and some few tears, that repentance and amendment can make them holy, and satisfy the demands of the broken law? If any of you entertain these unworthy ideas of God and of his law, you should consider that, although God does require you to be perfectly holy, yet he can require nothing of you but what is just. The law is just as well as holy, just in all its demands, and just in the rule of its process in rewarding obedience and punishing transgression. The scripture word for justice is taken from human affairs, and from thence is applied to divine. In the first ages of the world, money was paid and received by weight, and he who kept an even balance in paying and
receiving

receiving was a juft man. His juftice confifted in keeping the fcales even, in weighing all things with an equal balance, and in giving and taking only what was lawful and right. Now the law holds this balance of juftice in its hands, that it may prove the Judge of all the earth does right, and will be glorified in all that he requires of his creatures: for the holy obedience which he demands of them is a juft obedience. He had a fovereign authority to require it, and he gave them power to pay it him, and therefore they could not complain of any injuftice, if he fhould inflict the punifhment threatened to the difobedient, any more than if he fhould beftow the reward promifed to the obedient. Thus the law is juft. It is the exact copy of God's juftice, and is as perfectly juft as God is. It can no more require or do an unjuft thing, than God can: for the law only difcovers what is the infinitely juft mind and will of God concerning the behaviour of his creatures. The law fays, " Do this and thou fhalt live. " Tranfgrefs this, and dying thou fhalt " furely die." This is the will of the fupreme law-giver, and his juftice is engaged to fee the honour of his law maintained, as well

well in punishing transgression with death, as in rewarding obedience with life. The law cannot possibly do any injustice, because it is directed by the unerring will of God. God, and his will, and his law, are alike just; for it is written in the law, Deut. xxxii. 4, " The Lord's work is perfect; for " all his ways are judgment, a God of truth, " and without iniquity, just and right is " he."

All his ways and dealings with the children of men are perfectly just, and they are also good. His law is good. It partakes of the goodness of its divine author, inasmuch as it tends to promote the welfare and happiness of his creatures. The creature was made to shew forth the glory of its great Creator, and the law was the rule by which it was to walk in order to promote his glory, and in this holy walking there was all good to be met with. It was the way of pleasantness, and the path of peace. It preserved the assurance of the divine favour, afforded a perpetual feast of conscience, and gave sure and certain hopes of a glorious immortality; for Moses thus describeth the righteousness which is of the law, that the man who
doeth

doeth these things shall live by them. If he do all the things written in the book of the law he shall live unto God, and shall live with God. He shall enjoy a life of happiness here in the love and communion of God, and he shall enjoy an endless life of glory. Surely then the law is good! Since the keeping of it would have produced all good, and since the transgressing of it has brought all the evil upon man which he can suffer in time and in eternity. Consider, my brethren, how good the law is from that deluge of evil which came in upon the breach of it. When the Lord God, at the end of his six days work, surveyed all that he had made, behold it was very good. There was then no evil of any kind to afflict either body or soul; but by sin the body became subject to sickness, pain, and death, and the soul to guilt and misery, and in the next life both body and soul were subject to the worm that never dieth, and to the fire that never shall be quenched.

Such is the goodness of the law. It is the allwise provision which God has made for his own glory, and for the happiness of his creatures; to whom he has published it. He made it known to our first parents in paradise.

paradife. It was their rule of action, while they ftood in the likenefs and image of God. They had no oppofition then to his good and acceptable and perfect will, but the underftanding had a clear view of it, the will chofe it, and the heart loved it, and they were able to do it with all their mind and with all their ftrength. And when fin entered into the world, the will of God was not changed, nor his law repealed. The law was in full force from Adam to Mofes, in whofe time the Lord God recorded it with the moft awful majefty on mount Sinai, and engraved it with his own hands upon two tables of ftone. And it ftands unrepealed to this day; promifing life to obedience, and threatening death to tranfgreffion.

Since then the law has been properly promulged, an holy, juft, and good law, that altereth not, let us hear what it requires. It is the will of the law-giver, that he who doeth the things written in the book of the law fhall live by them. But then he muft do all things without exception. He muft not fail in any one point. If he will enter into life, he muft keep all the commandments. He muft be univerfally holy, juft,

and

and good, as the law is. If he ever receive the promifed reward, he muft perform the condition; that is, he muft pay the law perfect uninterrupted obedience with every faculty of foul and body, in their utmoft ftrength and vigour: for it cannot fuffer any tranfgreffion ; but for the leaft inflicts the threatened punifhment.

This is an effential property of the moral law. Upon the very firft offence it cuts the finner off from all claim to the promifed reward, and as to any thing that he can do cuts him off for ever. It is not in his power to make himfelf innocent again. Having once failed in his obedience, the law knows nothing of mercy, cannot accept the greateft repentance, nor be fatisfied with the deepeft forrow for what is paft; but immediately paffes fentence according to what is written, " Curfed is every one that con-
" tinueth not in all things which are writ-
" ten in the book of the law to do them."
If you fail in one fingle inftance of obedience, you do not continue to perform all things, but fall under the curfe of the broken law, and are as much liable to punifhment, though not in the fame degree, as if you had
failed

failed in every instance. In which sense the words of St. James are to be understood, "He that offendeth in one point is guilty "of all."

I have now gone through the several parts of the definition before given of the moral law, and it appears to be the holy, just, and good will of God made known and promulged to his creatures in all those particulars, wherein he requires their perfect obedience in order to their happiness. Since this is the case, it highly concerns every one of us to enquire, whether we be under an obligation to keep this law, which is the second particular I proposed to consider, namely,

Whether the moral law be still in force, and still requires of them, who expect to be saved by it, perfect unsinning obedience. And upon the first proposal of this question it would occur to every attentive person, that the law, being as holy, just, and good as God is, can no more admit of any variableness or shadow of turning, than God himself can. He says, " I change not," and how then can his law, which is the discovery

very of his mind and will be changeable? Man may change, but the law is the fame yesterday, to-day, and for ever. It altereth not. If man does not keep it, it will lose none of its honour. Justice will be glorified, by supporting the holiness of the law, and by inflicting the deserved punishment on the transgressors of it. But let us consult the law and the testimony. The Psalmist says, Psalm cxi. 7, 8, " All his " commandments are sure: they stand fast " for ever and ever, and are done in truth " and uprightness." ALL his commandments, not excepting one, are fixed upon a sure, immoveable foundation: for they stand fast for ever and ever in full force, established by the unchangeable will of God, and are ordained in perfect harmony with all the divine attributes, being done in truth, which cannot lie, and uprightness, which cannot err. To the same purpose he says in another Psalm, cxix. 160, " Thy word is true from " the beginning; and every one of thy " righteous judgments endureth for ever;" these righteous judgments are the decrees of the moral law, and there is not one of them that can be repealed, but they shall all endure in full force for ever. Our blessed Saviour has thrown great light upon this subject. The whole moral law is summed up in the ten commandments, which he has reduced to these two, the love of God, and the love of our neighbour: on these two commandments, says he, hang all the law and the prophets; for love is the fulfilling of the law, and love never faileth, consequently the law of love can never fail, but its debt of gratitude will be paying, and happy is he, who shall be paying it to all eternity.— Thus the moral law stands established by the authority of our divine teacher. In his sermon upon the mount he reforms the abuses and false comments which the Scribes and Pharisees had put upon the moral law, and he begins with this remark, Matt. v. 17, " Think not that I am come to destroy the " law and the prophets; I am not come to " destroy, but to fulfil;" to fulfil the law by paying it infinitely perfect obedience, and by being obedient unto death, even the death of the cross; and by this active and passive obedience he shewed that it was easier for heaven and earth to pass away, than that one tittle of the law should fail. If the law could have abated any thing of its demands, there would have been no necessity for

Christ's

Christ's fulfilling it by his obedience and death. But the law was unalterable. It could not be satisfied with any obedience, but what was absolutely holy, just, and good; and as all men had failed in paying it this obedience, they must therefore have been punished in their own persons, unless God, out of the riches of his wisdom and grace, had found out a way, by which the honour of his law might be advanced, and yet the sinner might be saved. And that was by sending his Son to fulfil the law. He was equal to this work; because he was God, equal with the Father, and he took our nature, and God and man were united in one Christ, that he might be capable of doing and suffering and meriting in an infinite degree. Accordingly, in the fulness of time, he stood up in the place of sinners, and therefore he became liable to do and to suffer whatever law and justice demanded, that having magnified the law, by obeying its precepts, and made it honourable by suffering its penalties, the righteousness of the law might be fulfilled in them, who should believe on him to everlasting life; but the law is still in force to condemn every one who does not savingly believe

believe on him, and will be for ever in force to inflict the deferved punifhment.

It is evident then that the moral law ftands to this day unrepealed. Although man may be changed from what he was at firft, yet the law is not. It is ftill the holy, juft, and good will of God requiring perfect obedience.— And when the holinefs of the law is violated, the juftice of God is bound to fee the fanctions of the law executed upon the difobedient ; and the divine goodnefs cannot plead an arreft of judgment, becaufe it is a good law which is broken, and therefore it is a good thing to fee that the tranfgreffors of it be paid the wages of fin.

My brethren, are not thefe very alarming truths, and ought they not to fuggeft to every one of you fuch reflections as thefe? What, am I under the law, bound to keep it with a perfect unfinning obedience? Can the law abate nothing of its demands, but muft I love God always, and with all my mind, heart, foul, and ftrength, and my neighbour as myfelf, if I hope to enter into life by keeping the commandments? Surely then

then I ought to examine, whether I have always loved God and my neighbour, as the law requires? If thefe be the thoughts of your hearts, then you are prepared to follow me to a ferious confideration of the third head of difcourfe, namely,

Whether we all have kept the moral law. Its demands are very great. It will not accept of any obedience, unlefs it be continual. You muft continue, without the leaft interruption, to do all things, that are written in the book of the law. And have any of you walked with a ftedfaft courfe in the way of the commandments, without once turning afide? Confult confcience. Does it not accufe? Confult fcripture. Does it not fay, "ALL we like fheep have gone aftray, "we have turned every one to his own "way?" leaving the way of God's commandments.

The law alfo requires fpiritual obedience. It reaches to the inmoft thoughts and intents of the heart. You muft never have one finful thought in you, if you expect life from your keeping the law: for the law is fpiritual. It fearches the heart and the reins,

and

and strikes at the very first motion or rising of sin. One sinful desire cuts you off from legal righteousness, as much as ten thousand sins: for it is written, " Thou shalt not covet;" and he that covets offends in one point, and therefore is guilty of all.

Besides, the law is perfect, perfectly holy, just, and good: for it is the will of God, and can no more suffer the least iniquity in its sight, than God himself can. It will abate nothing of absolutely perfect obedience. All the strength and all the mind, every faculty of soul and body is to be exerted, and with their utmost vigour, in the observance of the law. The heart too is to love it, and the affections are to be delighted with obeying it.

This is what the law demands of every one of you. It will have a continual, a spiritual, and a perfect love of God, without one thought ever arising in opposition to his holy will, and the love of your neighbour must be like the love of yourself. And does any man or woman keep the law in this manner? Do any of you? Certainly you cannot suppose that you have never broken the law, because you have just now declared the contrary out of your own mouths. You have confessed this day, and on your bended knees before God—" We have offended against " thy holy laws. We have left undone those " things which we ought to have done: and " have done those things which we ought " not to have done."—And when you spake these words, did not your consciences assure you, that they were true? For have you not offended against the holy law of God, and have not you left undone what it required, and done what it forbid? Surely you did not prevaricate with God, when in another part of the service you confessed that you had broken all the commandments. The rubric says— " Then shall the priest, turning to the peo- " ple, rehearse distinctly all the ten command- " ments; and the people still kneeling shall, " after every commandment, ask God mercy " for their transgression thereof for the time " past, and grace to keep the same for the time " to come," and accordingly after every commandment you prayed God to have mercy upon you for breaking it, and to incline your hearts to keep it. And have you not all sinned, and come short of the glory of God, by robbing his law of its due obedience?

What!

What! would you make me a breaker of all the commandments, says some self-righteous formalist? I never murdered any body, nor committed adultery. No? Had you never one angry thought or word against your neighbour? This is murder. Or did not one impure and unclean thought ever arise in your mind? This is sin, according to the spiritual law of God. You look at your actions in the glass of man's law, and because you have not outwardly offended, you think you have kept the law of God. There is your mistake. Look at Matt. v. 21, &c. and at 1 John iii. 15, and you will see that anger and hatred are murder in the eye of God; and read Matt. v. 27, 28, where our Lord teaches you, that one lustful look is heart-adultery. God regards the heart, and heart-sin is as much sin against his spiritual law as outward transgression; and when the formalist sees his heart naked and open, as God sees it, he will not pretend that he has not broken all the commandments, but will rather desire God to have mercy upon him, and to incline his heart to keep his laws.

If

If any of you refuse to be determined by these authorities, hear what the Lord God has declared concerning you, and his decree will, I hope, be decisive. He is represented, in the 14th Pfalm, as looking down from heaven upon the children of men to see if there were any that did understand and seek after God. But they were all gone out of the way; they were altogether become filthy, there was none that did good, no, not one; there was not one of the children of men, that did good and sinned not. We have, in the third chapter of the Romans, the apostle's comment upon this pfalm. After having proved both Jews and Gentiles that they are all under sin, and transgressors of the law, as it is written, there is none righteous, no, not one, legally righteous, he says—ver. 19, " Now we know " that what things soever the law faith, it " faith to them who are under the law, that " every mouth may be stopped, and all the " world may become guilty before God." Thus God himself has declared, that you have not done good, that you are under sin, and in his sight guilty. And what can you object to these scriptures? Sirs, are you not greatly alarmed at hearing them? For they

come

come home to every one's case, and ought to reach every one's conscience. And what are the present apprehensions of your minds concerning them? Have you broken the holy law of God, and you know you have, and do you not dread the consequence of your transgression? What can tempt you to hope that you shall escape the threatened penalty? Has your sorrow for breaking the law, or your repentance, or your amendment, merit enough so far to undo the sin committed, as that law cannot demand, nor justice inflict punishment for it? Or have you some blind notions of absolute mercy in God, as if he would cease to be just, rather than not be merciful to you? Men and brethren, if any or all of these false notions tempt you to be secure under the breach of the law, and under the wrath of the almighty law-giver, let us bring them to the standard of scripture, and enquire,

Fourthly, What is the penalty due to the breach of the moral law?

When God published his law, he enforced it with proper sanctions. He promised reward to the obedient — " Do this, and
" thou

" thou shalt live." And he threatened punishment to the disobedient—" In the day " that thou transgresseft, dying thou shalt " surely die." This is the rule of God's process. If you keep the law, you shall have the life promised. But if you transgress, you shall be alienated from the life of God and subject to death, to the first and to the second death, to a death of nature, and to a death of grace: for both these kinds of death are the punishment of sin: " For as " by one man sin entered into the world, " and death by sin, so death passed upon " all men, for that all have sinned:" And besides this death of the body, there is a death of the soul—" The soul that sinneth, " it shall die," Ezek. xviii. 4, it shall be alienated from the life of God for ever and ever, and shall suffer the vengeance of eternal fire; so that the broken law not only cuts you off from the fountain of life, but also pours out its curses, and inflicts real torments upon the unholy, the unjust, and the evil, according to the description in Rev. xxi. 8, " And the fearful and the unbe-
" lieving, and the abominable, and murder-
" ers, and whoremongers, and sorcerers,
" and idolaters, and all liars, shall have their
" part

"part in the lake which burneth with fire and brimstone, which is the second death."

These are the penalties which every transgressor of the law deserves, and these God has threatened to inflict. His will herein is unchangeable. His truth requires the performance of his threatenings. His justice is bound to see them inflicted. His holiness and goodness call upon justice for the immediate execution of the penalties due to sin. And how can the sinner escape? What can he do to deliver himself? He has nothing in his own power wherewith to satisfy the demands of law and justice. Suppose him sorrowful for his sin; that sorrow proves him guilty, and leaves him so. Say, he tries to repent; the law knows nothing of repentance; its language is, Do this, or thou shalt die. Grant, he amends his life for the future, yet what becomes of his past sins? Is his doing part of his duty any satisfaction for neglecting part of it? The law makes no provision for any such groundless pleas, but insists upon perfect obedience, and for the least failure puts the sinner under the curse and under the wrath

of

of God, and there leaves him to suffer the just punishment of his sin.

But some persons perhaps may object, if this be the case, what flesh can be saved? None, no, not one, can be saved by keeping the law: for all have sinned and transgressed the law of God: therefore, by the deeds of the law there shall no flesh be justified in his sight.

But still some may ask, Why then do you preach the law? Because it is a school-matter to bring men to Christ. It teaches them the nature of sin, and convinces them of their want of a Saviour. " By the law is " the knowledge of sin," Rom. iii. 20, and vii. 7. Men are secure and careless in sin, until the law, that worketh wrath, reach their consciences, then they begin to know sin, and to feel the exceeding sinfulness of it: " for it is the ministration of condemna- " tion," 2 Cor. iii. 9. The law, spiritually understood and applied, convinces the sinner that he is a condemned creature, shews him in God's word the sentence past upon him, and makes him dread the execution of it. And thus it becomes to him " the minis-
" tration

"tration of death," 2 Cor. iii. 7, proving him to be guilty of sin, and to be deserving of death. The apostle's case is very common. I thought myself alive, says he, without the law; he had no doubt but he was alive to God, while he was a strict Pharisee, but when the holy spiritual nature of the law was made known to him, he found himself to be dead in trespasses and sins. This then is the office of the law. It brings transgressors to the knowledge of sin, condemns them for it, and puts them under the sentence of death, and when the law has thus convinced them of their guilt and of their danger, they then find their want of a Saviour. But without this work of the law, they would not have been sensible that they stood in any need of him. If they were never sick, they would never send for the physician. If they were never brought to the knowledge of sin, they would never desire the knowledge of a Saviour. If they never found themselves under guilt and condemnation, they would never sue for his pardon, and would never ask life of him, unless they found that they deserved to die the first and the second death. For these reasons the law must be taught. It is the school-master

master appointed of God to bring sinners unto Christ, and when the school-master comes in the name and power of the divine Spirit, and convinces them of their distressed state and condition, and makes them sensible of their guilt and of their misery, then he brings them to Christ, earnestly to ask, and humbly to receive mercy from him, who is the end of the law for righteousness to every one that believeth.

And now, men and brethren, let us hear this school-master, who is sent from heaven to teach us a divine lesson. He speaks to you, ye careless and secure in sin, and denounces the anger of the almighty law-giver against you. Oh! with what a terrible voice does he reveal the wrath of God from heaven against all your ungodliness, and unrighteousness. There is nothing dreadful in earth or hell, nothing to be feared in time or in eternity, but what is included in this most awful sentence, " Cursed be he that confirmeth not all " the words of this law to do them." Deut. xxvii. 26. Have you done them? Have you done ALL that the law required? And in the perfect manner required? I dare appeal to your consciences. You may try to stifle
their

their evidence, but they will speak; and do they not at this very time charge you with sin? You know that you have not kept all the law, and what then is the consequence? Why, the law pronounces you cursed, and it would make your ears tingle, and your heart melt within you, if you were to consider what it is to be under the curses of the law, and to have the wrath of God abiding upon you for ever and ever. Have you no sense of these things, and no fearful apprehensions about your present condition? Is not conscience alarmed at the greatness of your danger, and do not the terrors of the law stir you up to flee from the wrath to come? If not, if all be quiet therein, while you hear the law of the most high God, which ought to convince you of your guilt and to make you apprehensive of your misery, then you are indeed sleeping the sleep of death. Oh may the God of all mercy take pity on you and awaken you! lest you should sleep on, until the curses of the law be actually inflicted, and wrath come upon you to the uttermost.

Some persons may think it happy for them that they are not careless and secure in sin; for they endeavour to keep the law as well

as

as they can, and God is a merciful God, he will forgive them, when they do amifs. This is a common, but it is a very dangerous miftake: for it fuppofes that the law can abate fomething of its demands, and can accept of an imperfect obedience. Whereas the law is the holy, juft, and good will of God, which altereth not. It requires perfect and univerfal obedience; and in cafe of the leaft tranfgreffion condemns the finner, and paffes fentence. If he plead that he never offended but in this particular inftance, that is pleading guilty. If a man be indicted for murder, and the fact be proved upon him, and he be found guilty, and the judge pafs fentence, what would it avail him if he fhould make this plea, that he had never been guilty of high-treafon? The judge would obferve to him, that he was not accufed of high-treafon, but of murder, of which he was found guilty and condemned, and his not being a traitor was no reafon why he fhould not be executed for being a murderer. So your not having broken this or that commandment cannot fave you from the juft fentence of the law, if you have broken any of them. Suppofe you are not an adulterer, yet if you are a murderer, you deferve to die, and to receive the wages of sin: "for he that said, Do not commit adultery, said also, Do not kill. Now if thou commit no adultery, yet if thou kill, thou art become a transgressor of the law." *James* ii. 11.

But some will say, Shall we not be accepted, if we endeavour to keep the law as well as we can? No. The style of the law is, Do. It does not say, Endeavour to keep the commandment, but it speaks with authority, Do it, and do it perfectly, and in every point, and with all the mind, and with all the soul, and with all the heart, and with all the strength. Here's no room left for good resolutions or good endeavours, but an actual performance of the whole law is demanded. The least failing or short coming is a transgression, and therefore is an absolute forfeiture of legal righteousness, and of every blessing promised to the perfect keeping of the law.

Some persons go a little farther than good endeavours, and think God will accept them for their sincere obedience. Whereas the law has nothing to do with sincerity. When you come to be tried by the law, the only question will be, whether you have broken

it,

it, or not ?. If not, the promised reward is yours. You may claim it as your due: for to him that worketh is the reward not reckoned of grace, but of debt. But if you have broken the law, your sincere obedience cannot be accepted in the place of perfect obedience: because the law has made no provision for your case. It requires a continual performance of all its commands, and in a perfect manner; and if you fail, and then plead your sincerity in your favour, that is owning your guilt, and is a confession of your not having continued in all things which are written in the book of the law to do them, and therefore as your sincere obedience is not perfect, it leaves you still under the curse of the law, and under the wrath of God.

There are other persons who think that there is some kind of absolute mercy in God, and that although they have sinned, yet he is ready to forgive. But this is not the character of God as drawn in the law; for the law considers him as the sovereign Lord of heaven and earth, having absolute authority to enact laws for the government of his creatures; over whom he presides with unerring justice

justice to see his laws carried into execution. Justice is the ruling attribute of the supreme law-giver. As his law is just, so are its sanctions. It is equally just in him to punish transgressors, as to reward the obedient; for the judge of all the earth cannot but do right, and distribute impartial justice. Whether he can shew mercy to the guilty, is not the question, but whether he has made any provision in his law for shewing them mercy; and he certainly has not. God is not described in the law as a God of mercy, but as a sovereign judge, whose wrath, and not whose mercy, is revealed from heaven against all ungodliness and righteousness of men.

But if the law-giver has made no promise in his law, that he will shew mercy to sinners, yet will he not be prevailed on by their sorrow and tears, their repentance and amendment? There is not one word in the law to encourage a sinner to hope for mercy, because he is sorry for his sin. It is full of threatenings against the least offence, and for the least cuts the offender off from all claim to legal righteousness. When he is in this state, what merit is there in sorrow, that it should change the laws of the most high

high God, or what efficacy in tears, that they fhould caufe him to be reputed innocent, who is in fact guilty? He has forfeited all right and title to the happinefs which the law promifed to obedience, and when he fees this, he grows forry for what he has done amifs. So does a murderer, when found guilty, and condemned to fuffer; but does the judge pardon him becaufe he is forry for his crime? By no means. But he gives figns of true forrow. He weeps bitterly. Suppofe he does, yet the law demands obedience, and not tears for difobeying. Thefe tears flow from a fenfe of guilt, and if there were rivers of them they could not wafh the ftain of guilt out of the confcience: becaufe the law has not afcribed any fuch virtue to them, as to accept of many tears for having offended, inftead of unfinning obedience. And granting he goes a ftep farther. He repents and amends. But what becomes of the broken law and of the deferved penalty? Can fimple repentance undo the fin committed? Or can amendment for the future avert the penalty already deferved? No, thefe are things impoffible. The law will have obedience or punifhment, and juftice is engaged to fee that the law be obeyed,

obeyed, and the threatened punishment inflicted; and therefore, after you have disobeyed, the law can allow no place for repentance, nor no way to escape punishment, although you seek it carefully with tears.

But if the law cannot shew the offender mercy, does it leave him without hope? Yes. It can shew him no mercy, nor does it give him any hope. It convinces him of sin, condemns him for it, and sentences him to the first and to the second death.

What! must he despair then! Of being able to attain mercy by any means in his own power he must despair—despair of working out for himself such righteousness as the law demands—despair of escaping, by any sorrow or repentance of his, the punishment which justice is bound to inflict. And when he finds himself in this guilty and helpless state, then will he be glad to hear of a Saviour. Blessed be God, there is salvation for him, who despairs of being saved by the law. To him the gospel offers a free pardon. When he flies to the gospel, seeking to be saved by free grace, then there is mercy for him and plenteous redemption. When he cries

cries out, Oh wretched man that I am! who shall deliver me from the curses of the broken law, and from the justice of an offended God? The gospel points out unto him the victorious Saviour, who hath redeemed his people from the curse of the law, being made a curse for them, and hath satisfied all the demands of his father's justice, having made reconciliation for iniquity and brought in everlasting righteousness. And therefore he can save to the uttermost. If there be any of you, whom the broken law accuses, and whom justice is pursuing to inflict the threatened punishment, fly to this almighty Saviour, and you will find in him a safe refuge. He can save you from the condemnation of the law; for there is no condemnation to them that are in Christ Jesus. And he can deliver you from the stroke of justice; for who shall lay any thing to the charge of God's elect, since it is God himself that justifieth them?

This is the great salvation set before you, who despair of being saved by the law. It is a free, full, and eternal salvation. He who has it to give, has graciously convinced you of your want of it, and has made
you

you willing to receive it as a free gift. Afk it then of him, deeply fenfible of your unworthinefs, and of your helpleffnefs, and he will incline his ear unto your petitions : for he never caft out the prayer of the poor deftitute. Afk, and ye fhall have the precious gift of faith, and great joy and peace in believing that you are redeemed from the curfe of the law, and that you are enriched with the bleffings of the gofpel. You will be made the children of God, and will receive the adoption of fons through faith in Chrift Jefus, and if fons, then you will be heirs, heirs of God, and joint heirs with Chrift of an inheritance incorruptible, and undefiled, and that fadeth not away, referved in heaven for you : which may the Father referve for you all, for the fake of his beloved Son, through the effectual grace of the Holy Spirit, that to the three perfons in one Jehovah you may be happy in afcribing equal honour and glory, and bleffing and praife for ever and ever. *Amen.*

UPON THE

CEREMONIAL LAW.

DISCOURSE III.

The Song of Solomon, iv. 6.

Until the day break and the shadows flee away, I will get me to the mountain of myrrh, and to the hill of frankincense.

AFTER man had broken the moral law, and had fallen into a helpless state of guilt and misery, it pleased God to reveal the covenant of grace. As soon as the way to salvation was stopt by the law, he opened a new and living way by the gospel. The Messiah was promised, and the rites and ceremonies were instituted, which were to represent what he was to be, and to do do for the salvation of men. "Which things were a shadow, but the body, or substance, was Christ." They were expressive figures and shadows of his actions and sufferings, and in them the religion of the gospel was delineated to the senses of the believer. This law of ceremonies was revealed upon the fall, and afterwards republished in writing by *Moses*. It had God for its author, and was established by his divine authority, and therefore it deserves our particular consideration.

In my last discourse I endeavoured to explain the scope and design of the moral law, and to prove that by its works no flesh can be justified in the sight of God. The next body of law is the ceremonial, which preached salvation from the pains and penalties incurred by the breach of the moral law. It held forth this doctrine under a great variety of types and figures, and taught it in many plain passages. The words, which I have read, contain the Messiah's own sentiments of this subject. The commentators allow him to be the speaker, and he is addressing himself to the believer, with whom he holds sweet and spiritual discourse in this

this divine treatife. He particularly informs them, where he vouchfafed his prefence, and would be found of them that fought him, fo long as the ceremonial law was in force. Until the day break, fays he, until the day of my firft coming in the flefh fhall dawn, and the fhadows flee away, the types and fhadows of the law fhall vanifh, I will get me to the mountain of myrrh and to the hill of frankincenfe, to the mountain of the Lord's houfe, even to the holy hill of Sion, and there I will be fpiritually prefent in the temple fervice; I will there give my blefling to the ordinances, and will make them the means of grace: whatever your wants may be, apply to me in thefe inftituted means, and you will find an abundant fupply: for until the day break and the fhadows flee away, &c.

The confideration of this paffage will, I hope, by the affiftance of God, help us to comprehend the fcope and defign of the ceremonial law. And may the Holy Spirit, who infpired thefe words, accompany our prefent meditation upon them, that we may,

Firft,

First, Clearly underſtand their true ſenſe and meaning, and

Secondly, May be eſtabliſhed in the doctrine which they contain.

There are many parts of the ſong hard to be underſtood, eſpecially by the unlearned and unſtable, who wreſt it, as they do alſo the other ſcriptures, to their own deſtruction. But the paſſage which we have now before us is very eaſy. There is no difficulty in it to perſons, who have a little acquaintance with the ſcripture manner of writing, which conſtantly uſes and accommodates natural things to explain ſpiritual, ſuiting its inſtructions to man's preſent embodied ſtate, in which he cannot ſee the things of grace, but through the glaſs of nature. The language of the Old Teſtament is entirely of this kind. Every Hebrew word has a literal ſenſe, and ſtands for ſome ſenſible object, and thereby gives us a comparative idea of ſome ſpiritual object. As this is the nature of the language, ſo is it alſo of the ſubject-matter of the book of *Canticles*. It is drawn up in the manner of a dialogue, in which outward and material things are uſed to repreſent inward and ſpiritual things. This way of writing is very

abſtruſe

abstruse to them, who have not the senses of their souls exercised to discern the things of God, but to them who have, it is an easy book. He that runs may read it, if he has but a little acquaintance with the scripture-language, and some of that love in his heart, of which this book treats: for it is a song of loves, setting forth the mutual affection between Christ and the believer, who is united to him by saving faith. And in the words of my text, Christ informs the believer where he might at all times find his presence. He would be spiritually present, in the services and ceremonies of the temple. By these he would convey grace and strength to his faithful people, until his coming in the flesh.

Until the day break. The scripture mentions two days by way of eminence, and distinguishes them by two of the greatest events, which the Redeemer's love and power are to produce, the day of Christ's first coming, and the day of his second coming. The day of his first coming in the flesh is here spoken of—the day which *Abraham* earnestly desired to see, and which is often mentioned in the prophets under the expressions, " of the day of the Lord, or of the day of
" our

"our God," and sometimes it is very emphatically stiled "that day," that day's wonders raising it above all days from the beginning to the end of time. And in the New Testament our Lord calls it *my* day, the day of my incarnation, when I *Jehovah* should take a body of flesh, and God and man should be one Christ. This day many prophets and kings desired to see; for God manifest in the flesh was the foundation of their faith and hopes. They longed to see this day break, and to behold the sun of righteousness with his saving and healing influences arising upon the earth, and when he did arise, we find those, who were then looking for redemption, singing his praises with grateful hearts, "Blessed be the Lord "God of *Israel*, through whose tender mercy "the day-spring from on high hath visited "us;" they blessed God, because the substance was now to take place of the shadow, and all the legal ceremonies were to be succeeded by gospel realities. When the glorious day of Christ's appearance in the flesh was come, and the light of life was risen upon the earth, then

The shadows were to flee away. The legal ceremonies are called shadows in scripture, because they were the outward and visible signs of inward and spiritual objects. St. *Paul* says, the ceremonial law " had the sha- " dow of good things to come," *Heb.* x. 1. of the good things which are now come to us by the advent of Christ, and it had the patterns and examples of heavenly things; every one of which had God for its author, and was instituted by him to be an apt figure, and to raise a just idea of some spiritual object; as *Moses* was admonished of God, when he was about to make the tabernacle. " For " see, saith he, that thou make all things " according to the pattern shewed to thee " in the mount."—Every rite and ceremony was a pattern of some heavenly object, the real existence of which the pattern proved, as a shadow proves the reality of the substance from which it is cast, and the resemblance and likeness of which it set before the eyes, as the shadow of a body is a representation of it. The scripture has expressly determined, what all these shadows were to represent: for the Apostle, speaking of them in *Col.* ii. 17. declares " that they " were the shadow of things to come, but " the

"the body is of Chrift." Chrift is the reality of all the fhadows of the law the body, the fubftance, of whom they the pictures. If you take away their reference to him, they ceafe to be examples and fhadows of heavenly things; but if you fuppofe them to reprefent him and his actions, and fufferings, &c. then they anfwered many noble purpofes, until he came in the flefh to fulfil them: for then thefe fhadows were to flee away, one great end of their inftitution being anfwered. The obfervance of them was to be no longer in force; but they were to be entirely repealed and abrogated. However until this bleffed day fhould break, and thefe legal fhadows fhould thus flee away, the text fays they were to ferve a double purpofe, they were firft to be the outward and vifible figns of the inward and fpiritual grace given unto us, and ordained by Chrift himfelf, to be fecondly a means whereby we receive the fame, and a pledge to affure us thereof. This is plainly implied in the laft words of the text, in which Chrift declares, that until the ceremonies were fulfilled by his coming in the flefh, he would be fpiritually prefent in them.

I will

I will get me to the mountain of myrrh, and to the hill of frankincense. Where was this mountain of myrrh? Was it not the place in which the Lord was present, until the shadows were fled away? And where was he present but in the services of the ceremonial law, which could not be performed any where, when the text was spoken; but in the temple? There the Lord had put his name; and had sanctified the house by the presence of his glory. " I have chosen, " says the Lord, 2 *Chron.* vii. 16. and sanc- " tified this house, that my Name may be " there for ever, and mine eyes; and mine " heart shall be there perpetually:" there will I receive the sacrifices which I have forbidden to be offered any where else, there will I accept of the prayers of the faithful offerer, and there will I dwell between the Cherubim with visible tokens of my divine presence and glory. As he chose the people of *Israel* out of all the nations of the earth to be his people, so he chose his sanctuary in *Judah*, and the holy hill of *Sion* to be his dwelling place, manifesting his presence there in such a manner as he did no where else in the world; and therefore we may infer that when Christ says, I will get me to the mountain of myrrh, until the

shadows

shadows flee away, he certainly meant the mountain of the Lord's house. And the *Hebrew* word justifies this inference: for the word rendered myrrh is the very same root with *Moriah*, the mount upon which the temple stood. I will get me, says Christ, to the mountain of *Moriah*, and there will I dwell, because I have a delight therein. So that we have here a plain testimony of Christ's presence in the ceremonial services performed upon mount *Moriah*. In these he was to be found of them that sought him, until the day of his manifestation in the flesh. And the meaning of the word seems to me farther to confirm this interpretation: for it signifies *bitterness*, what is bitter to the taste, and bitter to the spirit, grievous and hard to be borne; and what was there to be seen or done upon mount *Moriah* to render this its proper name? Look at the chief part of the temple-service, and then judge. It consisted in making gifts and sacrifices for sin, in which you may behold a striking picture of the bitter sufferings of the lamb of God. In the sacrifices were represented every day things more bitter than death, the shedding of his blood, and the taking away of his life. He made his soul an offering for sin,

and

and to satisfy the infinite demands of law and justice. His agony and bloody sweat, his cross and passion shew what bitter things the Father had written against him. These were represented in the roasting of the paschal lamb with fire, and in the eating it with bitter herbs. And when Christ, our passover, was sacrificed for us, and really underwent the fire of the Father's wrath, there never was any sorrow like unto that sorrow, which forced him to cry out, in the bitterness of his soul, " My God, my God, why " hast thou forsaken me ?"

If all these circumstances be laid together they will evidently determine the place of Christ's presence while the ceremonial law was in force. He was spiritually present in the temple-service, to render the sacrifices and the other typical rites the means of grace, and effectual to the ends for which they were instituted : for after the moral law was broken, there was no way to salvation but faith in the promised Saviour, and the necessity of faith in him was taught by the services of the ceremonial law, as it is written, " thro' " faith they kept the passover," they acted faith upon Christ in the passover: they flew and roasted the paschal lamb with fire, and eat it with bitter herbs, knowing it to be a type of the future sacrifice of the lamb of God, of the benefits of whose death they were then, through faith, partakers. They found his spiritual presence strengthening and refreshing their souls at the passover, as we do now at the Lord's supper, and they knew that through his merits and mediation their persons and their services were acceptable to God the Father, which is, I think, the sense of the last words of the text,

I will get me to the hill of frankincense.

This is the same place mentioned before, only described by another name, to express a different property. Incense was, by divine command, a chief part of the temple-service. As the sacrifices offered in the temple were to represent the death of Christ, so the incense there offered was to represent the sweet favour of his meritorious death, which alone could reconcile God to sinners, and could render them and their services well-pleasing in his sight: and therefore that rich perfume, mentioned *Exod.* xxx. which was the type of the sweet incense of Christ's merits,

rits, was forbid, upon pain of death, to be used upon any other occasion, than in the service of God, and in any other place, than in the tabernacle at that time, and afterwards in the temple. The command is, *ver.* 36, "Thou shalt put of it before the testimony, in the tabernacle of the congregation, where I will meet with thee: it shall be unto you most holy, *ver.* 38. Whosoever shall make like unto that, to smell thereto, shall even be cut off from his people." This was to shew, that God the Father is seen to be propitious to sinners, only through the merits of his Son's sacrifice, and that he who seeks to be accepted in any other way or means, shall die in his sins. The incense then was a type of Christ's meritorious death, and the hill of frankincense was the holy hill of *Sion*, upon which incense used to be offered, and a pure offering. The offering was that great sacrifice of the lamb of God, shadowed out by all the sacrifices slain from the foundation of the world, and the incense was to represent the efficacy of his sacrifice. It is said of the typical offerings, that the Lord smelled a sweet favour, how much more was he pleased with the offering and sacrifice of Christ, which was indeed

indeed a sweet-smelling savour, acceptable and well-pleasing unto God?

But how was Christ present in the offering up of the incense? It was his institution, and he was spiritually present to render it effectual to the ends, for which he instituted it. He appointed it to be one of the means of grace; for he taught believers by this ceremony, that he could make them and their services acceptable to the offended Deity, and by his Spirit he gave them the comfortable knowledge of their acceptance. When therefore he mentions his presence on the hill of frankincense, it is as if he had said, When the high priest enters once every year at the great feast of atonement into the holy of holies, and there fumes the incense before the Cherubim of glory, and sprinkles the blood before the mercy seat, I will then enable believers to act faith upon my future fulfilling and realizing of this service: for after my sacrifice upon earth, I will enter into the holy of holies, and will there plead my merits before the mercy-seat in heaven, and by my all-prevailing intercession will render the persons and the services of believers well pleasing unto God the Father.

Thus

Thus Christ was present upon the hill of frankincense, and there the faithful expected to meet with him; for while the priest was offering up the incense in the temple, the people used to be at prayers without, hoping that the angel of the covenant, who had much incense given to him to offer it up with the prayers of all the saints upon the golden altar which was before the throne, would make the smoke of the incense ascend up with their prayers before God. In this hope we find the whole multitude of the people (*Luke* i. 10.) praying without at the time that *Zacharias* was burning the incense in the temple of the Lord.

From the sense and meaning of the words as thus in part opened and explained, the following doctrine may be established. Upon the breach of the moral law, the ceremonial law was instituted to prefigure the promised Messiah and his actions and sufferings, and to preach forgiveness of sins through him. Until the day of his coming in the flesh, the ceremonies served as shadows to raise ideas of him, and as means of grace to support the faith and hopes of his people: they were outward and visible signs of inward and spiritual grace in the very same manner as the sacraments are at present, signing and sealing to believers the benefits purchased by the obedience and sufferings of the lamb of God. This is the doctrine which I purposed, under my second general head, to establish.

The whole volume of scripture considers the ceremonial law in this same point of view. It was the scope and design of the Old Testament to reveal to sinners the covenant of grace, and to teach them how they might attain pardon for their breach of the moral law. Upon the first breach of it, the Messiah was promised, and the rites and services of the ceremonial law were instituted, to keep up faith and hopes in him, until his coming in the flesh; for they shewed what he was to be, and to do, and to suffer. The New Testament relates the accomplishment of the Old, proving *Jesus* of *Nazareth* to be the promised Messiah, and declaring how he did and suffered every thing prefigured by the types, and foretold by the prophets. Both testaments therefore treat of one and the same subject, namely of the way and method by which the transgressors of the moral law may be delivered from the guilt and punishment

ment, which they have incurred. This is the opinion of our church in her sixth article. " The Old Testament is not contrary to the " new, for both in the Old and New Testa- " ment everlasting life is offered to mankind " by *Jesus Christ*." The everlasting life forfeited by the breach of the moral law is offered to mankind in the Old Testament as well as in the New, and offered by the same Saviour, *Jesus Christ*, and offered by the same gospel of the grace of God: " for unto us, " says the apostle (*Heb.* iv. 2.) was the gospel " preached, as well as unto them." He is speaking of the *Israelites*, who, after their deliverance from *Egypt*, perished in the wilderness through unbelief, and he says, that what is preached unto us, was preached unto them. They had the same gospel which *Paul* preached, and what it was he thus informs the *Corinthians*, I declare unto you the gospel which I preached unto you, how that Christ died for our sins, according to the scriptures, and that he was buried, and that he rose again the third day, according to the scriptures. This is our gospel, and it was theirs under the Old Testament dispensation. Believers then had the same faith that we have, in the same Saviour. The gospel preach-

ed to them the coming of Chrift, his fufferings and death for their fins, and his refurrection; they believed he would come, and we believe he is come. In this fingle circumftance their gofpel differs from ours. Our reformers, in the fecond part of the *Homily* upon faith, fpeaking of the fathers, martyrs, and other holy men mentioned *Heb.* xi. have thefe remarkable words: " They did not only
" know God to be the Lord, maker, and go-
" vernor of all men in the world; but alfo
" they had a fpecial confidence and truft,
" that he was, and would be, their God, their
" comforter, aider, helper, maintainer, and
" defender. This is the Chriftian faith which
" thefe holy men had, and which we alfo
" ought to have, and although they were
" not named Chriftian men, yet was it a
" Chriftian faith that they had; for they
" looked for all the benefits of God the Fa-
" ther through the merits of his Son *Jefus*
" *Chrift*, as we do now. This difference is
" between them and us, that they looked
" when Chrift fhould come, and we be in the
" time when he is come; therefore, faith St.
" *Auguftine,* the time is altered and changed,
" but not the faith." Faith was always the fame. Ever fince the moral law was firft broken,

broken, there has been but one gospel, which preached salvation by one Lord, and one faith.

If you ask, How was it preached to the holy men of old? It was revealed to them by many plain prophecies ("for the testi- "mony of the *Jesus* is the Spirit of pro- "phecy") and by many significant types and expressive ceremonies; under which Christ was as clearly preached as he is under the sacraments of the New Testament: for all these were memorials, instituted on pur- pose to keep him in memory, and they were patterns serving as copies to convey ideas of their originals, according to what is written, *Exod.* xxv. 40. And look, says God to *Moses*, that thou make them, namely, the tabernacle and all its vessels, after their pattern, which was shewed thee in the mount; they were the patterns of heavenly things, as St. *Paul*, rea- soning upon this passage, has assured us, *Heb.* viii. 5. "Who serve unto the example and "shadow of heavenly things, as *Moses* was "admonished of God, when he was about "to make the tabernacle: for see, saith he, "that thou make all things according to the "pattern shewed to thee in the mount."

Here

Here is a plain description of the scope and design of the ceremonial law. An infallible interpreter assures us, that it served for an example and shadow of heavenly things. Its ceremonies were examples to set these heavenly things before men's eyes, and to raise ideas of them, and they were shadows to delineate them, and to give an outward sketch of them, and they were patterns like a good plan or design, representing them clearly and distinctly. This was the nature of the types; they were instituted to prefigure the heavenly things which were to be in Christ, and which were to be derived from him to believers.

In this sense Christ was present upon mount *Moriah*. He was there in the types and services. These were his representatives. They stood for him, and acted in his name, and by his authority were deputed to declare his gracious intentions towards the transgressors of the moral law: for they all preached Christ, and salvation through his infinitely meritorious sacrifice. The whole temple-service represented him in this light: for the temple itself was the type and figure of his body. Our Lord himself calls it so, so. " Deſtroy this temple, and in three days I will build it up." *John* ii. 19. But he ſpake, ſays St. *John*, of the temple of his body, of the true tabernacle which the Lord pitched and not man. And herein he ſpake agreeably to the well-known uſage of ſcripture, which calls the type and the thing typified by the ſame name. The temple was the type of his body, and every part of its furniture was a type and figure of what was to be in the humanity of the incarnate God. All its veſſels were apt figures and beautiful pictures of thoſe divine graces which were in him, and which believers were to receive out of his fulneſs. The holy place repreſented what he was to do upon earth, the holy of holies repreſented what he was to do in heaven for his people. At the entrance of the holy place ſtood the laver filled with water, with which the prieſts were to waſh, when they went in and came out of the temple. This was to ſet forth the infinitely purifying virtue which was in Chriſt, and with which he was to cleanſe ſinners from the pollution of ſin, as he ſays in the prophet; " Then will " I ſprinkle clean water upon you, and ye " ſhall be clean: from all your filthineſs " and from all your idols will I cleanſe you." *Ezek*. xxxvi. 25. Next to the laver ſtood

the

the altar of burnt-offering, on which the blood of the sacrifice was offered, hereby was represented the all-meritorious blood of the lamb of God, which alone taketh away the guilt of sin. On one side of the holy place stood the candlestick, with its lamps always burning, to represent that divine light which came into the world, that he who followeth it should not walk in darkness, but should have the light of life. On the other side stood the table of shew-bread, the figure of that bread of God, which came down from heaven, and of which if any man eat, he shall live for ever. At the upper end of the holy place, next the veil, stood the altar of incense, to represent the sweet-smelling favour of Christ's sacrifice, through faith in which the transgressors of the moral law are reconciled to God the Father, and rendered acceptable and well pleasing in his sight.

The most holy place, or the holy of holies, was the figure of heaven, and what was done in it once a year by the high-priest was to represent what our great high-priest does in heaven for us and for our salvation. This doctrine is very clearly taught in several parts of the epistle to the *Hebrews*. Thus we read that,

that, "into the second tabernacle went the high-priest alone once every year not without blood, which he offered for himself, and for the errors of the people. The Holy Ghost this signifying, that the way into the holiest of all was not yet made manifest, while as the first tabernacle was yet standing: which was a figure for the time then present." *Heb.* ix. 7, 8, 9. And what the Holy Ghost signified by this service could not but be known, while the tabernacle and temple stood, because it was a figure for the time then present. The 9th chapter and great part of the 10th treat entirely of this subject. The high-priest was the type of Christ, our great intercessor. His going in once a year into the holy of holies was the figure of Christ's appearing once in the end of the world, and opening a new and living way for us into the holiest. His carrying blood to sprinkle upon the mercy seat, and incense to fume before the Cherubim of glory was to represent Christ's pleading the merits of his blood at the throne of grace, which was an odour of a sweet smell, a sacrifice well pleasing and acceptable to the Holy Trinity. The high-priests coming out of the holy of holies to bless the people, was the figure of

Christ's

Chrift's coming from the holieft to blefs his people with an everlafting blefling—" Come "ye blefled of my Father, inherit the king- "dom prepared for you from the foundation "of the world."

It appears then, from all thefe authorities, that the ceremonial law preached Chrift, and falvation through him from the guilt and punifhment incurred by the breach of the moral law. All its fervices prefigured him, and were lively and expreffive pictures of what he was to be, and to do, and to fuffer, in order to make an atonement for fin. His facrifice for this purpofe was reprefented by all the typical facrifices: for without fhed- ding of blood there was no remiffion, and it was not poffible that the blood of bulls and of goats fhould take away fins; therefore be- lievers hoped for remiffion through his moft precious blood, and facrificed in faith, rely- ing on the future offering of the lamb of God. So that it was plainly the fcope and defign of the ceremonial law to preach re- miffion of fins through the fhedding of blood. When any perfon had offended, and his con- fcience accufed him of fin, he was required to bring his facrifice to the prieft, and to lay

his

his hands upon its head and to confefs his fins over it: after this its life was to be taken away and its blood fhed inftead of the finners life. And this was to be done, even when a perfon had offended through ignorance. But in what did the merit of the facrifice confift? Did its blood take away fin? No. It was not poffible the blood of bulls and of goats fhould do that. The facrifice was only a memorial inftituted to bring the Meffiah into mind, as if he had faid, Do this in remembrance of me, remembering in every facrifice the future facrifice of the lamb of God; and believers did remember him. When they eat of the pafchal lamb, by faith they difcerned the Lord's body, and enjoyed communion with Chrift, our paffover, as we do now at the Lord's fupper. They found him prefent in the ordinances, according to his moft true promife in the text. Until the day dawn, fays he, the great day of my appearing in the flefh, and the fhadows flee away, the fhadows of the ceremonial law be realized and fulfilled in my life, obedience, fufferings, death, refurrection, and afcenfion, until thefe things be, I will be fpiritually prefent upon mount *Moriah*, in the temple worfhip, and upon the hill of frankincenfe, to render the persons and the services of my people well-pleasing and acceptable unto God the Father.

Since then it was the scope and design of the ceremonial law to prefigure Christ under its expressive types and shadows, do you, my brethren, look upon it in this light? Are you convinced, that the Old Testament contains the gospel, and the evidence for its doctrines? And have you read it carefully, in order to collect this evidence, and to establish yourselves in your most holy faith? Or, instead of making this use of the Old Testament, have you greatly neglected it, supposing it to contain a religion different from Christianity? This is the opinion of too many among us. But it is very unscriptural. The New Testament is so far from being contrary to, that it is in perfect harmony with, the Old. They both preach one gospel, one Saviour, and one faith: for both in the Old and New Testament everlasting life is offered to mankind by *Jesus Christ*. And this life by him was preached by the ceremonies of the Old Testament, as well as by the sacraments of the New, with only this difference, the New is the fulfilling of the Old; the Old Testament

promises

promises the Messiah should come and dwell among men, and the New proves that he did come, and that God has been manifest in the flesh. Consider what has been said at present in proof of this point. Weigh it carefully; and then I hope you will read the Old Testament with great pleasure and profit, finding it testifying throughout of Christ, and of salvation through him.

But what have we to do, may some say, with the *Jewish* types and ceremonies? Are they not all now repealed and abrogated? Yes. Christ has fulfilled them, even to the least jot and tittle; but they still stand upon record to teach us what he was to fulfil. They still continue to bear evidence for Christ, although the observance of them hath ceased; therefore we are still concerned to search what witness they bear of him. " Search " the scriptures, says Christ, for these are " they which testify of me." There were no scriptures, when he spake this, but the Old Testament, and it testified of Christ. It did bear witness of him, by its types, for they were shadows of good things to come, of which Christ is the body, and by its prophecies, for the testimony of *Jesus* is the spirit of prophecy. This testimony it still bears, witnessing to us what Christ was to be, and to do, and to suffer, as the New Testament witnesses to us that *Jesus* of *Nazareth* was the promised Messiah: for he was, and did, and suffered what the Old Testament had foretold. Thus they mutually support each other. The Old Testament looks forward to the accomplishment of its ceremonies and prophecies, referring its readers to some person, who was to fulfil the law and the prophets, and the New Testament proves *Jesus* of *Nazareth* to be the person; and thus all the scriptures testify of him.

If you ask in what particular respect does the ceremonial law testify of him? It considers him chiefly in this point of view. The moral law being broken, and the transgressors of it being under guilt and liable to punishment, Christ was proposed to them by the types as the sacrifice and atonement for their sins. All the sacrifices pointed at his sacrifice, and the atonement made by them had no merit, but what was derived by faith from his all-perfect atonement: for he was the lamb fore-ordained to be slain by the

the covenant of the ever-blessed Trinity, which was made before the foundation of the world, and he was the lamb typically slain from the foundation of the world in all the sacrifices after the fall, and slain really in the fulness of time, when he appeared to put away sin by the sacrifice of himself. In this respect all the sacrifices pointed to the lamb of God, referring the transgressors of the moral law to his most precious blood, without the shedding of which there could be no remission: because it was not possible that the blood of beasts could take away sin.

Upon this state of the doctrine there arises an important question, in which, my brethren, you are all nearly concerned, namely, Whether you look upon Christ in the same light that the ceremonial law places him. All the ceremonies pointed to him, and when any one had offended against the moral law, the ceremonial law required him to bring his sacrifice to make an atonement for his sin: for without shedding of blood there was no remission; and thus he was taught to hope for remission only through the shedding of the blood of the lamb of God.

God. Now, my brethren, Do you act as the ceremonial law enjoins? Are you convinced of your offences against the moral law, and sensible of your guilt, and apprehensive of your danger? Have you put your trust in the sacrifice of the immaculate lamb of God? Have you placed all your hopes of pardon on the merits of his most precious blood? If not, What besides can you rely upon? You have sinned, and the wages of sin is death. The almighty law-giver has declared, that you shall die—" The soul " that sinneth, it shall die." Under this sentence you lie, as to any thing you can do, either to respite it or to revoke it, until it be executed upon you. Your life is forfeited, and you must die the death. And while justice spares you, how do you resolve to act? You hear there is a Saviour, and redemption in his blood. He laid down his life, and died to purchase life for all transgressors, who will come unto him for it: either, therefore, you must receive life of him, or die. Consider then seriously, which of these two is your choice. Which would you have; life or death? If you refuse to come to Christ for life, you must die. Your blood must be shed, and your soul must perish;

rish: for the Lord God, who cannot lie, hath spoken, that without shedding of blood there is no remission; unless, therefore, you are saved by the blood of Christ, there is no remission for you. You must die in your sins.

But if you seek to be saved by the blood of Christ, and desire the life purchased by his death, you have all possible encouragement to hope for his favour. He has begun, and he must carry on the work. Wait upon him then for his grace in the ways of his appointment, and you will find him still present in them. Seek his face in prayer. Hope to find his good Spirit in hearing and reading his word, and continue thus in his service, and he will give you to experience the truth of the doctrine preached by the ceremonial law. All its sacrifices taught remission of sin through blood, and all pointed to the bleeding lamb of God, and to his atonement; and, by faith, believers of old received the benefit of his atonement, as we do at present: for by faith they kept the passover and the sprinkling of blood, lest he that destroyed the first-born in *Egypt* should touch them. Wait upon God, and he will enable you also to act faith upon Christ your passover, and when his blood has been sprinkled upon your heart, the destroying angel cannot then touch you. This blood will keep you from death and from him that hath the power of death. Through faith in it, you will live in the comfortable knowledge of what this scripture means, " He " that believeth in me, says Christ, though " he were dead, yet shall he live, and who- " soever liveth and believeth in me shall " never die," (*John* xi. 25, 26.) Happy are they who thus believe and live in him. They have redemption in his blood, even the forgiveness of sins, and they are passed from death unto life. They know the infinite value of his atonement, not only for the forgiveness of their past offences against the moral law, but also for their present failings. They want the benefit of his most precious blood every day: for all that they do wants to be cleansed in the fountain, which was opened for sin and for uncleanness. They are forced to bring their very duties to be cleansed here: because these do not come up to the perfect demands of the moral law. There are short comings in their most holy things, for which they want an atonement.

Oh

Oh how precious then muſt the blood of Chriſt be to ſuch perſons! With what love will their hearts burn towards him? With what gratitude will they ſerve him? How dear will the ordinances be to them, ſince there they find their Lord ſpiritually preſent, comforting, ſtrengthening, and eſtabliſhing their hearts. Theſe perſons want no arguments to perſuade them to a conſtant attendance upon the ordinances: for they know that they ſhall in them find him, whom their ſoul longeth for, and ſhall in them enjoy ſweet communion with him, until the day of glory break, and the earthly ſhadows flee away. Then they ſhall ſee him face to face, and ſhall be for ever happy with their Lord. Oh that this happineſs may be yours and mine. Grant it, Holy Father, for thy dear Son's ſake, to whom, with the eternal Spirit, three perſons in one Jehovah, be equal honour and glory, praiſe and worſhip for ever and ever. *Amen.*

UPON THE

LAW of FAITH.

DISCOURSE IV.

Romans iii. 27.

Where is boasting then? It is excluded. By what law? of works? Nay, but by the law of faith.

HAVING already considered the nature of the moral and of the ceremonial law, I am now to treat of the law of faith mentioned in my text. The moral law is the holy, just, and good will of God, to which he required, and does require, perfect obedience: for his will is like himself, always one and the same without variableness, or shadow of turning: but there is no salvation now to be expected from this law, because all have

sinned

sinned against it, and are liable to the threatened penalties. Upon the first breach of it God was graciously pleased to reveal the ceremonial law, the design and scope of which was to point out the promised Messiah, and to be the means of grace to the people of God: for by its services, which were shadows and types of Christ, and of the good things to come through him, the eye of faith was kept looking earnestly upon him, and waiting for the happy time, when the day should break and the shadows flee away, and he should come in the flesh, to deliver his people from the curses of the moral law. At the end of 4000 years he came, and having fulfilled the ceremonial law, and accomplished every thing signified by its typical services, it was then repealed, and the law of faith alone was established, by which believers have been saved from the beginning, and are to be saved to the end of the world.

If we take a short view of the Apostle's reasoning in this chapter, we shall easily discover what this law of faith is. He is treating of the corruption of mankind, of the *Jews* as well as of the *Gentiles*, and he proves that they

they are all under fin: for they have all broken the moral law, and are guilty in the fight of God, and are thereby become abfolutely incapable of ever attaining inherent legal righteoufnefs. After the moral law has been once broken, it can never afterwards juftify the finner: becaufe it requires perfect uninterrupted obedience, and allows of no failing, no not in thought. Its ftyle and language is—" Do this, and thou fhalt live,"—" If "thou tranfgrefs, dying thou fhalt furely " die." And when any one tranfgrefles, it knows nothing of mercy, nor has made any provifion for pardon, but calls aloud for juftice to inflict the deferved punifhment. And fince all men have tranfgrefled, therefore the Apoftle concludes, that by the deeds of the law there fhall no flefh be juftified in the fight of God. Thus every mouth is ftopped, and all the world is become guilty before God. But now the righteoufnefs of God without the law is manifefted in the covenant of grace, in which the honour and dignity of the moral law is fecured, and a wonderful way is revealed, whereby the finner may be pardoned, and infinite juftice may be glorified in fhewing him mercy. The Lord Chrift being God equal with the Father

ther freely covenanted to take man's nature; and in it to act and suffer as his reprefentative, to pay the law perfect and infinitely meritorious obedience, and to endure fatisfactory and infinitely meritorious fufferings, yea, to bear the wrath, and to die the death, which man deferved, and thus he wrought out an all-perfect righteoufnefs, even the righteoufnefs of God, which is by faith of *Jefus Chrift* unto all and upon all them that believe. And this method of juftifying finners by his being made fin for us, who knew no fin, that we might be made the righteoufnefs of God in him, is thus opened and explained by the Apoftle in the words going before the text. All have finned, fays he, and come fhort of the glory of God, being juftified freely by his grace, and if by grace, then it is not by works, but it is all a free gift through the redemption that is in *Chrift Jefus*, whom God hath fet forth to be a propitiation through faith in his blood, his blood made the propitiation, and faith applies and receives it, and thereby declares the righteoufnefs of God for the remiffion of fins that are paft. And in this way of juftifying finners through the righteoufnefs of the Lord Chrift, God the Father proves himfelf to be be juft, and the juftifier of him who is of the faith of Jefus. He vindicates his juftice and the honour of his law, and thefe being fecured, he can then juftify him that is ungodly, if he believe in Jefus: for then his faith will be imputed unto him for righteoufnefs.

When the carnal man hears this doctrine, he is apt to take offence at it. He has fuch a high opinion of himfelf, and of his own boafted abilities, that he cannot conceive how God fhould juftify finners by his free grace, without any of their works and merit, and he is ready to afk, What! muft I do nothing towards my juftification? No. You can do nothing: becaufe while your fins are unpardoned, you are under fentence of death. You are dead in law, and you can no more do any act that is good and valid in the court of heaven, than a condemned criminal can do any act that is good and valid in one of our courts of juftice. What! am I not to work out, fays he, and to merit fome part of my juftification? No, none at all. The fcripture gives all the glory to God, that it may cut off all boafting from man; for if God juftify finners

ners freely by faith, without any works, where is boasting then, says the Apostle? Man would have room to boast, if he was justified wholly by his own works, or partly by faith, and partly by his works; if *Abraham* were justified by works he hath whereof to glory; but since he is justified entirely by free grace, through faith, in the righteousness of another, all boasting is excluded. By what law? By the law of works? No, by the works of the law shall no flesh be justified, and therefore no flesh can boast: for how absurd would it be to boast of the works of that law, which brings sinners in guilty and condemns them? But all boasting is excluded by the law of faith; for faith receives justification freely from *Jesus Christ*, without any merit or works of man, and therefore is obliged to give all the glory to God; so that faith effectually excludes boasting, and the law of faith, the obligation that a sinner is under to go out of himself for righteousness, and to believe in the righteousness of another, in order to his being justified, still farther excludes boasting; for the Lord God has made a decree, and heaven and earth shall pass away rather than it shall

not

not be carried into execution, that a sinner shall be justified no other way, but by faith. This is the law of the most high God, which he hath revealed from heaven, that ye believe in him, whom he hath sent, for righteousness. Under this law we now live, and by it only can we be saved, and may he, who teacheth man wisdom, teach you the nature of it. May he accompany with his grace and blessing what I shall observe from the text,

First, Concerning the law of faith, and

Secondly, In defence of the Apostle's doctrine, and

Thirdly, By way of application.

As to the first head, the Apostle has thus explained the law of faith. The moral law is still in force, but there is no salvation by it: because it requires perfect uninterrupted obedience, and will not allow of the least failing, no not in thought. If you offend once, you have lost all claim to legal righteousness for ever; so that by the works of the moral law no flesh can be justified, since all have sinned and come short of the glory of God. And as the moral law cannot save the sinner, neither can the ceremonial: for it is now repealed. Christ the substance is come, and has fulfilled all the legal types. These shadows of good things are now fled away, and to observe them at present would be denying that Christ has been manifested in the flesh, and has completed them. And therefore since the moral law brings us all in guilty, and condemns us for transgressing it, and the observance of the ceremonial law is now repealed, there remains only the law of faith, by which a guilty sinner can be saved. This way of salvation by faith is established by law. The Lord God has made a decree, and has enacted, by his sovereign authority, that he who with his heart believeth unto righteousness shall be saved. This is the great charter of heaven, by which all the divine graces and blessings of time and of eternity are conveyed to transgressors. The law of faith says to them, you have broken the moral law, and are under sentence of condemnation, but behold the lamb of God, believe in him, and you shall be be juſtified. And thus the law of faith takes a poor ſinner off from working and ſtriving to merit his juſtification, and requires him only to believe what Chriſt has done and ſuffered for him and in his ſtead. It commands him to rely entirely upon the righteouſneſs of the Lord Chriſt for his pardon and acceptance with God the Father. This is the only way of juſtification now eſtabliſhed by law. All other ways are illegal, and are expreſsly forbidden by a divine ſtatute in this caſe made and provided, in which are theſe words—" Therefore we " conclude, that a man is juſtified by faith " without the deeds of the law," either moral or ceremonial. The moral law is broken and it condemns him, and the ceremonial law is repealed, therefore we conclude, that he cannot be juſtified but by the law of faith ; and by this he is obliged and bound to accept of juſtification by believing, and not by working, ſo that if he ſeek to enter into life, he muſt keep this commandment, he muſt renounce all merit of his works, all righteouſneſs of his own, and accept of the Saviour's righteouſneſs as a free gift, and have it, by faith, imputed to him for his juſtification. This is the law of faith,

faith, upon which the scripture is very full. The Apostle has discussed this point at large in his epistles to the *Romans* and to the *Galatians*. In the third chapter of the *Romans*, he proves both *Jews* and *Gentiles*, that they are all under sin and guilt, and cannot by any of their own works be justified before God; and then he speaks of the manner of their justification, which is freely by grace, through the redemption that is in *Christ Jesus*, whom God hath set forth to be a propitiation through faith in his blood to declare his righteousness. In the fourth chapter, he proceeds to illustrate this doctrine from the case of *Abraham*, who believed God, and it was imputed unto him for righteousness. Now unto him that worketh, the reward is not reckoned of grace, but of debt. But to him that worketh not, but believeth on him that justifieth the ungodly, his faith is counted for righteousness, and since this is entirely of grace, then it is no more of works; for it is a manifest contradiction to maintain, that we are justified freely by the grace of God; and yet that the work of man is some way needful to merit our justification. Is not this something like purchasing a free gift? Equally inconsistent is the grace of God bestowing freely, and the

works

works of man meriting, righteousness. Man has nothing to do but to believe, and this too is the gift of God's free grace: for righteousness is imputed to him who worketh not, but believeth, even as *David* also describeth the blessedness of the man unto whom God imputeth righteousness without works, saying, Blessed are they whose iniquities are forgiven, and whose sins are covered, blessed is the man to whom the Lord will not impute sin. In these scriptures our justification before God is ascribed to faith without works. These two, faith and works, cannot stand together. The righteousness of Christ freely received by faith, is inconsistent with man's working in hopes of attaining a righteousness of his own: for he hopes to attain an impossibility. The Apostle in his most excellent sermon, preached at *Antioch*, recorded *Acts* xiii. declares that we *cannot* be justified by the works of the law. After he had finished the argumentative part of his discourse, he makes this application: "Be it known unto you, therefore, men and "brethren, that through this man is preach- "ed unto you the forgiveness of sins, and "by him all that believe are justified from
"all

"all things, from which ye *could* not be jus-
"tified by the law of *Moses*," neither by the works of the moral, nor yet of the ceremonial law, so that the whole of a sinner's justification is put upon his believing—"All that
"believe are justified."

I might bring many more passages of scripture to confirm this doctrine, but they would be needless, because it is already abundantly confirmed by the articles and homilies of our church. The title of the eleventh article is,

"Of the justification of man.

"We are accounted righteous before God
"ONLY for the merit of our Lord and Sa-
"viour *Jesus Christ* by faith, and not for our
"own works or deservings, wherefore that
"we are justified by faith ONLY is a most
"wholesome doctrine and very full of com-
"fort, as more largely is expressed in the
"homily of justification."

In which homily we have these words:

"This

"This saying, that we be justified by faith ONLY, freely, and without works is spoken for to take away clearly all merit of our own works, as being unable to deserve our justification at God's hand, and thereby most plainly to express the weakness of man and the goodness of God, the great infirmity of ourselves, and the might and power of God, the imperfection of our own works, and the most abundant grace of our Saviour Christ; and therefore wholly to ascribe the merit and deserving of our justification unto Christ ONLY, and his most precious blood shedding. This faith the holy scripture teacheth us is the strong rock and foundation of the Christian religion; this doctrine all old and antient authors of Christ's church do approve; this doctrine advanceth and setteth forth the true glory of Christ, and beateth down the vain glory of man; this whosoever denieth is not to be accounted for a Christian man, nor for a setter forth of Christ's glory, but for an adversary to Christ and his gospel, and for a setter forth of man's vain-glory." These remarkable words are in the second part of the homily; in the third part we have this passage:

"The very true meaning of this proposition or saying, We be justified by faith in Christ ONLY is this; we put our faith in Christ, that we be justified by him ONLY, that we be justified by God's free mercy, and the merits of our Saviour Christ ONLY, and by no virtue or good works of our own, that is in us, or that we can be able to have, or to do, for to deserve the same, Christ himself ONLY being the cause meritorious thereof."

These authorities are very plain and very decisive. They declare that we are justified by faith ONLY without any of our works or deservings. What words can be more full to the point than these are? "We put our faith in Christ, that we be justified by him only, and by no virtue or good works of our own that is in us, or that we can be able to have or to do for to deserve the same." And are these the words of our established church? Are they indeed part of one of our homilies? What! does she teach, that no good works, which we can be able to do, deserve our justification? Surely then, my brethren, the law of faith is here with great plainness enforced, and you cannot, as good members of our church, refuse your assent to this proposition, that in the way of justifying a sinner by faith in the righteousness of Christ all boasting is excluded.

The natural man cannot receive this proposition, although it comes recommended to him by the highest authority. His heart rises against it. To leave him nothing to boast of, no work, no virtue to glory in, Oh it is too humbling to be borne! Scripture may be plain, and our church's comment upon it still plainer, but he cannot allow himself to be quite helpless. It appears strange to him, that he should have no hand or merit in justifying himself. His carnal reason cannot conceive how this should be, and therefore whenever he hears of justification by faith only, he always fastens the idea of licentiousness to it, and is ready to object, " If this doctrine be allowed, what a wide " door is here opened for all manner of " wickedness? At this rate, men may do " just what they please: for if they are to be
" justified

"justified by faith only without works, is
"not the moral law hereby made void and
"all obedience to it? Can there be any ne-
"cessity for their obedience, unless they are
"to merit heaven by it?" The apostle was
aware of this objection, and has answered it
in this chapter: "Do we then make void
"the law through faith?" Do we repeal
the moral law by shewing that it cannot
justify a sinner? Is this making it void?
God forbid. "Yes, we establish the law."
It stands established by faith, and by no other
method, that has been revealed from heaven,
or can be contrived on earth, as I proposed
to shew under my

Second general head, wherein I was to prove
the truth of the Apostle's doctrine in my text.
The doctrine is this. In the way of pardoning and justifying a sinner God was willing
to shut out all boasting, that the whole glory
might be ascribed to his free grace, and therefore he chose the law of faith, which obliges
the sinner to acknowledge himself justly condemned for breaking the moral law, and to
rely upon the righteousness of the Lord
Christ as the only means of his pardon and
acceptance; for if the sinner's justification
had

had been altogether of works, or partly of faith and partly of works, then he would have had whereof to glory, becaufe he would have done fomething whereby to merit; but now that righteoufnefs which is the matter of his juftification being freely wrought out for him, and given to him by fovereign grace as a free gift, and then apprehended and received by faith only without works, in this cafe all boafting is utterly excluded. This is the Apoftle's doctrine, which I will endeavour to eftablifh by the following arguments. And

Firft, There has been no other way or method difcovered of eftablifhing the moral law after it had been broken, and of repairing its honour and dignity, but by the law of faith. The moral law is holy, juft, and good. It is the will of the moft high God, and therefore partakes of the divine holinefs, juftice, and goodnefs. It is as holy, juft, and good as God is, and can no more behold the leaft iniquity, than he can; fo that when all flefh was become guilty before God upon account of the breach of the moral law, there could be no longer any falvation expected from it; for the decree is pofitive and abfo-
lute—

lute—" By the works of the law shall no
" flesh be justified."

In what way then, or by what means may
they be justified, whom the law condemns?
As all have sinned and robbed the law of its
glory, it pleased God, of his infinite grace,
to contrive a way, whereby the sinner might
be saved, and yet his law and justice might
be maintained in their full honour and dignity.
The Son of God, equal with his Father
in every perfection and attribute, undertook
to stand in the place of sinners, and as
their representative, to do and suffer for
them, whatever law and justice demanded.
The Father was well-pleased for his righteousness
sake, because he knew that his beloved
Son would magnify the law, and bring
honour to his justice. When the fulness of
time was come, and the word was made
flesh, for us and for our salvation he wrought
out that righteousness, with which his Father
was well-pleased. His obedience to the
moral law was for sinners, that by the obedience
of one many might be made righteous,
and he kept the law in all things, continually,
perfectly, in thought, word, and deed,
in its spiritual nature, and in its utmost extent,

tent. This obedience was such, that he challenged the enemy to find the least failing in it, *John* xiv. 30. "The prince of this world cometh, and hath nothing in me." Yea, he could appeal to the all-searching eye of infinite justice for the absolute perfection of his obedience. Just before his sufferings begun, he said, "Father, I have finished the work which thou gavest me to do." *John* xvii. 4. The work of his active obedience being finished, he then undertook to suffer for sinners the pains and penalties due to their breach of the moral law. He suffered once for sin, the just for the unjust, he took their griefs, and carried their sorrows, he was wounded for their transgressions, and was bruised for their iniquities, the chastisement of their peace was upon him, and by his stripes they are healed. He bled, he was made a curse, he died, that by his death they might live: for he who did and suffered these things was God. He was truly a divine and infinite person, self-existent, co-eternal and co-equal with the Father: for as our church well expresses it, "that which we believe of the glory of the Father the same we believe of the Son, and of the Holy Ghost, without any difference or inequality."

And

And since there is no difference or inequality between the persons of the ever-blessed Trinity, consequently what the Lord Christ did and suffered was as infinitely meritorious, as if the Father had done and suffered it. When the Lord our righteousness stood up to pay the law obedience, the dignity of his person brought more honour to the law, than the obedience of all created beings, angels and men, could possibly have done: because their obedience would have been only finite, whereas his was divine and infinite, and they could only have wrought out a righteousness sufficient to save themselves; whereas he has brought in an everlasting righteousness to save even the ungodly. The prophet *Isaiah* speaking of this subject, says, xlii. 21. "The Lord is well pleased "for his righteousness sake, he will magni- "fy the law, and make it honourable;" and he did magnify it by completing it. He paid it both an active and a passive obedience in the most perfect degree, and established it in his highest honour and dignity; by which means even that justice, from which the sinner had most to fear, may now be glorified in justifying him; for God may now be just,

and

and yet be the justifier of him, that believeth in Jesus.

The righteousness, which is the ground and matter of our justification, is called in scripture the *righteousness of faith*, because faith receives and applies it, and *the law of faith*, because the sinner is obliged to accept of this righteousness by faith only, and the manner of his receiving it is by imputation. As Christ took our sins upon him, and was a sinner by imputation—He was made sin for us, who knew no sin, so we are made the righteousness of God IN HIM, not righteous in ourselves inherently, but in him; we are righteous only in him: his righteousness is imputed to us, and made ours by faith, even as *Abraham* believed God, and it was imputed unto him for righteousness. And in this way of justifying a sinner by imputed righteousness, the moral law is so far from being made void, that it is established, and the great end of it is answered: for the Apostle says, " Christ is the end of the law for " righteousness to every one that believeth." The end of the law was to justify those who keep it, " Do this, and thou shalt live," but we attain not to this end, because through

the

the corruption of our nature, we do not keep the law perfectly; but Chrift fulfilled the law for all thofe who believe in him, and thereby he became the end of the law for righteoufnefs to every one that believeth. By believing we receive his righteoufnefs, and then we anfwer the end of the law. Thus the law of faith does infinite honour to the moral law, and the believer is continually glorifying it: for his language is this— I acknowledge the law of God to be perfectly holy, juft, and good; it requires nothing but what is for the glory of the great law-giver, and for the good of his creatures, and no fatisfaction can be made to its honour and dignity, after it has been once broken, but what is infinitely meritorious, which no finner can poffibly pay. But thanks be to God for the unfpeakable gift of Chrift's righteoufnefs, which, by faith, is mine. His active and paffive obedience are imputed unto me for righteoufnefs, and I can now give glory to the moral law of God by acknowledging myfelf to be juftly condemned by it, and by placing my whole truft and confidence in *Jefus Chrift*, who of God is made unto me righteoufnefs.

Thus the moral law is established. It was fulfilled in Christ, and the end of it is answered in believers; from whence it appears, that the law of faith has provided a full security for the honour and dignity of the moral law, and has magnified it and made it honourable, not only in the way of justifying sinners, but also in their walk and conversation after they are justified, which is the second argument I shall bring in defence of the Apostle's doctrine.

2. The law of faith absolutely excludes all boasting, and all confidence in our works, but it does not make void the moral law: for although Christ does deliver the sinner through faith in his righteousness from the guilt and condemnation of sin, and thereby justify him, yet he does not give him a discharge from all obedience to the moral law, but by many gracious motives inclines and enables him to keep it. He sends his good Spirit to enable the justified believer to exercise all his faculties in paying a grateful obedience to the will of his God.

His understanding was before in darkness. He knew not the will of God, and therefore formed

formed a very wrong judgment of it, but now the Holy Spirit enlightens his underſtanding, and lets him ſee the goodneſs and equity of all God's commandments. He uſed to think ſome ſins were very little and might eaſily be pardoned, and in the commiſſion of others he lived ſecure without any remorſe of conſcience, hoping to make amends by repentance and reformation, and ſome ſorrow and tears. But now the caſe is altered. He ſees the law in its ſpiritual nature and extent, in its holineſs and juſtice, and confeſſes that the leaſt breach of it deſerves everlaſting miſery, and although Chriſt has delivered him from the curſe of the law, yet with his unſtanding he aſſents to its being for God's glory, and for his own intereſt, to walk in the law of the Lord.

And, as the Holy Spirit enlightens his underſtanding to ſee what the law of the Lord is, ſo he takes away the prejudices, and ſubdues the oppoſition, which were in his heart againſt it. The commandments ceaſe to be grievous unto him. The love of God being ſhed abroad in his heart conſtrains him to love God, and to love the will of God: for God and his will are one. He that loves God

God cannot hate God's will. Love cannot beget hatred. And therefore when the Holy Spirit gives that faith, which worketh by love, he then reconciles the believer's will to God's will, and he can truly say—Lord, what love have I unto thy law! I see the holiness, and goodness, and justice of it, my will approves of it, and my affections love it; yea, I love it above gold and precious stones. Oh! give me strength that I may keep it with my whole heart. And the Holy Spirit does wonderfully strengthen believers in keeping it. He makes them strong in the Lord, and in the power of his might: for he sets their hearts at liberty, and then they run in the way of the commandments. So far then is faith from making void the moral law, that it establishes it as a rule of life for the believer, who endeavours, by his holy walking, to glorify it. As he has received *Christ Jesus*, the Lord, so he desires to walk in him unto all pleasing: And this he would do, not to procure himself a right and title to heaven; for he received that when the Redeemer's righteousness was imputed to him for his justification, and gratitude for this inestimable gift constrains him to love God who so exceedingly loved him, and to evidence this love in the way which God has required, and that is in a grateful obedience. This love, which casteth out all other fear, brings in a filial fear of displeasing his loving Father. He dreads nothing so much as sin, because he knows nothing else can offend his Lord and his God; and therefore he would resist unto blood striving against sin. He would rather die than sin. This fear of offending God influences his whole life and conversation, and keeps him continually watchful, that he may walk worthy of God, who hath called him unto his kingdom and glory.

Upon these two arguments we may rest the truth of the Apostle's doctrine in my text. The law of faith excludes boasting, because it excludes all man's work and merit in his justification. His keeping of the moral law cannot in the least justify him before God, because after he has once broken it, it becomes to him the ministration of death and condemnation. In this state Christ finds the sinner, guilty and condemned, under the curses of the broken law, miserable and helpless. He takes pity on his distress, and determines to save him. With a love truly divine

divine and infinite, he comes from his eternal throne, appears in the likeness of sinful flesh, and God and man are united in one Christ. This was necessary in order to his working out in our nature a divine and infinite righteousness for believers, against which law and justice might have no exception. He attained this righteousness by obeying the law, by suffering its pains and penalties, even unto death, and by being put into the prison of the grave. He was kept there three days, but it was not possible he should be holden any longer. On the third day he rose triumphant from the dead, and thereby demonstrated that law and justice had no farther demands upon him: for they had certainly received full satisfaction when they released him out of prison. The law was magnified infinitely by his obedience and sufferings, and it is made honourable, whenever a sinner is brought to submit to be justified through the righteousness of Christ; because he then acknowledges the law to be holy, just, and good, allows himself to be justly condemned by it, and is convinced that no righteousness can save him, but what is infinitely perfect. Such is the Redeemer's. The benefit of this he seeks, and when he receives it, and it is imputed unto him by faith, he then stands justified in the righteousness of God which is by faith of *Jesus Christ*, and has the Spirit of Christ to guide, strengthen, and sanctify him. This good Spirit enlightens him to understand the law, to love it, and gives strength to keep it; and thus by his holy walking the law gets honour: so that the law of faith does not make void the moral law, but establishes it, both in the justification of a sinner, and also in the holy walk and conversation of a believer.

It is evident then, that ever since the moral law was broken, there has been but one way, in which a sinner could be saved, and this was the law of faith, which stands established by the sovereign decree of the most high God. He has solemnly provided and enacted, that whoever would enter into life must believe in the name of the only-begotten Son of God. Have you then, my brethren, kept this commandment and believed in him? Apply this to your own hearts, and examine them strictly. Do you believe the record which God hath given of his Son? If not, how do you expect to be saved? Against God's will you cannot be saved.

You cannot refift omnipotence. And his will is, that you fubmit to the law of faith, and with the heart believe unto righteoufnefs. The moral law condemns you to death for finning againft it, and no tears or forrow, no repentance or amendment can repair the injury you have done it, and therefore by it you cannot be faved. There remains then only the law of faith. This offers you a free pardon, and obliges you to accept of it upon pain of dying in your fins. The offer is, "He "that believeth fhall be faved," but, oh! how dreadful is the fentence which follows the kind offer, "He that believeth not fhall "be damned."

Perhaps fome of you may be convinced of the neceffity of believing, but you cannot fee how faith in the righteoufnefs of another can gain you acceptance with God. You think that your works and Chrift's muft go together to your juftification. This is the opinion of too many among us, who will not fubmit to the righteoufnefs of Chrift, but will go about to eftablifh their own righteoufnefs along with his. Their miftake arifes from their ignorance of the moral law; they know not its infinite holinefs, and what its demands are, and from their ignorance of the gofpel, which by the law of faith obliges the finner to accept of that righteoufnefs as a free gift, which is to fatisfy all the demands of the moral law. Such a righteoufnefs Chrift has wrought out, and he offers it freely, and the finner by accepting it receives juftification to life. He is made alive to God, and then can act and work in fpiritual duties, but before this he was dead legally and fpiritually, dead under the fentence of the law, and dead to all motions and acts of fpiritual life. While he lies in this ftate, he can do no more than a dead corpfe can ; but by the gift of righteoufnefs he is legally alive. The fentence of death is taken away, and he is freely pardoned ; and then he becomes fpiritually alive, and can perform the offices of fpiritual life. Being made alive at the root, he produces the fair bloffoms and brings forth the ripe fruits of righteoufnefs. But thefe fruits do not make him legally alive ; they only evidence him to be fo. They are the proper effects and confequences of his being, fpiritually alive, as the bringing forth the bloffoms and fruit prove the tree to have life, but do not give it life. Oh ! beware then, my brethren,

of

of the dangerous miſtake of making up a righteouſneſs, which is to be your juſtification to life, partly with your own works and partly with Chriſt's. Theſe two cannot ſtand together in your juſtification. The prophet ſeparates them entirely, " I will " make mention, ſays he, of thy righteouſ- " neſs, even thine only," *Pſalm* lxxi. 16. and yet he had as much righteouſneſs to make mention of as any of the Old Teſtament-ſaints. And the Apoſtle, whoſe praiſe is in the goſpel for his labouring more abundantly than all the Apoſtles, yet prayed to be " found in Chriſt, not having his own " righteouſneſs which is of the law, but that " which is through the faith of Chriſt, the " righteouſneſs which is of God by faith." *Phil.* iii. 9.

What! ſhall we not do good works, will ſome ſay? Yes. Work from life, but not for life. You cannot work any thing acceptably, until you who were dead in treſpaſſes and ſins be quickened, and when you are made alive unto God through *Jeſus Chriſt* our Lord, then you will ſtudy to walk worthy of the Lord unto all pleaſing, being fruitful in every good word and work.

This

This careful walking, my Christian brethren, is in a more especial manner incumbent upon you. You are called unto liberty, only use not your liberty for an occasion of sin: for you are still under the law to Christ. Although you are freed from its condemning power, yet it is still a rule for your life and conduct: because it is the holy, just, and good will of God your reconciled Father, whom you love, and whom you are exceedingly desirous of pleasing. And it is the will of Christ, your Saviour, to whose image you seek to be conformed, and in whose steps you would gladly tread. And it is the will of the Holy Spirit, who is your guide, your sanctifier, and your strengthener: By him being led you can take up your cross daily, mortifying sin, resisting the world's allurements, overcoming the temptations of Satan, and subduing the risings of your carnal minds against the moral law. Under the teachings of this good Spirit you will be led right, and under his influence you will be enabled to bring forth much fruit. Oh that this Spirit of the Lord may rest upon you, the Spirit of wisdom and understanding, the Spirit of counsel and might, the Spirit of knowledge and of the fear of the Lord, that you may

may always walk worthy of the vocation wherewith you are called. May he help you to adorn the doctrine of God your Saviour in all things, and so to walk before him as to demonstrate publickly, that you do not make void the law by faith, but do perfectly establish it in its full force and vigour. Grant this, holy Father, for *Jesus Christ* his sake; to whom with thee and the eternal Spirit be equal honour, praise, and worship for ever and ever. Amen.

UPON

IMPUTED RIGHTEOUSNESS.

DISCOURSE V.

2 COR. V. 21.

He hath made him to be sin for us, who knew no sin, that we might be made the righteousness of God in him.

It is the great and merciful design of the gospel to acquaint a sinner, who is guilty and condemned by the holy law of God, how he may be pardoned and justified. Every one of us is a sinner: for all have sinned, and therefore all of us stand in need of pardon, and ought to receive it with thankful hearts as soon as the gospel preaches it

to

to us. But the greatest part of mankind are not sensible of their guilt, nor apprehensive of their danger. Sin has nothing in it terrible to them. They love it, dream of happiness in the enjoyment of it, and while this delusion continues, they see not their want of, and therefore have no desire for, the gospel salvation. But when one of these persons awakes and opens his eyes, he is then terrified at the sight of his present state. Sin appears to him in a new light: he finds it to be exceeding sinful, and the wrath of God revealed from heaven against it to be beyond measure dreadful. His guilty conscience alarms him with an awful sense of his danger, and makes him feel some of the punishment due to sin, and then he cannot be easy, until he know that his sins may be pardoned, and he cannot be happy, until he has some evidence of their being pardoned. Now Christianity is the only religion which can give such a person relief: because it alone teaches him by what means he may be pardoned and justified, and have peace with God. He may be pardoned freely through the grace of God, and justified through the righteousness of *Jesus Christ*, whom God the Father hath made sin

for

for us, although he knew no sin in himself, that we might be made the righteousness of God in him, and being thus justified by faith in him, we might have peace with God through our Lord *Jesus Christ*.

Although this doctrine be clearly taught throughout the scriptures, yet there are at present two sorts of men, who are great enemies to it, and who strive to keep convinced sinners from the comfort of it; I mean the Papists, who go about to establish their own righteousness, and the Pharisees among us, who will not submit to the righteousness of God. The notion of the Papist's concerning merit is the foundation of all their errors. They teach, that Christ merited the grace for them, which is in them, and then this grace in them merits their justification, and for this inherent grace God doth justify them. And thus they make a Saviour of inherent grace, and put it in the place of Christ, and give his glory to their own works. But if inherent grace be our righteousness before God, then how does God justify the ungodly, who have no grace, or how can he justify a man for those graces which are imperfect,

imperfect, and which want the benefit of Christ's atonement? Absurd as this opinion of theirs is, yet they must defend it. Their cause rests upon it: for if you take away their doctrine of merit, down falls the whole superstructure of their superstition, all their indulgencies, pardons, pilgrimages, masses, fasts, penances, and the mighty *Babel* of man's inventions. When this doctrine was grown to a monstrous height, it pleased God to raise up *Luther* and the rest of the reformers to preach against it. Their principal aim and design was to overthrow the merit of works, and to establish justification by faith only, and they succeeded. Several nations were converted from the errors of popery, and among the rest the inhabitants of this island. Our forefathers threw off the *Romish* yoke, and received the pure doctrines of the gospel, which amidst our several changes and revolutions of government have been happily preserved, until there has been of late years a manifest departure from them. Great multitudes of *Protestants* are going fast back again to *Popery*, and seemingly without knowing it; for it is a received opinion in *England*, as much as in *France*, that man's works are effectual and

meri-

meritorious towards his juſtification before God. This is the fundamental hereſy of the *Papiſts*, and how many nominal *Proteſtants* have fallen into it, our enemies can tell. They ſee, with pleaſure, that there is very little appearance of religion left among us, and that ſome of our moſt decent profeſſors are become *Papiſts* in that leading principle, which ſeparates the *Popiſh* from the *Proteſtant* communion.

Things being in this unpromiſing ſtate, the friends of the reformation ſhould beſtir themſelves. They ſhould try to point out the old land-marks. This is more eſpecially incumbent upon the clergy. It is high time for them to hold forth to their people the fundamental doctrines of the eſtabliſhed church, and to warn them againſt the errors of *Popery* and *Phariſaiſm*. With this view, I have choſen the words now read for your preſent meditation; and may the Lord give his bleſſing to what ſhall be ſpoken upon them. Oh that he may accompany with the effectual working of his power, what ſhall be ſaid,

First, Concerning Chrift's unfpotted innocence. He knew no fin. Yet,

Secondly, God made him to be fin for us, and

Thirdly, For this reafon, that we might be made the righteoufnefs of God in him.

And firft, our Lord's fitnefs to be made fin for us is here fet forth by his knowing no fin. He knew it not in the fcripture fenfe of the word. He had no practical knowledge of fin, either in thought, word, or deed. Speculatively he knew it well, but that could not defile him: for it was the fin of others which he knew, and hated, and came to put away by the facrifice of himfelf. Chrift was perfectly acquainted with the holy, juft, and good law of God; he faw clearly into the purity and fpirituality of it, which could not fuffer the leaft offence, being as holy, juft, and good as God himfelf is, and being the copy of his moft perfect mind and will. In this view our Lord beheld the odious nature of fin, and the exceeding finfulnefs of it. He knew the hatred which the all-pure God had to it, the punifhment it deferved, and
the

the everlasting fire which it had kindled in the nethermost hell. No one ever understood these things so clearly as Christ did. He saw the destructive effects of sin, what disorder it had brought into the world, and to what temporal and eternal evils it had subjected the bodies and the souls of men. He knew also, that there was no help upon earth, and that no creature in heaven, of the highest order of angels, could deliver any one sinner from his distress, and much less a multitude; therefore, his eye pitied us, and his compassion was moved at the sight of our lost and helpless state. Behold what manner of love he hath bestowed upon such sinners as you and me; a love which led him to do greater wonders to save, than he had before done to create us: for he, the most high God, blessed for ever, humbled himself to be made man. He, whom angels and arch-angels had been worshipping from the moment of their creation, took upon him the form of a servant, and came to save his people from their sins. Adore, my brethren, and praise this infinite condescension of the incarnate God: for it was for you who believe it by true faith, and for your salvation that the word was made flesh. He was equal to this great work: because he was perfect God and perfect man in one Chrift, and as fuch he was abfolutely free from fin— " he knew no fin," he knew it not in practice. No fin, no inclination, no motion, or rifing of fin ever entered into his heart, and therefore he was pure from the leaft fpot or ftain of pollution.

The fcripture is very plain upon this point. Chrift was known in the times of the Old Teftament by the titles of the Holy Name, the Holy One, the Holy One of *Ifrael,* and the prophet *Ifaiah* fpeaks of the Lord the Redeemer of *Ifrael* and his Holy One, and when the fulnefs of time was come, that this Holy One fhould be made flefh, he was conceived and born without the leaft taint of corruption, conceived of the Holy Spirit, and born of a pure virgin. Yea, the angel *Gabriel* pronounced him to be holy before his birth, in the meffage to the virgin, *Luke* i. 35. " The Holy Ghoft fhall come upon thee, " and the power of the higheft fhall over- " fhadow thee; therefore alfo that holy " thing which fhall be born of thee fhall " be called the Son of God." He was born holy, and fuch was the life of the holy

child

child *Jesus*, as his birth had been. We may see clearly how pure he came into the world, from the purity with which he lived in it. How different was his life from ours? He knew no sin in thought, word, or deed. The prophet says, " He had a clean heart," all his thoughts were clean; " He had pure " hands," all his actions were pure; " and " he had a mouth without guile," no idle, false, or sinful word ever passed through his lips. He was altogether holy, harmless, and undefiled, and separate from sinners. In the law of the Lord was his study and his delight. He came to glorify it, and by keeping it in its spiritual nature, and in its full extent, with every faculty of soul and body, and at all times he made it honourable. He paid it that obedience which it demanded, and continued in all things that were written in the book of the law to do them. Thus in him was no sin, sin being the transgression of the law. And accordingly we find him challenging his bitterest enemies upon this point, " which of you, says he, (*John* " viii. 46.) convinces me of sin?" Nay, he went farther, and defied Satan himself, as well as the *Jews*, " The prince of this world
" cometh,

"cometh, and hath nothing in me," no sin of mine own to lay to my charge.

From these passages it plainly appears, that Christ knew no sin. He was a pure and spotless lamb, holy and without blemish; and it was necessary he should be so: because if he ever had any sin of his own, he could not have obeyed and suffered for the sins of others. The infinite purity of God's law can pass by no sin. Upon the least transgression, if it be but a thought or motion in the heart, the law passes sentence and condemns, " Cursed is every one who con- " tinueth not in all things that are written " in the book of the law to do them." And if you continue not to do them, justice calls aloud for the inflicting of the threatened curse, and waits to see it fully executed; therefore, unless Christ had continued to do all things which are written in the book of the law, he could not have obeyed and suffered for the sins of others; because he would then have suffered for his own, which must not be imagined. It would be blasphemy to suppose any such thing. When the last scene of his sufferings began, he was led like a lamb to the slaughter, a
lamb

lamb without blemish and without spot, such as the ceremonial law required. You know, my brethren, that no creature could be offered in sacrifice to the Lord, if it had the least blemish or deformity. By this type was prefigured the perfect sinless purity, which was to be in the great sacrifice for sin. He was to be a lamb without blemish, without the least spot or stain of sin, either in his nature or in his life, and such an one was the lamb of God. The Apostle says expressly, 1 *Pet.* ii. 22. "He did NO sin," and St. *John*, 1 *Ep.* iii. 5. speaks to believers, "Ye know, that he was manifested to take "away our sins, and in him is no sin:" this was a known and established truth, that in Christ there was NO sin. If judgment was laid to the line, and righteousness to the plummet, there would be found in him a perfect conformity to the law. And this his active obedience was necessary to prepare him for his passive, that having obeyed the law actively he might suffer passively whatever was due to our disobedience. And that righteousness, by which we are accounted righteous before God, is the effect of his being obedient unto death, of his obedience to the preceptive part of the law, which was his fulfilling the righteousness of the law, and of his obedience to the vindictive part of the law, which was his bearing the curse of it. His active obedience was absolutely perfect. He knew NO sin, and therefore was every way fit and qualified to suffer for sin, " to be made sin for us," as the Apostle expresses it in my text, which words I am, in the second place, to consider.

Although Christ knew no sin, yet he was made sin. How could that be? How could he be made sin, who knew no sin? He was made sin not practically, but by imputation. He had no sin inherently in him, but had sin imputed to him, when the Lord laid upon him the iniquities of us all. In his own person there was no inherent spot or stain of sin, or any such thing. He could not touch the pollution of sin, nor could he practically know its filthy defiling nature. He was not a drunkard, a whoremonger, a thief, or whatever you call a sinner as such. He neither was a sinner practically, nor had he ever the least inclination to be so: because his will was always in perfect harmony with the will of God. From whence it it appears, that Chrift was not made a polluted finner, nor yet a guilty finner as to the merit and defert of fin. In this refpect he was not capable of being made fin. He did not, as to himfelf, deferve the punifhment of fin, for which he fuffered. Punifhment is due to tranfgreffors, but Chrift had not tranfgreffed. Even when he fuffered, according to St. *Peter*, he was juft and righteous in himfelf, (1 *Pet.* iii. 18.) " Chrift " alfo hath once fuffered for fins, the juft for " the unjuft." He was perfectly juft, and therefore capable of undertaking to fuffer for the unjuft, that as no fuffering was due to him, the merit of what he fuffered might be imputed unto them. And fo it was. He freely entered into an obligation to ftand in the place of the unjuft, and to undergo the punifhment due to them, and this with his own confent the Lord laid upon him, and in this fenfe he was made fin for us. He was made fin in the fame way that we are made righteous. Now the righteoufnefs by which we are juftified is not inherent in ourfelves, but it is in Chrift, and is made ours through God's imputing it to us. In like manner our fins were not inherent in Chrift, but imputed to him and laid upon him.

him. He was willing to become our surety and to answer for our sins, and to have them imputed to him, so as to be obliged to bear the punishment of them, even the wrath and curse, which, if he had not endured them, would have sunk every one of us into the pit of hell. But Christ his own self bore them in his own body upon the tree. As the surety of all that shall believe in him he undertook to answer all the demands which law and justice had upon them. And he was willing to have all their sins imputed to him, and placed to his account, that he might satisfy for them. Accordingly we read that he was once offered to bear the sins of many, and that by his own blood he obtained eternal redemption for them. When their iniquities were laid upon him, although he knew no sin, yet he knew what it was to suffer for sin. He died the death and endured the pains, which were in nature and proportion due to them for their sins, and for the full satisfaction of law and justice.

In this sense Christ was made sin; but what would this avail, if he was a mere man? He might be made sin, and might suffer,

suffer, but not *for us*. The Apostle says in my text, he was made sin *for us*. What was effectual to us, must be more than human, and could be nothing short of divine. Christ's undertakings were too great to be performed by any person less than the most high God. And accordingly the scripture teaches us, that Christ was Jehovah, the true self-existent God, a co-equal and co-eternal person with the Father and the Holy Spirit, and in his person God and man were united in one Christ. By this personal union, what the manhood did and suffered partook of the infinite merit of the Godhead. The manhood of Christ had no sin in it, and therefore what it suffered for the sin imputed to it, was infinitely meritorious, because he who suffered was God as well as man. This most wonderful method of bringing many sons unto glory, was contrived by the ever-blessed Trinity, and settled by the covenant of grace. God the Son was pleased to become their surety, and to stand up in their nature to act and to suffer for them. And what he undertook he could not fail of accomplishing; for all things are alike possible to his almighty power. When he acted for his people, he was God as well as man,

man, his obedience was therefore divine and infinite, and by the merits of it shall many be made righteous. When he suffered for his people, his sufferings were of such infinite merit and efficacy, that by his stripes they are healed and freed from suffering. He took their griefs and carried their sorrows, that they might never feel them. When he died, and paid the debt to justice, which they ought to have paid, he soon brought them a discharge: for although he was buried and descended into hell, yet on the third day he rose again from the dead, and thereby demonstrated, that all the ends were answered, for which he was made sin for them.

Here, my Christian brethren, let us stop and adore the free love and rich mercy of our Divine Redeemer. He, the most high God, blessed for ever, condescended to be made man for us, and for our salvation. Oh wonderful condescension! that there should be any mercy for such enemies and rebels as we have been, and how did he magnify his compassion, that when he might in justice have destroyed us, yet he humbled himself and stooped down to save us!
But

But how great was his humiliation in vouchsafing to take on him the form of a servant, and to live in poverty and contempt. Considering who it was that became a man of sorrows, and acquainted with grief, we see the greatest wonder of all, the depth of his humiliation. He that was the lowest upon earth was the highest in heaven. He came down to be made sin for us, to have our sins imputed to him, and to answer for them to law and justice. Accordingly they were laid upon him, and he bore them in his own body on the cross, and thereby saved us from our sins. Blessed, for ever blessed be the name of our dear Redeemer. Glory, and honour, and thanks never-ceasing be to him, who took all our sufferings upon himself, because he could bear that which we could not, and because he could satisfy for that in a short time, which we could not in eternity, and who having thus delivered us from sin and suffering, has righteousness to impute unto us, in which we may stand blameless at the bar of justice. Oh let us praise him with our lips and lives, who was made sin for us, that he might be made righteousness to us, which is the third point I was to consider.

He was a spotless lamb, and therefore capable of being made sin for us, that we might be made the righteousness of God in him. Righteousness is a perfect conformity to the law and will of God, and without this no man shall see the Lord: " For the " unrighteous shall not inherit the king- " dom of God," 1 *Cor.* vi. 9. and we are all unrighteous, because we have all sinned and robbed God of his glory. The question then is, In what way or by what means can we attain righteousness? Can we attain it by the works of the law? No, it is impossible: because if it was attainable by our own works, then we should be inherently righteous, and should have such a righteousness as the law demands; but the law demands perfect unsinning obedience, which we have not paid it. And upon our failing to pay it, the law pronounces us guilty, passes sentence, and leaves us, as to any thing we can do, for ever under the curse, it being the irreversible decree of the almighty law-giver; that since all flesh has sinned and broken the law, therefore, by the works of the law shall no flesh be justified.

But

But if sinners cannot be justified by any inherent righteousness, what righteousness have they to plead at the bar of justice? They have a righteousness absolutely perfect and complete, called in scripture, the righteousness of God, because the Lord our righteousness contrived and wrought it out. He came into the world, and took flesh in order to fulfil all righteousness. By his obedience and sufferings he satisfied all the demands of law and justice, and paid that immense debt which none of us could pay, and hereby he was made of God unto us righteousness: God the Father constituted and ordained him to be the perfect righteousness of believers. In him is their righteousness, "Their righteousness is of me, saith "the Lord." (*Isai.* liv. 17.) For Christ is the end of the law for righteousness to every one that believeth.

If you ask how the righteousness of another can be made yours? It must be in the same way that Christ was made sin. He had no sin of his own, and yet he was made sin by imputation; and believers have no righteousness of their own, and yet are made righteous by imputation. Christ had no inherent sin of his own, nor have they any inherent righteousness; but he was made sin by having their sins imputed to him, and they are made righteous by having his righteousness imputed to them. The manner of God's proceeding is the same in both cases. When the Psalmist says, " Blessed is the " man to whom the Lord imputeth not ini- " quity," How is this to be understood? Has he no iniquity in him? Yes, he has original and inherent sin, and if he says he has no sin, he deceives himself; but he is a blessed man, because the Lord does not impute sin to him, nor charge him with it. So when *David* describeth the blessedness of the man to whom God imputeth righteousness; has the man this righteousness in himself, and is he inherently righteous? No, but by an act of grace God accounts him righteous, and imputes righteousness unto him, and therefore he is blessed. And thus God imputes righteousness to them who believe, not for a righteousness which is in them, but for a righteousness which he imputes to them. As their iniquities were laid upon Christ, and satisfaction for them required of him, as a debt is of the bondsman, although he had none of the money, so is

the

the righteousness of Christ laid upon them. In like manner, as their sins were made his, so is his righteousness made theirs. He is sin for them, not inherently, but by imputation; and they righteousness through him, not inherently, but by imputation.

This is the righteousness in which alone a sinner can stand acquitted at God's bar. There he must make mention of this righteousness, even of this only: for none but this can answer the demands of the law, and expiate the curse of it, and this righteousness can be made his by no other way than by God's imputing it to him; which, as it is the great truth held forth in my text, I will endeavour more fully to explain and defend by the following reasons.

And first, the ceremonial law taught this doctrine very clearly. Whenever a person had sinned, he was to bring his sacrifice to the priest, and to lay his hands upon its head, confessing his sins over it, and then the guilt was transferred to the sacrifice, and its blood was shed instead of his. This is mentioned several times in *Leviticus* iv. And of the scape goat we read, *Lev.* xxvi. 21.

M " *Aaron*

"*Aaron* shall lay both his hands upon the head of the live goat, and confess over him all the iniquities of the children of *Israel*, and all their transgressions in all their sins, putting them upon the head of the goat." All the sins of the children of *Israel* were passed over to the goat, but were they put into the goat, or were they inherent in him? No. This is too absurd to be supposed, but they were put upon the goat. And this was a very expressive image of our sins being laid upon Christ; for all the sacrifices represented him. As the scape goat had imputed to him all the people's iniquities, so had Christ all his people's iniquities imputed to him; and as the goat did bear upon him all their iniquities, so Christ did bear all their sins in his own body upon the tree. What was prefigured by the type was fulfilled by the reality, when Christ suffered once for sin, the just for the unjust; for then he was made sin for us, that we might be made the righteousness of God in him. Our righteousness is *in him*, this is a

Second argument, That righteousness which is our justification before God is IN Christ. Believers

Believers have it not in themselves. They have not an inherent righteousness, wrought out and attained by their own works, but their justifying righteousness was wrought out by another, and it is *in* him. How then can it be made theirs in any other way than by imputation? Must it not be transferred to them in the same way that their sins were transferred to him? And how were they transferred to him? They were imputed, not inherent; they were laid upon him, not into him. So his righteousness is in him, as their sins were in them, and it is imputed, not inherent; it is not put into them, but upon them. Their righteousness is in him, and he is the Lord their righteousness, and consequently that righteousness for which they are justified, cannot be in them; but it is made theirs when God imputes it to them, and they by faith receive it. The manner of receiving it, which is by faith, is the

Third argument, I shall bring in support of the Apostle's doctrine. Faith is the only instrument which God is pleased to use in applying Christ's righteousness. The Apostle calls

calls it the righteousness of faith, because faith alone is employed in the application of this righteousness. It is never called the righteousness of any other grace, but of faith. We never read of the righteousness of humility, meekness or charity; these are of great price in the sight of God, but they have no office in justifying a sinner. This belongs solely to faith: for to him that worketh not, but believeth, is righteousness imputed. It is not by working, but by believing, that sinners are justified. When they are convinced of sin, find no righteousness in themselves, hear the dreadful sentence of the law against the unrighteous, and feel in their guilty consciences some of the miseries which they deserve, then they are stirred up to seek for a righteousness in which they may stand acquitted before the judgment-seat of God. The scripture offers to them such a righteousness in Christ, and when God enables them to rest and to rely upon it for their justification, they then by faith have peace with God through *Jesus Christ* their Lord. Thus the convinced sinner is forced to seek a righteousness out of himself, and to rely upon the righteousness of another, and how can this be made or accounted

counted his in any other way, than by imputation? How can he be made righteous in Christ, but by having Christ's righteousness imputed to him?

If these arguments be well considered, they will, I hope, establish the doctrine of the text: for they clearly prove, that God hath appointed the Lord *Jesus Christ* to be the only righteousness of his people. He was made sin for them, their sins being laid upon him, as the sins of the children of *Israel* were laid upon the scape goat. And he was made of God unto them righteousness, and their righteousness is in him, not an inherent, but an imputed righteousness, and received by faith, which submits to be justified by the righteousness of another, and rests with full trust and confidence upon it. This is the fundamental doctrine of Christianity, and the direct contrary is the fundamental doctrine of Popery. At the reformation, the Lord raised up faithful witnesses to bear their testimony against that reigning heresy of the *Papists*, which places merit in man's works; yea such merit as to justify a sinner before God; yea still greater merit, for they maintain, that a man can do more than the moral law requires, and can perform works of supererogation, the merit of which may be imputed to another person, and yet, at the same time, they deny the imputation of Chrift's merits. The firft reformers preached boldly againft thofe blafphemies, and that bleffed fervant of God, *Luther*, was bold indeed. He knew well the dangerous tendency of the doctrine of merit, and therefore he principally wrote and preached againft it, and God gave him great fuccefs. A finner made righteous by the righteoufnefs of Chrift, is, as he ufed to fay, the doctrine upon which a church ftands or falls. Upon it our church was eftablifhed, and has long ftood; but do we ftand upon it now? Are we all champions for the *Proteftant* doctrine, or are we in general departed from it? Alas! our enemies can tell, with triumph they tell of the increafe of the *Popifh* intereft among us. And why does it increafe? Whence is it, that they make fo many converts? Is it not, becaufe our people are not well eftablifhed in this *Proteftant* doctrine? If it was taught and preached more, our churches would not be fo empty, as they are, nor the mafs-houfes fo full. Many of our people know not what it is to be a *Proteftant*,

and

and therefore they become an easy prey to the *Papists*, who are so busy and successful in making converts, that they pretend they have on one Lord's day more communicants at the mass-house in *Lincoln's-Inn-Fields*, than we have on the same day at all the churches in *London*. I fear this may be true; but is it not greatly alarming, and ought it not to stir up the *Protestant* clergy, to try to put a stop to the spreading of *Popery?* But how can they do this more effectually, than by laying the axe to the root, and striking at the doctrine of merit, which is the fundamental error of the *Papists?* Overthrow this, and *Popery* cannot stand. A man cannot be a *Papist*, who believes that his justifying righteousness is in Christ, and whoever does not believe this, is not a *Protestant*. May the Lord raise us up faithful and able men (for we greatly want them) to defend his righteousness against them who have established a meritorious righteousness of their own, and will not submit to the righteousness of God.

But besides the *Papists*, we have other enemies to the doctrine in the text. The careless sinner treats it with great contempt;

for he does not see its value, nor his own want of it, and therefore he lives easy and secure in the practice of sin. The scripture has revealed the wrath of heaven against all his unrighteousness, but he does not regard the revelation. The law brings him in guilty and condemns him, but he gives himself no concern about the threatenings of the law. The gospel offers him mercy, and its ministers intreat him to accept of it, but he stops his ears. Neither the grace of the gospel, nor the terrors of the law can prevail upon him. Although he has no righteousness of any kind, yet he lives as if he was in no danger. Oh deluded man! if thou didst but know thy state, thou wouldst cry earnestly to the Redeemer, and seek to be accepted in his righteousness. May he take pity upon thee, and send his good Spirit to convince thee of sin, and to convince thee of righteousness.

The formalist is another enemy to the doctrine in the text. He will not receive justification by imputed righteousness, but will have his own righteousness seated on the throne along with Christ. He falls into this great mistake from his ignorance of the

perfect

perfect nature of God's law, which has made no provision for any failing, but for the very first passes sentence, " Cursed is every one " who continueth not in ALL things, &c." and since all have failed, consequently all are under the curse, and can never be justified by that law which has condemned them. And his mistake arises also from his ignorance of the gospel. He takes the gospel to be a proposal of terms and conditions, mitigating the rigour of the law, and so he makes Christ only a milder law-giver than *Moses*, requiring not perfect but sincere obedience of his creatures. Whereas Christ came to redeem us from the curse of the law, by obeying its precepts, and by suffering its penalties, and our righteousness comes to us from him as the fulfiller of the law, and is received by faith without any of our works or deservings.

If any of you, my brethren, have fallen into this mistake, weigh and consider attentively what has been before said upon the moral law, and upon the law of faith, and if you are not convinced, can you ask God to direct you in the right way? If you can, he has promised to give you wisdom; he will teach you

you the true doctrine, and will enable you to submit to the righteousness of God. But if you are convinced, are you waiting for the precious gift of faith, or have you received it? If you are waiting for it, remember whose gift it is. The Holy Spirit alone can work faith in your heart. It requires his power, even that almighty power, which raised up *Jesus* from the dead. The scripture ascribes to him the office of convincing sinners of Christ's righteousness, and of giving them faith to rest upon it for their justification. Look up to him for this blessing. Wait in his appointed ways, hoping for it. And when the Spirit shall be poured upon you from on high, then you will be justified by faith in Christ's righteousness, and the work of righteousness shall be peace, and the effect of righteousness, quietness and assurance for ever.

Happy are you, my Christian brethren, who have received the righteousness of faith, and know in whom you have believed. Since Christ's righteousness is yours, bring forth its proper fruits, and shew publicly, that there is an inseparable connection between justifying faith and sanctifying grace. By justifying faith the believer is united to Christ,

Christ, and receives life from him, as a graft does from the stock upon which it grows. By virtue of this union, Christ liveth in the believer, and enables him to put forth the proper acts of spiritual life, as the stock upon which the graft grows supplies it with sap and juices to put forth leaves, and blossom and fruit. This is the certain effect of the abiding of a branch in the vine; it will bring forth fruit; and if any one fancy himself to be a believer, and neither brings forth, nor is seeking to bring forth any fruit, he only deceives himself, and the truth is not in him: for whosoever has Christ for a Saviour, will have the Holy Spirit for a sanctifier, and will bring forth fruit to the glory of God.

See then, my Christian brethren, that ye value and prize this righteousness, and give it its proper honour, both with your hearts and lives. While you are bringing forth its peaceable fruits, you will continually find the comforts of it. This righteousness is one of the pieces of Christian armour. It is called a breast-plate: because it is the proper armour for the vital parts. Your life is always safe while you have your breast-plate on, on, you need not fear the terror by night, nor the arrow that flieth by day. Let thousands fall you are safe. You are defended from outward attacks : for although many be the afflictions of the righteous, yet the Lord delivereth him out of them all; and you are kept in inward peace : for the work of righteousness is peace, and the effect of righteousness quietness and assurance for ever. In time of sickness this righteousness will be a perpetual cordial. It will not suffer the heart to sink, although the body grows weak and faint; for this breast-plate is not only proof against the pains of sickness, but also against the weapons of death. "Righte-"ousness delivereth from death;" *Prov.* xi. 4. not by keeping the justified person from dying, but by keeping him from the fear of the first, and from the power of the second death. The righteous man, armed with this invulnerable breast-plate, can challenge all his enemies. Who shall separate me from the love of Christ? shall tribulation or distress, or persecution or death? Nay, cloathed in the robe of Christ's righteousness I shall not be afraid to go through the valley and shadow of death, nor yet to stand at the awful bar of God's infinite justice. Why should

should he fear to stand there to be tried? For who shall lay any thing to the charge of God's elect? It is God himself that justifieth. Who is he then that condemneth? It is Christ that died, yea rather that is risen again for their justification, and in his righteousness they shall stand holy and unblameable and unreprovable before the judgment-seat of God.

Since these are some of the benefits of having on the breast-plate of righteousness, let us, my Christian brethren, keep it always in use. Since we are fighting under the captain of our salvation, let us be ever armed with his righteousness; and may we all wear it upon our breasts, that neither guilt within, nor troubles without, may ever separate us from the love of *Christ Jesus* our Lord; but may we, in life and death, find the blessedness of this armour, by its protecting us from the threatenings of the broken law, and from the vengeance of almighty justice; and may we in time and in eternity live to his glory, who humbled himself to be made sin for us, that we might be made the righteousness of God in him. Grant this, holy
Father,

Father, for the sake of thy dear Son, *Jesus Christ*: to whom, with thee and the Holy Spirit, three persons in one Jehovah, be honour and glory, and blessing and praise for ever and ever. Amen.

UPON BEING

RIGHTEOUS OVER-MUCH.

DISCOURSE VI.

Eccles. vii. 16.

Be not righteous over-much.

The generality of men think it a very easy matter to get into heaven. They have never tried in earnest to get in, and therefore they are not sensible of any difficulty. Scripture may speak contrary to their opinion, but they will not hear it. Plain matter of fact may be against them, but they will not regard it. They sit down easy and unconcerned about their eternal state, resolved to enjoy the present world, like the fool upon record, " Soul, take thine ease, eat, drink, and be " merry," live jovially at present. Give

thyself

thyself no trouble about religion, and let not one thought of death disturb thee. It will be time enough to prepare for eternity at some future period. Thus they think and act. Nay, many have arrived at such an absolute indolence, that they are angry and provoked, if any one tells them they are certainly in the wrong, and they will not bear it, no not from their minister, whose office and duty it is to try to convince them of the necessity of striving to get into the kingdom of heaven. But if such careless creatures will not hear us, yet they ought to hear him who has the power of life and death, and who says, " Strive to enter in
" at the strait gate: for wide is the gate,
" and broad is the way that leadeth to de-
" struction, and many there be who go in
" thereat. Because, strait is the gate, and
" narrow is the way that leadeth to life,
" and few there be that find it." Matt. ix. 13, 14.

As soon as these great numbers, who are going through the wide gate and in the broad way, see any of their acquaintance beginning to strive to enter in at the strait gate, and to walk in the narrow way, immediately

diately they are offended, and they try to stop them with urging the authority of the text—" Be not righteous over-much"—Why, say they, cannot you be content with the religion of your forefathers; you used to keep to your church, and you lived as good a life as any of your neighbours, and you was righteous enough, what occasion is there then for so many prayers, and sermons, and sacraments? Indeed you carry things too far, and if you do not stop in time, you will quite ruin your character.

This is their manner of talking to every man, who is determined to save his soul. As soon as he begins to live different from his neighbours, and refuses to join with them in their way of murdering their time, they mark him out for a precise godly fellow. They think he makes more ado about religion than need be, and if, after many trials, they cannot laugh him out of his oddities, they heartily despise him for an over-righteous fool.

But if the same man should be convinced of the great change which Christianity ought to make in him. If he begin to talk of the necessity of the new birth, and of the Holy Spirit's beginning and carrying on a saving work of grace in his heart, without which no man is a Christian, more than in name, then worldly men are thoroughly provoked: they cannot bear this enthusiastic stuff. But if he insist farther upon the necessity of Christ's righteousness, without which no sinner can be accepted and justified before God, and that his righteousness is imputed to the sinner by faith only, without any previous good works; although it be productive of all good works; for they are all the fruits of righteousness: these seem to worldly men the wild notions of a distempered brain. If he prove these points and enforce them from plain passages of scripture, they are ever ready to object, What! shall we not be accepted if we do all the good we can, if we do no body no harm, but pay every one his own, and keep strict to our church, and go to the sacrament, as often as we have time to prepare, is not this being righteous enough? And although we fail sometimes, as who does not, yet is not God merciful, and will he not for Christ's sake forgive us? These wordly men know of no righteousness, but what consists in outward duties, in a mere

outside

outside conformity to some parts of the law. They forget that the law is spiritual, reaching to the very thoughts of the heart; and perfect, allowing of no offence, nor offering a pardon for the least, but pronouncing him guilty who offendeth in one point, and under guilt he must lie for ever, as to any thing he can do, unless he be justified freely by grace through the righteousness of the Lord Christ. Whoever insists upon these things is sure to be reckoned in the number of the over-righteous, and will certainly have this caution given him—" Be not righteous over-" much."

It is certain then, that the meaning of the text is generally mistaken. Natural men fancy it commands them not to take too much pains about saving their souls, nor to be singularly religious, but to be content to live according to the course and fashion of the world. More than this, is being righteous over-much. Besides, many serious persons do not understand the text, and therefore have not an answer ready for their adversaries, who are at every turn misapplying this scripture, and putting a wrong sense upon it. The doctrine, which it teaches, ought

ought also to be frequently inculcated and enforced, being one of the fundamental articles of our most holy faith. For these reasons, I have determined to give the passage a particular consideration, and will endeavour to shew,

First, Negatively what the words do not mean;

Secondly, What is their positive and precise meaning, and

Thirdly, I shall bring some arguments to prove the doctrine contained in them. And while I am speaking to these points, may the Lord God open all your understandings clearly to see his mind and will in this scripture, and prepare your hearts to practise the duty which it enforces. May his good Spirit be with us for these gracious purposes, while I am

First, Shewing what the words do not mean. They are generally understood in a wrong sense. People fancy they contain a caution against attaining too much of the righteousness which is of the law; whereas that is impossible. A man cannot have too much legal righteousness. Let him keep the law always and perfectly, in its spiritual nature, and in its full extent, yet he can be but righteous. He does not perform more than the law requires, he only pays it its just demands: for the love of God and the love of our neighbour comprehend the whole law. On these two commandments hang all the law and the prophets. Now we cannot love God too much, nor yet our neighbour, since we are required to love him as ourselves; and therefore if we love God with all the heart and soul, and mind and strength, and our neighbour as ourselves, yet we only do our duty, we do no more than is commanded us, and consequently we are only righteous, but not righteous over-much. But,

Secondly, The scripture declares, there is no man living who so perfectly loveth God and his neighbour, as to attain the righteousness which is of the law. All have sinned, and have thereby robbed God of that love, and his law of that service, which are their due, and all are therefore unrighteous. The psalmist declares, (Psalm liii. 1.) "there "is none that doeth good," which words the apostle cites in this manner, (Rom. iii. 9, 10.) "We have before proved both Jews "and Gentiles that they are all under sin, "as it is written, there is none righteous, "no, not one." Now since there is none so righteous, and much less more righteous, than the law requires, consequently there can be none, no, not one, righteous overmuch.

Thirdly, To this agree the words of our blessed Saviour, Luke xvii. 10. When ye "shall have done all these things which are "commanded you, say, we are unprofitable "servants, we have done that which was our "duty to do." Who does all those things which are commanded him? Not one: for all have sinned. But supposing he did, yet he would be only as righteous as the law requires. He would not be righteous overmuch, because he would only do that which was his duty to do.

A *fourth argument* may be taken from hence: That any man living can be over righteous, and do more than the law requires is a Popish tenet, exploded by the whole Protestant church.

church, and particularly by the church of England in her 14th article.

Of works of Supererogation.

"Voluntary works, besides, over and above God's commandments, which they (the Papists) call works of Supererogation, cannot be taught without arrogancy and impiety: for by them, men do declare, that they do not only render unto God as much as they are bound to do, but that they do more for his sake, than of bounden duty is required; whereas Christ saith plainly, When ye have done all that are commanded to you, say, we are unprofitable servants." This article condemns the general interpretation put upon the text, and declares that it cannot be maintained without arrogancy and impiety. To these arguments, I will add a

Fifth, Taken from the character given in this verse, of the men who would be over righteous, namely, that they thereby destroy themselves; the righteousness which they are seeking will bring upon them destruction. " Be not righteous over-much · Why shouldest thou destroy thyself?" This single

single circumstance will help us to determine, what kind of righteousness it cannot be: for it cannot be the righteousness of the law. This promises life to him that keeps it—"Do this and thou shalt live," and therefore this cannot be a destroying righteousness. Indeed, if after a man has broken the law, he afterwards turns to it for righteousness, and hopes, by his keeping of it, to be made righteous, then he will destroy himself; because the law promises life only to perfect obedience, and threatens to put them, who offend in one point, under the curse: for he that offendeth in one point, is guilty of all. This indeed is a destroying righteousness, opposite to which is the righteousness of the gospel. It is to save sinners from being destroyed by the law. It was wrought out for them by the God-man, Christ Jesus, and is imputed unto them by faith, and when they with the heart believe in it, they are then saved from destruction. Of this saving righteousness it is impossible a man should have too much. He must have all that is needful for his justification, and more than he needs he cannot have. He wants righteousness in an infinite degree, such as none can give him but the Lord our righte-

righteousness, and without this he cannot be saved.

It is evident then that the text speaks of a righteousness, to which if a man trust, it will destroy him, which cannot be the righteousness of the law, for this promises life to them who keep it, nor yet the righteousness of the gospel, for this promises pardon and life to them who have broken the law, but believe in the name of the only begotten Son of God. And since it is neither the righteousness of the law, nor of the gospel, I come now under my second general head, to consider what is the positive precise meaning of the text, and what is the false pretended righteousness of which it treats.

The context may lead us to the true meaning. In what sense a man is commanded not to be righteous over-much, may appear from the following words, " Neither make " thyself over wise." How can a man be over wise? Certainly he cannot know too much. Knowledge is part of the image of God in the soul, as the apostle teaches, " The " new man is renewed in knowledge, after " the image of him that created him." (Col.
iii.

iii. 10.) A man cannot be too wife, but he may think and fpeak of his own wifdom more highly than he ought, and that is making himfelf over wife. In like manner, righteoufnefs is part of the image of God in the foul, Eph. iv. 24. "And that they put on "the new man, which after God is created "in righteoufnefs." A man cannot poffibly be over righteous, he cannot do more than the law requires, but he may think and fpeak of his fancied righteoufnefs more highly than he ought, and that is making himfelf over righteous. It is fuppofing him to be what he is not, which is felf-righteoufnefs. In this fenfe Theodore Beza, one of the great lights of the reformation, underftood the paffage: for, in his note upon it, he fays, "Boaft not too much of thine own righte- "oufnefs and wifdom;" he fuppofed a man's boafting of his righteoufnefs was making himfelf righteous over-much; and this is really the cafe. A man cannot poffibly have too much righteoufnefs, but he may fancy himfelf to be righteous when he is not, and if he fpeak and act according to his own fancy, then he is one of the over righteous. And

Secondly,

Secondly, The true sense of the words agrees with the context. Strictly rendered they read thus, " Be not thou a great self-" justifier," the original word, which is translated righteous, is in the conjugation Hiphil, which in the Hebrew tongue signifies, to make righteous, or to justify, and being here used personally, it stands for a justifier, one who would make himself righteous, and he does it to excess, he justifies himself over-much, pretending to a greater righteousness than he has. This is the meaning of the text, " Be not thou a great self-justifier:" for there is not a righteous man upon earth, who doeth good and sinneth not, and consequently there is not one man upon earth righteous enough, much less righteous over-much, except in his own proud conceit. And against this self-righteousness the text cautions us, advising us not to think of ourselves more highly than we ought to think. But granting this to be the meaning of the text, some will say, What necessity was there for this caution. My answer to this is a

Third argument, By which the meaning of the words may be settled. It was always necessary to give men this caution, because

no man can be righteous over-much, and yet men have been always trying to make themselves so. It is impossible to do more than the law requires, and it is impossible for fallen man to do all that it requires, and yet his pride puts him upon trying impossibilities. There is a self-righteous spirit in him, which leads him to hope he can, by his keeping of the law, attain to such a righteousness as God will accept, and for it justify him. This appears from the history of the Jews in the Old Testament. Moses often dissuades them from the opinion of their own righteousness, and the prophets enlarge upon this particular. The book of Job treats entirely of it, being written professedly to shew, that no man could be justified before God by any righteousness of his own. Job insists upon it in his debate with his three friends, that his life and conversation had been such, that he could maintain his own ways before God. " Let me " be weighed in an even balance, that " God may know mine integrity; for till I " die, I will not remove mine integrity " from me. *My* righteousness I hold fast " and will not let it go, my heart shall not " reproach me so long as I live. I am
" clean,

"clean, without tranfgreffion, I am inno-
"cent, neither is there iniquity in me." But
he foon changed his opinion, after Elihu
had found a right indictment againſt him,
and charged him with having faid, that he
was righteous, and fhould be found fo, if
God was to weigh him in an even balance.
Elihu's arguments brought down and humbled his proud felf-righteous fpirit, and he
confeffed, " I have uttered what I under-
"ſtood not, things too wonderful for me,
" which I knew not. Behold, I am vile,
" I abhor myfelf, and repent in duſt and
" aſhes." The Lord God knew the temper
of the Jews, and that they would be always leaning to felf-righteoufnefs, and therefore he left this book upon record to filence
all the pleas which they fhould ever make
for the fufficiency of their works towards
their juſtification at his bar. How neceffary this book was, we may fee clearly from
the great degree, to which a felf-righteous
fpirit prevailed in our Lord's time; for then
the Pharifees, and all that made a great
fhew of religion, knew of no righteoufnefs,
but what they could attain by their own
works, and not fo much by the works of
the moral, as of the ceremonial law. They

fuppofed

supposed the observance of the ceremonies to be meritorious, and hoped to be made righteous by keeping them strictly. In consequence of this opinion, the learned doctors, rabbies, and scribes, introduced a vast number of traditions, and thought that by keeping them with the ceremonies, they should be holier than others, and they condemned our Lord, because he would not practise the traditions of the elders, but opposed them, and said that they had made the law of God of none effect by their traditions; they had made the moral law of none effect, because they thought to atone for their offences against it, by keeping the ceremonial law, which also they rendered of none effect, because it was instituted to point out the Messiah, who was to make an atonement for the sins committed against the moral law. Our Lord often preached against the Scribes and Pharisees, and he never spake such sharp words against any sort of sinners as against them, for he says, they were farther from the kingdom of God than publicans and harlots. In all his ministry, he never made such a severe discourse as in the 23d chapter of St. Matthew, where he is exposing the errors of the Scribes and Pharisees, rifees, and notwithstanding their many long prayers, and alms, and fastings, and pains to make proselytes, and frequent washings, and many other such-like things, which they thought made them righteous, yet he says to them, "Ye serpents, ye generation of "vipers, how can ye escape the damnation "of hell?" How necessary then was the caution in the text to such persons, who thought themselves righteous and despised others, and is it not still necessary for those who are seeking righteousness by the works of the law? How many thousands and tens of thousands are there now in the world, Protestants as well as Papists, who place righteousness in duties, in living up to the law as near as they can, in keeping clear of gross sins, in going to church, and in hearing and reading the scripture, and if they do all this, they then think themselves safe. But there are some more strict than these who enjoin themselves a round of duties, set forms of prayers and times of fasting, and give many alms, and never miss the sacrament once a month; and perhaps have some family worship; upon which account they think themselves very good, and can thank God that they are not like other men. If any minister dares attack this false righteousness, they cry out against him, as the Pharisees did against Christ. If he tell them, that he does not speak against what they do, but against the motive upon which they act, not against the thing done, but against the end they propose in doing it, this provokes them more; because it tends to lay open the rottenness of their hearts, which being not cleansed from sin, all their outward and pretended righteousness is only like painting a sepulchre, or washing the outside of a cup, while there is left within all manner of uncleanness.

Since then a self-righteous spirit has prevailed, and still prevails in the world, the wise man's caution has been, and is still necessary. He calls to persons of this temper, who are seeking righteousness by the works of the law, and says to them, Why will ye try to justify yourselves by your duties? You are attempting an impossibility: for the law requires absolutely perfect obedience which you have not paid it. You have sinned, and you are none of you righteous, no, not one. There is not a righteous man upon earth, that doeth good, and sinneth

eth not, and consequently there is not one, who has that unsinning righteousness which the law demands, and without which none can be justified by it. Trust not then to your imperfect obedience. It can only destroy you, but seek a better righteousness, even the righteousness of God.

If these arguments be carefully considered, they will, I hope, lead you to the true meaning of the text. The wise man is not speaking against the righteousness of the moral law, nor against the righteousness of the law of faith, but he is dissuading sinners from seeking righteousness by the works of that law, which they have broken, and which condemns them. But trusting to this false righteousness they must inevitably be destroyed; for it is the righteousness of a sinner, which is a contradiction in terms. It is an unrighteous righteousness. The law knows nothing of it. The righteousness of the law consists in perfect obedience; and one single failing renders the sinner ever after absolutely incapable of being made righteous by his keeping the law. This is the doctrine of the text, which, because of the great opposition made to it, I proceed to defend

defend under my third general head. And I will only mention two arguments, the first taken from the righteousness of the law, and the second from the righteousness of the gospel.

The righteousness of the law consists in paying it its due, and that is unsinning obedience. Whoever is legally righteous must keep the law in its most perfect degree, not offending even in a single thought. He must continue to do all things always and perfectly, as the law requires, and then it will pronounce him righteous and give him the promised life. But who is thus righteous? Not one: for all have sinned. And how then can any one be righteous overmuch? So far from it, no one can be righteous at all, by his keeping the law, after he has once broken it; because it immediately brings him in guilty and condemns him. Having offended in one point, he has thereby lost his claim to the righteousness of the law, as much as if he had offended in all, and therefore he cannot be made righteous by the deeds of that law, which has passed sentence upon him, and given him up into the hands of justice to suffer the first and second

second death. While he lies in this miserable, helpless state, he can no more do any act which is good and valid in law, than a malefactor can under sentence of death, and yet he is so proud as to fancy, that he can merit heaven by his dead works. Poor vain creature, he is so full of self, as to think he can do all that the law requires, although he has broken it, and although he can do nothing but sin, until he be pardoned and believe in the name of the only begotten Son of God: for whatsoever is not of faith is sin. What great numbers are there among us of this self-righteous spirit? Who, because they are somewhat stricter in their lives than others, and are more constant attenders upon ordinances, therefore take state to themselves, and expect you should give them place according to their own fancied rank of merit. They are still proclaiming, as the Pharisees used to do, Make way there, stand by, I am holier than thou. Against this mock righteousness the text is levelled. The design of it is to strip the self-righteous of all their borrowed plumes, and to convince them that after they have broken the law, they cannot be made righteous by a partial keeping of it. The wise man would lead them to consider what the moral law is, how far short they come of the obedience it requires, and how imperfect, yea sinful, their works and duties are, and thus he would convince them of their want of a better righteousness than their own. The Jews were exceedingly prone to trust to their own righteousness, and therefore he tried to beat them off from any reliance upon it. When our Lord came, he found them under the influence of the same self-righteous spirit; and in all his preaching he spake with great sharpness against the pretended righteousness of the Scribes and Pharisees. We have still men of the same spirit among us, whose righteousness does not exceed the righteousness of the Scribes and Pharisees, and yet they hope to enter into the kingdom of heaven. To all such persons the wise man directs his advice, and counsels them not to trust to their works and duties for a righteousness, in which they may be justified before God—" Be not ye great self-justifiers. Why " will ye destroy yourselves?" Your false righteousness will destroy you, if you venture to put your trial upon it at God's bar: for he has already decreed, that since all have sinned, therefore by the deeds of the

broken

broken law shall no flesh be justified in his sight.

It is certain then, that the text does not speak against the righteousness of the law, nor yet, secondly, against the righteousness of faith. The law of God is as holy, just, and good as he is, and cannot pass by the least sin. It has made no provision for a pardon, nor given any promise to repentance or to amendment; but requires absolutely perfect unsinning obedience, and upon the first offence it puts the sinner under the curse, and leaves him in the hands of justice to inflict upon him the threatened and deserved punishment. In this state the gospel finds him, and offers him the righteousness of the Lord Christ; but the proud sinner will not submit to be justified by it, until the Holy Spirit preach the law to his conscience, and convince him of its holy, spiritual, and perfect nature, upon which he feels guilt, conscience accuses and condemns him, and he sees no righteousness in his fancied good works to rely upon, but finds he must go out of himself for a righteousness, in which he may appear before God. Then the Holy Spirit convinces him of Christ's righteousness, how infinitely perfect it is, and how safely he may trust to it, and gives him faith to apprehend it, and to apply it to himself for his justification. And then he no longer goes about to establish his own righteousness, but submits to the righteousness of God. Against this the wise man cannot caution us. We all want it, and over much of it we cannot have. It is the righteousness of God, as perfect as God is, and the divine person, who wrought it out by his obedience and sufferings, humbled himself to be made sin for us, that we might be made the righteousness of God in him. Believers are not only righteous in him, but righteousness, and that the righteousness of God too, against which law and justice cannot make any exception; therefore of this righteousness, though not of their own, may they boast all the day long. The merits of it are their justification, the fruits of it are their sanctification, and when they come to heaven, this righteousness will be their everlasting robe of glory, and to sing his praises, who cloathed them with it, will be their employment and happiness for ever and ever. Surely then, the wise man's caution in the text was not levelled against this all-perfect

and

and glorious righteousness? No. He knew the inestimable value of it, and intended to recommend it by detecting that false righteousness, upon which sinners are apt to rest and see not their want of a better. This was his design, which having proved and established by several arguments, I shall only add two or three practical observations upon what has been said.

This greatly mistaken text is, I hope, now set right, and the meaning of it is made plain and clear. The wise man did not intend to speak against the righteousness of the law, nor against the righteousness of faith, but against a false righteousness, which was then and is still in the world. How many are there, who after they have broken the law, think of being justified by keeping it better, and hope to make themselves very good and righteous enough by their works and duties? To every such person, the wise man says, " Be not thou a great self-justifier: Why " shouldst thou destroy thyself?" But very few will take his advice. There is a generation of men, proud and self-righteous, who think their own works can recommend them to God. Although they have sinned, yet they fancy that duties can atone for fins. The Jews were much addicted to this error, and the apocryphal books are full of it. In our Lord's time we find the religious among the Jews placing righteoufnefs in works. Our modern Pharifees copy exactly after them, and refufe to attend to the wife man's caution in the text. Thefe over righteous ones make a faviour of their duties, and hope to merit heaven by their works; and yet, alas! their works are but few, and thefe very imperfect. Their righteoufnefs is chiefly negative, confifting in doing no harm, in not murdering, or ftealing, or getting drunk, or breaking the commandments outwardly. Then they are what you call very good fort of people. But if they keep clofe to their church, and go to prayers on Wednefdays and Fridays, and on a faint's day, if they have nothing elfe to do; and will not play at cards, or go to the playhoufe on Saturday night before the facrament, although they have no objection againft going on Monday after they received. Oh, thefe are your mighty good people indeed! Who are righteous, if they are not? But if they go to the facrament once a month, and ufe the *new week's preparation*, and follow it ftrictly; or if they mifs any of the prayers

through

through an engagement in the evening, they will be sure to say them all the next morning; and if they have some new book of devotion, out of which they say their formal task, morning and evening, like the stupid Papists gabbling over the bead-roll of their Ave-Mary's and Pater-nosters; these are our great saints: Who shall go to heaven, if they do not? These, like their predecessors of old, think themselves righteous and despise others. Their pride deceives them, and hinders them from submitting to the righteousness of God. They are too proud to submit. The knowledge of the law and the knowledge of themselves would humble them. But they are so ignorant of the law, as to believe that by doing some of its duties they shall be made righteous enough; and they are so ignorant of the plague of their own hearts, as to see no necessity for an inward change. They cannot be persuaded but they have very good hearts, and therefore they have no reason to pray with the psalmist, Create in me a clean heart, O God, and renew a right spirit within me. Without this clean heart and right spirit, they have only the form and outside of Christians. The life and power is wanting, and Christ

may

may fay to them, as he did to the church of Sardis, "I know thy works, that thou haft a name that thou liveft, and art dead."

But if this be the cafe, fome will be apt to fay, Why need we do any good works, if they be not meritorious? Why need we go to church, and pray, and hear and read the word, and go to the facrament, and do good, if all this be no part of our righteoufnefs before God? It certainly is not: "for by grace are ye faved, fays the apoftle, through faith: not of works, left any man fhould boaft." And to this doctrine the whole Proteftant church fubfcribes, and all the Papifts deny it. The reformers were called Proteftants, becaufe they protefted chiefly againft this blafphemous tenet of Popery, namely, that works merit towards a finner's juftification before God. This is the grand diftinction between us and the Papifts, and yet, alas! this diftinction is wearing out. What great numbers have we among us, who truft to their own fancied good works for acceptance with God? In this point, and it is a very leading one, they are perfectly agreed with the Papifts. They are both great felf-juftifiers, having at leaft equal, if

not

not superior merit to Christ in the matter of their justification. Hear the form of a monkish absolution, in which the doctrine of merit is thus taught.

"God forgive thee, my brother, the merit of the passion of our Lord Jesus Christ and of blessed saint Mary, always a virgin, and of all the saints, the merit of thine order, the strictness of thy religion, the humility of thy confession, and contrition of thy heart, the good works which thou hast done and shall do for the love of our Lord Jesus Christ, be unto thee available for the remission of thy sins, the increase of desert and grace, and the reward of everlasting life. Amen." What a deal of self-wrought stuff is here, the merit of which, instead of the merit of Christ alone, is said to be available for the remission of sins? And is it not the same with our half Papist Protestants? Are there not multitudes of them who think that the merit of their church-going, and the strictness of their lives, and the merit of their prayers and alms, and other good works, will justify them before God, or if they dare not trust wholly to them, yet they hope Christ will supply what is in
them

them deficient; but this is mixing grace and works, which the scripture will not allow to stand together: for if works, wholly or in part, merit our justification, then there would be room for boasting, which God in his way of justifying sinners by the righteousness of Christ has absolutely excluded, that no flesh might glory in his presence, Christ being made of God unto sinners all that they want, even wisdom, righteousness, sanctification, and eternal redemption: that, according as it is written, he that glorieth, let him glory in the Lord.

Since then Christ has made an atonement for sin, and brought in everlasting righteousness, why will you glory in yourselves, rather than glory in the Lord? Why will you trust to your own fancied righteousness, since nothing but pride could tempt you to glory in it? Your ignorance of Christ's righteousness hinders your seeing, how infinitely perfect it is, and your own self-sufficiency will not let you submit to be saved by it, and therefore you go about to establish your own righteousness. You may work for a time upon this plan, and think yourselves safe. You may lull conscience asleep, and deceive
yourselves,

yourselves, and deceive others with your fair outside. But the cheat cannot last long. God sees your hearts, and the corruption in them is naked and open to him, although you study to hide it from yourselves. He has declared of you, although you will not believe him, that you are not righteous: for there is none righteous in himself, no not one. This is his sovereign decree. Oh! that your consciences may submit to it, and seek for a righteousness which God will accept at his bar. Dreadful will be the time, if you appear there without a complete and infinitely perfect righteousness. Such there is in Christ, and in none else, and it is offered freely, even to you, ye self-righteous Pharisees. You may receive the free gift of his righteousness, if you will renounce your own. And what is your own? What merit can there be in these duties, which are done out of pride, done in sin, and done in opposition to the word of God. If you can reject all dependance upon these, the gospel offers to you freely the righteousness of God for your justification. Oh that he may dispose you to accept of it, that being justified by faith, you may have peace with God through Jesus Christ our Lord, and may live in the comfortable fenfe and enjoyment of this peace, until you receive a crown of righteoufnefs, which fadeth not away. Grant this, Holy Father, for the all-perfect righteoufnefs fake of thy beloved Son Jefus Chrift; to whom, with Thee and the Holy Spirit, three perfons in one Jehovah, be equal praife and honour, and glory and dominion, and power, in time and in eternity. Amen, and Amen.

UPON THE RIGHT KNOWLEDGE of GOD.

DISCOURSE VII.

MARK xii. 28, 29, 30, 31.

And one of the Scribes came, and having heard them reasoning together, and perceiving that he had answered them well, asked him, which is the first commandment of all. And Jesus answered him, The first of all the commandments is, Hear, O Israel, the Lord our God is one Lord; and thou shalt love the Lord thy God with all thy heart, and with all thy soul, and with all thy mind, and with all thy strength: This is the first commandment. And the second is like, namely this, Thou shalt love thy neighbour as thyself; there is none other commandment greater than these.

OUR blessed Saviour had been disputing with the chief priests, and elders, and the Scribes, and after he had silenced them, they left him and went their way. But they departed with enraged

enraged and malicious hearts, determined to take the firſt opportunity to deſtroy him, and they ſend certain of the Phariſees and of the Herodians to catch him in his words; theſe hypocrites pretended to believe him to be a faithful teacher of the way of God, and to come to him with no other view than to deſire his opinion upon a very difficult caſe, namely, Whether it was lawful to give tribute unto Cæſar, or not? Our Lord ſolved this difficult queſtion in a manner that aſtoniſhed his very adverſaries; for he knowing their wicked hearts, ſaid unto them, Why tempt ye me? Bring me a penny; and when they brought it, he ſaid, Whoſe image and ſuperſcription is this upon it? And they anſwered, Cæſar's. Then, ſaid he, render therefore to Cæſar the things that are Cæſar's, and to God the things that are God's. As ſoon as he had ſilenced them, certain of the Sadducees came with a caſe out of the law, which they thought he was not able to ſolve; but he preſently ſhewed them, that their error aroſe from their ignorance of ſcripture, and he put them to ſilence. While he was confuting them with the authority of Moſes, the Phariſees were gathered together againſt him, and one of them being a Scribe,

Scribe, learned in the law, having heard him reasoning with the chief priests, then with the *Herodians*, and afterwards with the Sadducees, and perceiving that he had answered them well, was willing to try him with a question out of the law. The Scribe asked him, Which is the first commandment of all. And *Jesus* answered him, the first of all the commandments is, Hear, O *Israel*, the Lord our God is one Lord, and thou shalt love the Lord thy God, &c. And the Scribe said unto him, Well, master, thou hast said the truth: for there is one God, and there is none other but he, and to love him with all the heart, and with all the understanding, and with all the soul, and with all the strength, and to love his neighbour as himself, is more than all whole-burnt offerings and sacrifices. And when Jesus saw that he answered discreetly, he said unto him, Thou art not far from the kingdom of God. And no man after that durst ask him any question.

In this passage we have the sum and substance of vital and practical religion. The first and greatest commandment is the love of God arifing from the right knowledge of his effence and perfonality, and the fecond is like unto it, namely, the love of our neighbour founded upon the true love of God. There is none other commandment greater than thefe: for upon thefe two hang all the law and the prophets; and fince thefe two are the greateft, they therefore deferve our greateft attention. Our Lord demands it of us in the text. What he enjoins for the two greateft commandments we ought to efteem fuch, and to ftudy them moft, and to practife them beft. To that end let us confider them carefully, and may his good Spirit open our underftandings to comprehend them, and difpofe our hearts to love them, and give us grace and ftrength to practife them agreeably to his holy will.

The firft commandment confifts of two parts, the knowledge of God, and the love of God. The true knowledge of God is contained in thefe words—Hear, O *Ifrael*, the Lord our God is one Lord. And the nature and degree of love to God is thus defcribed.—Thou fhalt love the Lord thy God with all thy heart, mind, foul, and ftrength. I fhall confine myfelf at prefent

to

to the firſt of theſe particulars, purpoſing through divine aſſiſtance to explain and enforce what is laid down in the text concerning the true knowledge of God, reſerving the other parts of the text for ſome future opportunity.

The firſt and chief point in our religious enquiries is, to diſcover what God is. This is the fundamental article, upon which all the reſt depend. We muſt know the nature and perſonality of God, before we can ſerve and love him, and therefore our bleſſed Saviour very properly places the knowledge of God before the love of him. We cannot love what we know nothing of. Ignorance of God cannot poſſibly beget love of him. If there be very dark and confuſed ideas of him in the underſtanding, there cannot be much true love of him in the heart: for which reaſon the text determines and fixes the proper object of worſhip, before it requires the love and ſervice, which is to be paid him. Our Lord begins with the knowledge of the true God, and does not propoſe any thing new upon this point, but goes to the law and to the teſtimony. He cites a paſſage from *Deut*. vi. 4.

in which the divine essence and personality are clearly stated, "Hear, O *Israel*, the Lord our God is one Lord." This is a command to the whole *Israel* of God, whether *Jews* or *Gentiles*, to hearken to what the Lord God says concerning himself. He calls to them and requires them to hear him—" Hear, O *Israel*," by which means it becomes a matter of duty, and we are indispensably bound to attend to this revelation of his will. He has not left us at liberty to think what we please about his essence and his personality, because he has revealed what we are to believe about both. And it was necessary he should do this, because there is no religion without a God, and no true religion without the true God. How should we know what religious service to perform, if we were ignorant of the proper object of worship? It being absolutely necessary that we should know God, the knowledge of him is therefore revealed, and settled in the first part of the greatest commandment. We are not left to reasoning about the being of God from the light of nature, or from philosophy or metaphysics; but the scripture has fixed our creed, and we must abide by it; otherwise we cannot keep the following parts of the text;

text; we cannot love God and our neighbour aright, unless we first know what God is. Since this is a material point in our present enquiry, and not thoroughly understood, I will endeavour to prove the necessity of settling the proper object of worship, before the worship due to him can be paid. It is very certain there can be no salvation without belief in God. An *Atheist* cannot be saved. He that cometh to God must believe that he is; but the *Atheist* denies his very being, denies that God is, and thereby withdraws all allegiance from him. Now, if a man cannot be saved without believing in God, consequently he cannot be saved without believing in the true God: for a false God is no God at all, it is a mere idol, a nothing in the world. Whoever pays his service and worship to this false god is an idolater, and guilty of high-treason against the supreme Majesty of heaven. If any of you, who owe your allegiance to king *George*, were to go to *Rome* and pay it to the Pretender, in what light would the law consider your proceeding? Would not it try you for a capital offence, and if found guilty, would not it deprive you of your fortune and life? The law of the most high

high God treats those, who withdraw their allegiance from him in the same manner, having already passed sentence upon them, and decreed, that idolaters shall not inherit the kingdom of Christ, and of God.

Since then the true object of worship must first be known before we can worship him aright, how are we to come to the knowledge of him? This is the next step in our present enquiry. And who shall determine this point for us? What authority shall we abide by? Shall scripture or reason decide? If scripture be judge, its determination is clear. What words can be plainer than these are? " Canst thou, by searching, " find out God? Canst thou find out the Al- " mighty to perfection? No. It is as high " as heaven, what canst thou do? deeper " than hell, what canst thou know? The " measure thereof is longer than the earth, " and broader than the sea," (*Job.* xi. 7, 8, 9.) entirely out of the reach of our faculties. The reason of this is assigned in *Matt.* xi. 27. " No man knoweth the Son but " the Father; neither knoweth any man the " Father, save the Son, and he to whom- " soever the Son will reveal him," no man therefore,

therefore, be he ever so wise and learned, knoweth God the Father, but by the revelation of his Son. And to this agree the words of the Apostle, 1 *Cor.* i. 21. " The " world by wisdom knew not God." The world by such wisdom, as it could attain, was not able to discover the true God.

If these testimonies of holy writ be not suffered to determine the point, it is not because they are of doubtful interpretation: for words cannot speak plainer, but because you would have the matter tried before some other judge. Well then, let us hear what reason says; but we will not hearken to its proud boastings of what it can discover; we will examine matter of fact, and enquire what it has discovered. Did reason ever find out God, and did any reasoners ever find out the almighty to perfection? Who were the men? When, where did they live? In the refined and enlightened ages of *Greece?* Tell us, ye disputers of this world, did your *Aristotle*, or any of his followers, with their subtle reasoning, attain to the knowledge of God? It is an undoubted truth, that they did not. And did any of the other *Greek* philosophers succeed better in their enquiries? No, not one of them. Professing themselves to be wise they became fools, and fell into gross idolatry along with the ignorant vulgar: for they changed the glory of the incorruptible God into an image made like to corruptible man, and to birds, and to four-footed beasts, and creeping things. But if the *Greeks* failed, did not the learned *Romans* find out God? No, not one of them ever discovered what God was. The *Roman* philosophers, aided and assisted with all the discoveries of the *Greeks*, yet remained as ignorant of God as they had been. *Tully* has left us a curious treatise upon the nature of the gods, in which he has demonstrated the apostle's proposition, that the world by wisdom knew not God: for in this volume, there is not a conjecture or a hint about the nature of the true God. After the fruitless enquiries of such a genius, I need not bring any other arguments to prove, that the *Romans*, with all their learning and refinement, knew not God. Their reason was not equal to the task. And where shall we find greater reasoners? Did any man ever make a better use of his reasoning faculties than *Tully?* and yet with all his searching he could not find out God.

In these instances we see the utmost stretch of reason, and what it can discover. Indeed it boasts great things, and pretends, by the help of metaphysics, to discover the secrets of the spiritual world; but these are vain boastings. Matter of fact disproves them: for there was not one reasoner in *Greece* or *Rome* who discovered the true God. These men came the nearest to the truth, who erected an altar to the unknown God; by which they held forth and exposed the weakness of human reason, since in one of the most famous universities of the heathen world the philosophers worshipped an unknown God. How weak and groundless then are the boastings of our modern unbelievers, who pretend to discover what God is by the mere dint of reason? What have our *Arians* and *Deists* discovered of him? Do they know more of God, than the philosophers did? No. They have indeed greater helps, but by rejecting them, their pride is greater, and their ignorance appears more manifest: for they have left revelation, and have invented to themselves as empty an idol as any heathen philosopher ever worshipped. They rejected the Godhead of Christ, and of the Holy Spirit, and have imagined to themselves

selves a god existing in one person, infinitely extended, filling infinite space, with many other such like chimerical attributes. And this idol, this nothing in the world, is become the fashionable divinity of our times; but its worshippers are all traitors. Every act of worship paid to this idol is high-treason; for by such act men withdraw their allegiance from the true God, and pay it to what has no more divinity than stocks and stones. And ought not the servants of the most high God kindly to admonish their fellow creatures of their guilt, when they see them seduced by this dangerous heresy? And if the watchmen give them not warning, will they not be partakers with them in their sins? If we hold our peace, they will perish, but their blood will God require at our hands. So that as well for the sake of our own souls, as of theirs, we ought to speak plainly upon this subject, and bring it to a matter of self-examination. Let each of us put these questions to himself: Is it so, then, that there can be no true worship or love of God, unless it be paid to the true God, have I then the right object of worship for my God? How was I brought to the knowledge of him? for this is the best way

way to discover the certainty of what, I think, I know of him. Did I find him out by the light of reason? And did metaphysics help me to find him out to perfection? If I have taken this method, I have been deceiving myself, for the world by its reason never found out God. Or was I brought to the knowledge of him in this way? Was I convinced of sin, and humbled under the sense of it, and did I then find myself fallen from God, and alienated from the life of God, so that I had no means of discovering his nature and perfections, but as revealed by his word and by his Spirit? Did I read the word, and pray for the Holy Spirit to open and to explain it, that I might come to the knowledge of the only true God and of *Jesus Christ*, whom he hath sent? And am I still in this humble, teachable frame of mind, reading the word, and praying for the teachings of the Spirit of God? If this be your case, happy are ye. God has promised, and his word cannot be broken. Ask and ye shall have. Ask and ye shall have this great promise of the new covenant fulfilled to you, *Jer.* xxxi. 34. " And they shall
" no more teach every man his neighbour,
" and every man his brother, saying, Know
" the

" the Lord: for they shall all know me
" from the least of them to the greatest of
" them, saith the Lord." He will teach you
the knowledge of himself, and will manifest
to you his essence and his personality. You
shall know him as he has been pleased to
reveal himself in the text, in which we have
the whole of what is contained in the sacred
volume: for here he declares what his essence is, he is one Jehovah, and what the
persons in this one Jehovah are, they are
Alehim, Jehovah our *Alehim* is one Jehovah.
This proposition is one of the deep things of
God which he hath revealed unto us by his
Spirit, and which contains more than can
be written in many volumes. Each word
has a rich copiousness, and explains to us
many treasures of divine truth. May that
Lord and God, in whom are laid up all the
riches of grace and knowledge, open them
to you at this time, that you may understand the will and mind of the Lord in his
great and glorious name Jehovah.

The word translated Lord, is in the original Jehovah, which signifies a manner of
existence peculiar and proper to the most
High God. He is the only self-existent
essence.

essence. All other beings owe their existence to his will and pleasure, and depend on him for life and breath and all things; but he exists by a necessity of nature, and this necessary existence is the meaning of the word Jehovah. We cannot fully comprehend the idea conveyed by this word, because we are not acquainted with the manner of necessary existence. The wisest man upon earth cannot describe in what manner any material object exists: for the atoms of which bodies are composed fall not under the observation of our senses. We know that gold differs from water, but we are ignorant of their constituent particles, which make them differ, so that we confessedly know not the manner of their existence; and the plain reason is, gold and water do exist in a different manner, but our senses cannot discover how their particles or atoms differ. And since we know not the manner of the existence of the material bodies with which ourselves are conversant, how absurd would it be for any man to pretend to know the manner of the existence of a spiritual being? How presumptuous then would it be for any man to undertake to describe how Jehovah exists, and rashly to affirm that he exists in a manner which excludes all perfonality, while this very man does not know the manner of the exiftence of any one thing in the world. And yet every little philofopher, who has but juft learned to reafon upon the objects which are within his reach, pretends to reafon about the nature and attributes of God, and every minute infidel undertakes to prove by metaphyfics, and one of them more proud and ignorant than the reft thought he could prove *a priori*, that Jehovah exifts in one perfon, although Jehovah himfelf declares he does not. If thefe men would attend to the meaning of the name Jehovah, it might correct fome of their miftakes. It fignifies neceffary exiftence. Now from whence fhall we form a perfect idea of this word? We have no ideas but from our fenfes, and there is no object within the reach of our fenfes, which exifts by a neceffity of nature. All thefe Jehovah hath formed and made: confequently they can only give us ideas of dependent exiftence. There is but one Jehovah, the text fays, and he exifts in a manner, of which no other thing can give us a perfect idea, and therefore we can have no reafon to reject the account which God has given us

of

of the manner of his exiftence, but if we act confiftently, we muft receive and abide by the revealed account, which teaches us that Jehovah is the felf-exiftent effence, and that this effence is one, one Jehovah, but the *Alehim*, the perfons in Jehovah, are three. There was no doubt in thofe ancient times about the perfonality, the fcripture guards moft the unity of the effence, and while it affirms the Father, Son, and Holy Spirit to be of the felf-exiftent effence, it, at the fame time, teaches us that thefe three are one, one in effence, but three in perfons.

The perfonality in Jehovah is defcribed in the text by the word *Alehim*, which is in the plural number, and acknowledged to be fo by the *Jews* as well as *Chriftians*, and if they had not owned it, yet the fenfe of the paffage would lead us to feek for a plural interpretation, becaufe there was no need for a revelation to teach us, that Jehovah our one *Alehim* is one Jehovah, which is no more than that one is one. But the word *Alehim* being plural, the Father, Son, and Holy Spirit being *Alehim*, it was necef- fary to reveal to us the unity of the effence,

and

and to teach us that these three persons were one Jehovah, and therefore being of the self-existent essence, none is before or after other, none is greater or less than another, but the whole three persons are co-eternal together and co-equal. Each of the persons is Jehovah. The Father is Jehovah, as we read *Isai.* lxiv. 8. " But now, O Jehovah, " thou art our Father." The Son is Jehovah, *Isai.* xlv. 21. " Who hath declared " this from antient time? Have not I Je- " hovah? and there is no God else beside " me, a just God and a Saviour;" here the Son our Saviour is called Jehovah. And the Holy Spirit is Jehovah, *Isaiah* xi. 2. " The Spirit Jehovah shall rest upon him, " the Spirit of wisdom and understand- " ing, &c."

Each of the persons is called *Alehim*. The Father is so called, 1 *Chron.* xxix. 10. " And " *David* said, Blessed be thou Jehovah, " *Alehim* of *Israel*, our Father, for ever and " ever." The Son is *Alehim*, *Isaiah* xlv. 21. " There is no *Alehim* else beside me, a just " God and a Saviour." The Holy Spirit is *Alehim*, *Exodus* xxxi. iii. " I have filled *Be-* " *zaleel* with the Spirit *Alehim*," not of the

the *Alehim*, the *Hebrew* is, with the Spirit *Alehim*, so that the Spirit is the *Alehim*.—
These scriptures confirm the doctrine of the text, namely, that Jehovah is one, and that in the unity of Jehovah there are three *Alehim*, which word does not signify their manner of existence. Jehovah denotes that, but it is a relative word, descriptive of the gracious offices of the eternal three in the œconomy of man's redemption. And neither the personality expressed by its being plural, nor its meaning, are retained by our translators in the singular word *God*. God is no more the sense of *Alehim*, than goodness is. And if the translators could not find a proper word in our language, they should have given a definition of it in the first place they met with it in the Bible, and then have retained the *Hebrew* name ever afterwards. By their neglect our people are kept in ignorance of this gracious name, under which Jehovah would have himself to be known. It belongs to the covenant of grace, and is descriptive of the acts and offices of the eternal three in the glorious plan of man's salvation, and it signifies the binding act of the covenant, the obligation entered into upon oath to fulfil it. This is the sense of

Q *Aleh.*

Aleh, the root from whence *Alehim* is derived, and there is no other root from whence it can be derived, without offering great violence to the established rules of the *Hebrew* tongue. The oath of God is often mentioned in scripture, and the people's entering into it is beautifully described, *Deut.* xxix. 10, 11, 12. " Ye stand this day all of you
" before the Lord your God, your captains
" of your tribes, your elders, and your of-
" ficers, with all the men of *Israel*, your
" littles ones, your wives, and thy stranger
" that is in thy camp, from the hewer of
" wood unto the drawer of water, that thou
" shouldest enter into covenant with the
" Lord thy God, and into his oath." God is here said to have made an oath, emphatically stiled *his* oath, because it was the oath of the covenant from whence the name *Alehim* is taken.

If you ask, when was this covenant made by oath, and by whom, and for what end? the scripture answers those points very clearly.

The covenant was made before the world began, as *Titus* i. 2. " In hope of eternal
" life

"life which God that cannot lie promised before the world began." Was not this promise the oath of the covenant? What else could it be? God who cannot lie promised before the world began, and fore-ordained (as 1 *Peter* i. 20) that Christ should be the lamb, who should take away sin by the sacrifice of himself. This was fore-ordained by an eternal purpose, which he purposed in Christ Jesus our Lord, *Eph.* iii. 11. What is called in these scriptures the purpose, the promise, and fore-ordination of God, was the covenant of grace which was made before the world began, yea, by an eternal purpose, and from which the divine persons who confirmed this covenant by an oath, are called *Alehim*, and as the covenant was made before the world began, they therefore took their name from it, and are described by it before the creation in the first chapter of *Genesis*. They had done some act before, from which this name was taken. Now it signifies, to confirm any thing by oath, therefore they had confirmed something by oath before the world began; and what it was these scriptures determine, which speak of the purpose, counsel, promise, and fore-ordination of God made before all worlds, to bring many sons unto glory by *Jesus Christ*. This was the design of the purpose, counsel, &c. and the persons who designed this, are the three in Jehovah: for each of them is called Jehovah, and each of them is called *Alehim*, because each person in Jehovah had a distinct office in the œconomy of the covenant. The Father undertook to demand full satisfaction for sin; therefore he is called a jealous God and a consuming fire. Christ undertook to pay this satisfaction, and is therefore called God the Saviour, and the Holy Spirit covenanted to apply and to render effectual the benefit of Christ's satisfaction to believers; and therefore his constant name is Spirit, which word signifies the air that we breathe, on which our animal life depends, as our spiritual life does on his inspiration. Now since the divine persons have entered into a covenant, and do sustain those distinct offices in it, and since our salvation depends upon the knowledge of these truths, was it not an act of infinite love and condescension for the divine persons in Jehovah to take the gracious name of *Alehim*, and to reveal themselves to us, as persons bound by the obligation of an oath to carry the covenant of grace into execution?

If

If you afk, what neceffity there was for this oath ? It was neceffary only on our parts, and it was an act of aftonifhing mercy, and will demand our everlafting tribute of praife, that God would vouchfafe to give convinced finners fuch encouragement to hope for mercy, as to bind himfelf by two immutable things to fave them. The Apoftle, Heb. vi. 16, 17, 18, thus fpeaks of this wonderful inftance of God's love. " An oath for con-
" firmation is among men an end of all ftrife;
" wherein God, willing more abundantly to
" fhew unto the heirs of promife the immu-
" tability of his counfel, confirmed it by an
" oath, that by two immutable things, in
" which it was impoffible for God to lie, we
" might have a ftrong confolation, who have
" fled for refuge to lay hold of the hope fet
" before us." In this fcripture the Apoftle defcribes the counfel, or covenant of God to fave finners, and this was confirmed by an oath ; and the reafon of the oath, was for the fake of the heirs of promife, that they might have two immutable things to reft their faith upon, namely, the immutable counfel and the immutable oath of God, and thefe ought to filence all doubts in the heirs of promife,

becaufe

becaufe it is impoffible that either of them fhould be broken.

These authorities may fuffice to determine the meaning of the divine name *Alehim*. It is expreffive of the perfonality in Jehovah, and denotes what the Father, Son, and Holy Spirit, the three *Alehim*, have covenanted upon oath to do for the falvation of finners. *Alehim* fignifies the Trinity in covenant, and particularly expreffes the oath, which was the binding act of the covenant, and thereby it denotes the moft merciful relation, in which divine love could manifeft itfelf; a relation productive of the richeft bleffings of time and of eternity. Jehovah is a name of majefty and greatnefs. *Alehim* is a name of grace and mercy. Jehovah expreffes the felf-exiftence of the Godhead, and the infinite difference between his manner of exifting and that of his dependent creatures, and after they had finned it was to them a name of terror. Whereas *Alehim* expreffes nothing but tender love and abundant mercy to returning finners: for the covenant was made for fuch, and it was confirmed by an oath, that they might place their whole truft and confidence on what
the

the Trinity had covenanted to do for them and for their falvation: for the Father, although he be the avenger of fin, yet has been fatisfied with the obedience and fufferings of his co-equal and co-eternal Son, and will be fatisfied with all thofe who fubmit to be faved by his righteoufnefs, and the Holy Spirit will influence them to accept the righteoufnefs of God for their juftification, and he will work mightily in them to enable them to bring forth the fruits of righteoufnefs, until he bring them fafe to glory.— Thefe are the mercies promifed in the covenant of grace, and expreffed by the divine name *Alehim*. How greatly then fhould this name encourage convinced finners to come and afk the covenant mercies? And what ftrong confolation does it give them, when they flee for refuge to *Jefus Chrift*, to lay hold of the hope fet before them in him?

From what has been faid, it appears that the firft part of the commandment, relating to God, is the right knowledge of him, and what we are required to believe concerning his effence and perfonality is defcribed in thefe words:—" Hear, O *Ifrael*, " Jehovah

"Jehovah our *Alehim* is one Jehovah." Jehovah the self-exiftent effence, who is our *Alehim*, our Trinity, bound by the oath of the covenant to fave finners, thefe three in covenant, Father, Son, and Holy Spirit, are not before nor after other, greater or lefs than another, but they are of one and the fame felf-exiftent effence, thefe three are one Jehovah, the holy, bleffed, and glorious Trinity are one Jehovah.

This, my brethren, is the doctrine of the text, which the Lord God himfelf calls upon you to hear—"Hear, O *Ifrael*." And have you heard him? Have you received his account of the divine effence and perfonality? If not, why do you reject it? Is not his command a law, and are you not bound to believe what the Lord has revealed concerning himfelf?

Perhaps you think the revealed account is not eftablifhed upon fufficient authority. This point does not come under confideration at prefent. We are only treating of the doctrine, and what can you object againft it, as it has been now ftated? Why, fay fome, I ftill think, after all that you have faid, the

doctrine

doctrine is inconsistent: for you are forced to maintain that three are one. Nay, we maintain no such contradiction: for the Trinity is not three and one in the same respect, but three in person and one in essence. The air which is reduced to atoms in the action of fire, and the light which comes from it, and the gross spirit of the air which feeds the fire, these three conditions of the air are one in essence, and is it any contradiction to say, these three are one? No surely. Just so we speak of the essence as one, and of the persons in it as three.

Supposing this to be a good illustration of the doctrine, yet still we cannot receive it, say some, because it is unintelligible. What is unintelligible? The proposition itself is plain, in the self-existent essence there are three persons. You cannot object to the difficulty of the terms, or of your forming a clear idea of what they convey. But you cannot conceive how there can be three persons in one essence. And is this the cause of your unbelief? If you will not believe the doctrine of the Trinity, until you comprehend the manner of the divine existence, consider how absurdly you act: For do you know how

how a spirit exists? No. And yet you believe the existence of an immortal spirit within you. Can you comprehend how an infinite Spirit exists? No. You know not how your own spirit exists, and yet while you are confessedly ignorant of a finite object, you pretend to be so well acquainted with the mode and manner of existence of an infinite Spirit, as to reject what is revealed in scripture concerning it. Whether this be not acting an absurd part, I leave it to yourselves to judge.

But still you cannot think the scripture-doctrine of the Trinity is rational. If you go to try it by reason, you forget that the world by reason knew not God. It did not know him formerly in the learned ages of *Greece* and *Rome*. And if then this enlightened age has discovered how Jehovah exists, let our reasoning infidels demonstrate, that he exists in such a manner as absolutely excludes all personality. But this they cannot demonstrate, they know they cannot, and yet they pretend the scripture-doctrine of the Trinity is not rational, although they have no reason against it; no good reason, however, none that they dare publicly own.

The

The cause of their unbelief must be ascribed chiefly to their sins. While they live in wilful sin they cannot know God, because their minds are in total blindness, and will continue so, as long as they continue alienated from the life of God. They must be convinced of sin, and humbled under the sense of it, and sue for mercy, and receive it, and then they will know the blessed Trinity is Jehovah: for no man knoweth the Son but the Father, neither knoweth any man the Father, but the Son, and he to whomsoever the Son will reveal him by the teaching of his good Spirit. May he, who has the residue of the Spirit, send him to take away ignorance from all unbelievers, hardness of heart and contempt of his word, that they may be converted, and believe to the saving of their souls.

But besides these more open deniers of the doctrine, we have several of our own people, who attend upon the ordinances of the church, and yet are ignorant of this fundamental doctrine. For their sakes we ought to insist upon it, and to explain it as taught in scripture, and in the liturgy of our church, with which the state of the doctrine, as now

laid

laid down, is perfectly confiftent. The firft of the thirty-nine articles treats of faith in the Holy Trinity, and fays that in the unity of the Godhead there be three perfons of one fubftance, power, and eternity, the Father, Son, and Holy Ghoft: and the proper preface in the communion-fervice for Trinity Sunday is more clear and determinate. "It is very meet and right that we "fhould give thanks to thee, who art one "God, one Lord, not one only perfon, but "three perfons in one fubftance, for that "which we believe of the glory of the Fa- "ther, the fame we believe of the Son, and "of the Holy Ghoft, without ANY DIF- "FERENCE or INEQUALITY." Thefe are the teftimonies of our church, and they are very full in confirmation of the doctrine which you have now heard. Confider them carefully, my brethren, and beg of God to enlighten your underftandings with the knowledge of the truth. Oh that he may manifeft it fo clearly, as that you may know the Father to be your reconciled Father, the Son to be your Almighty Saviour, and the Holy Spirit to be your counfeller and comforter, your ftrengthener and fanctifier unto the end.

Happy are they who thus know God, or rather are known of God. You, my Christian brethren, enjoy this happiness: for you know in whom you have believed. By faith you have come to God, believing that he is Jehovah, the self-existent essence, and that he is a rewarder of them who diligently seek the mercies of the covenant, which was made by the blessed three in Jehovah, and which is expressed by the gracious name *Alebim*. You know Jehovah your *Alebim*, and thus you keep the first part of the great commandment of all—Hear, O *Israel*, Jehovah our *Alebim* is one Jehovah. You believe in and worship Jehovah, one in essence and three in person. You are thankful for what is revealed concerning the personality, and the merciful offices sustained by the divine persons in the covenant of grace. With your lips and with your lives you are ready to shew forth the thankfulness of your hearts, and to follow me to the next part of my text, which treats of the love of Jehovah *Alebim*. But this I must reserve for the subject of another discourse, only desiring you at present to look up to that Lord and God of whom we have been speaking, and to beseech him to render useful what has been

said

said to all of us. O that he would enable us all to make ufe of the words of our church upon the occafion, and with the prayer of faith to fay,

Almighty and everlafting God, who haft given unto us, thy fervants, grace by the confeffion of a true faith to acknowledge the glory of the eternal Trinity, and in the power of the divine majefty to worfhip the unity; we befeech thee, that thou wouldeft keep us ftedfaft in this faith, and ever more defend us from all adverfities, who liveft and reigneft one God, world without end. Amen.

UPON THE RIGHT
LOVE of the LORD GOD.

DISCOURSE VIII.

MARK xii. 28, 29, 30, 31.

And one of the Scribes came, and having heard them reasoning together, and perceiving that he had answered them well, asked him, which is the first commandment of all. And Jesus *answered him, The first of all the commandments is, Hear, O Israel, the Lord our God is one Lord; and thou shalt love the Lord thy God with all thy heart, and with all thy soul, and with all thy mind, and with all thy strength: This is the first commandment. And the second is like, namely this, Thou shalt love thy neighbour as thyself; there is none other commandment greater than these.*

OUR blessed Saviour has delivered in these words, four very important truths:

First, He teaches us the right knowledge of the Lord God.

Secondly,

Secondly, The right love of him.

Thirdly, The right love of our neighbour arising from the right love of God; and

Fourthly, The greatness of these commandments, there is none other commandment greater than these.

The first of these particulars has been already treated of. It is contained in these words: Hear, O *Israel*, Jehovah our *Alehim*, is one Jehovah. There are three that have entered into covenant in heaven, Father, Son, and Holy Spirit, and these three are one, three persons of one essence. This is the revealed account, and this, my brethren, you are bound to receive if you believe in God: for if you withdraw your allegiance from the three persons in one Jehovah, and pay it to an absolute God existing in one person, you are as guilty of idolatry as if you had twenty thousand gods. This is the case of every *Deist*, who, by rejecting the scripture-doctrine of the Trinity in unity, is in as bad a state as the *Atheist*: for what is the difference between him who has no God, and him who has a false god? They are both without the true God in the world,

both

both traitors againſt the majeſty of Jehovah, and both have turned away their ears from hearing his laws. He has commanded them to believe in him as Jehovah *Alehim*, but they refuſe to believe in him. The *Atheiſt* ſays there is no Jehovah, and the fool upon record, the *Deiſt* hath ſaid in his heart, there are no *Alehim*; and how then can they eſcape his vengeance, ſince he has threatened that they who only forget him ſhall be puniſhed in everlaſting fire, " the wicked ſhall be " turned into hell, and all the people that " forget God." The crime is ſmall to forget God, compared to theirs who deny his very being, or who refuſe to worſhip him as the true God. In either caſe they are guilty of high-treaſon: for the Lord God calls upon them to hearken to him. He is about to deliver the firſt and great commandment, and he requires his people to attend and to receive the law from his mouth—Hear, O *Iſraël*—*Iſrael* ſignifies all the people of God in whatever age or country they live, whether they be *Jews* or *Gentiles*. " Hear, O *Iſrael*, Jehovah " our *Alehim* is one Jehovah," Jehovah is one, but *Alehim* is plural, more than one, namely, the three in covenant, Father, Son, and Holy Spirit, who took this name becauſe

R   the

the covenant was confirmed by an oath for the fake of the heirs of promife, that they might have two immutable things to reft their faith upon. The right knowledge of God then confifts in believing, that in Jehovah the felf-exiftent effence there are three co-equal and co-eternal perfons, between whom there is no difference or inequality, but what is made by the covenant of grace. Their names, Father, Son, and Holy Spirit, are not defcriptive of their nature, but of their offices, they are not to teach us in what manner they exift in Jehovah, but they are covenant names, belonging to the offices which the divine perfons fuftain in the covenant. The fcripture does not ufe thefe names to teach us how the divine perfons exift, but how they act; how they ftand related to the heirs of promife, and not what they are in themfelves, as perfons in Jehovah. This is a truth of great importance, which I have endeavoured to defend both from the pulpit and from the prefs; and particularly in a printed difcourfe upon the felf-exiftence of *Jefus Chrift*. The true object of worfhip then, to whom our obedience and love are due, is Jehovah *Alehim*, according to what is faid in the Creed, " the
" unity

"unity in Trinity and the Trinity in unity is to be worshipped." And is this, my brethren, the object of your worship? Do you pay your allegiance to a God in one person, or to Jehovah in Trinity? If you have not been determined to worship Jehovah *Alehim*, but have broken this first part of the great commandment of all, you cannot keep the other parts: for the love of God depends upon the knowledge of God. How should you love the true God until you know him? But if you know him as he has been pleased to reveal himself to us in the text, as three persons in one essence, and are desirous of paying him that tribute of love which he requires, then you will gladly follow me to my second general head, namely, to the consideration of the right love of the Lord God. And may he be present with us, while we are treating of his love. Oh that he would send his good Spirit to stir up longings in their hearts, who have as yet no desire to love the Lord God, to shed his love abroad in their hearts, who are hungering and thirsting for it, and may both speaker and hearers find their love to God increase from what shall be said upon these words—" Thou "shalt love the Lord thy God with all

" thy heart, and with all thy foul, and with all thy mind, and with all thy ftrength." In difcourfing upon which I fhall

Firft, Shew the nature of the love here commanded.

Secondly, I fhall confider, whether all men keep this commandment.

Thirdly, If they do not, in what way the gofpel directs us to attain the love of God, and then in order to ftir us up to attain it, I will lay before you

Fourthly, Some of the exceeding great and precious promifes made to them, who love God.

Firft, The text treats of our love to the Lord God, requiring our love to arife from our knowledge of him. When the underftanding perceives what he is, the heart ought to receive him for its chiefeft good. As Jehovah, he is the fountain of all good; he is the felf-exiftent effence, through whofe power and goodnefs all other beings exift, and therefore to him they all owe their tribute of love and obedience. As Jehovah *Alehim*

Alehim the Trinity in covenant, he has engaged to bestow upon his redeemed people every grace and every blessing, which they stand in need of in time and in eternity, and on this account he has an undoubted claim to their allegiance. When they view him in this light, their hearts should be determined to love him, and when they partake of the graces and blessings of the covenant they ought to love him out of gratitude. The debt of gratitude is so immense, that they can never repay it, and therefore they are the more obliged to make every possible acknowledgment of their thankfulness. They ought to love Jehovah their *Alehim* with all their heart, with all their soul, with all their mind, and with all their strength. And yet when they do love him in this perfect manner, they can only acknowledge the debt, for they leave it still unpaid; and it will be for ever unpaid, as to any return in kind, that they can make. They can only love, (and what less can they do than love) the Lord their God for his infinitely rich blessings, and this love he demands. As Jehovah, he has a right to demand it of all his creatures, and as *Alehim* he may claim it of every one who partakes of the benefits of the covenant. They ought to love him

With all the heart. The heart is the feat of affection. All the affections belong to the heart, and the Lord God here claims them all. They are all to centre in him. He is to reign fole monarch of the heart, and the affections are to be his willing fubjects, loving him above all things and in all things. Whatever any of them defire as good, they are to defire it out of love to God: and they are not to give any object a place in their efteem, unlefs their love to it be a proof of their love and obedience to God. My fon, says he, give me thy heart, all thy heart, and let me have no rival to fhare in thy affections. And as he thus demands the love of the immortal fpirit within us, fo does he in the next words claim the affections of the human frame. " Thou fhalt " love the Lord thy God

" *With all thy Soul.*" The *Hebrew* word here rendered *foul*, does not fignify the immaterial and immortal Spirit, but is generally ufed in fcripture for the parts concerned in carrying on the circulation of the blood, and in which

which the appetites of the human frame are placed. These are to be regulated by the love of God, and they are all to be used in his service. The heart, being the commanding and ruling faculty, ought to influence them at all times to act upon a principle of love to their infinitely kind creator and benefactor. Every desire and craving, every instinct and passion of the animal faculties should be brought into such a chearful subjection to the Lord God, that to do his will should be their delight. There should not be a motion or stirring of desire in any of the appetites, but what took its rise from love: for all the soul, the whole human frame was to be governed and influenced by the perfect love of God. There should not be a desire in any one instinct or appetite, but what sprung from divine love, and when carried into act and gratified, it ought to be invariably directed by the same principle. And the Lord God not only demands the service of all the affections of the immortal spirit, and of all the appetites of the human frame, but the text goes on to claim the service of all the rational faculties: for that is the sense of the *Greek* word which is rendered

With all thy mind. It denotes that power of the mind, whereby it deduces one thing from another. It is what the logicians call discursus, or the art of reasoning: the mind having before received ideas by simple apprehension, and formed a judgment of them, is then enabled to reason upon them, and this faculty of reasoning is here meant. So that every thing which the mind can reason upon ought to lead it up to God, and to increase its love to God. Reason with all its powers, should be under the influence of divine love. And thus the Lord God expects us to keep the first and great commandment: he requires all the affections of body, soul and spirit, and all the reasoning faculties to be invariably fixed upon him; and he would not only have them to be influenced by his love, but he would also have each of them to exert their whole strength in manifesting their love in him,

And with all thy strength. The love of God must be perfect in kind, in degree, in duration. Whatever strength there is in man, divine love should have the command of it, and the continual use of it. All the powers of soul and body, and of all their faculties, should

should be directed in every thought and word and work by the love of God; and there should be no abating of their vigour in any refpect; but they fhould be continually carried out with their whole ftrength into grateful acts of love and obedience.

This is the nature of the love required in the text, and it is required by the Lord God, to whom we are all under infinite obligations, and whom we are bound, by innumerable ties, to love with all the affections of the immortal fpirit, and of the human frame, with all our reafoning faculties, and with all our ftrength. This is the firft and great commandment, and whoever keeps it in this perfect manner, fulfils the law of the firft table. He cannot have any other God as an object of love or worfhip, neither can he fet up any falfe worfhip, nor difhonour the divine name, by taking it in vain, nor forget the time appointed for enjoying communion with his God. How can he break any of thefe commands, while the love of God reigns in his heart, and commands all his affections? But if he breaks any one of them, does he not thereby by withdraw his love and service from God? and if this be done only once, he has not kept the first and great commandment, but is become a transgressor of the law, and liable to suffer the punishment due to his transgression.

Here then there arises an important question, in which you are all nearly concerned, and every one of you should ask his own heart, Have I kept this first and great commandment? The Lord God has an undoubted right to this tribute of perfect love, have I paid it him? Whether you have or not shall be now enquired under my

Second general head, and it was proposed to consider, whether all men keep this commandment.

Let us examine these two faithful witnesses upon the point, scripture and matter of fact, and by their concurrent testimony let the truth be established. Look around you, my brethren, and see what men's affections appear to be most set upon. What are they coveting with all their hearts, wishing for with all their souls, and pursuing with all their

their strength, and in the enjoyment of what do they account themselves happy? Is God in all their thoughts? Is he the chief object of their love, and the great end of all their pursuits? Is gratitude to him the ruling principle of their lives, and do they think themselves most happy when they love him most and serve him best? A very little acquaintance with mankind will soon convince you, that God does not reign in their hearts, altho' his hands have made them and fashioned them, and their life and breath and all things come from his bounty, and the use of them depends upon his good pleasure. They have forgotten all his benefits, and turned traitors to their sovereign Lord. They have taken up arms, and have entered into rebellion against his lawful government. They have enlisted freely in the service of sin to fight under the banner of satan. Their love to sin has drawn them into this unnatural rebellion, and their strong attachment to its pleasures has made them reject the happiness which God offers them. While they are at war with him, he publishes an act of grace, and out of his infinite mercy declares his willingness to forgive them, if they will throw down their arms; but they

refuse

refuse to receive his free pardon, being not only lovers of pleasure more than lovers of God, but also such desperate lovers of pleasure, that they are haters of God. They hate him for denying them the sweet enjoyment of their beloved sins; and they hate him the more for threatening to punish them. And this hatred shews itself openly, by their hating his will, his ordinances, his people; yea, by their hating every thing, that God loves.

Well might the prophet say, Lord, what is man? What is he indeed! What a most wonderful creature is he, that he should not be afraid to fight against the Almighty, and that he should dare to hate an infinitely perfect God! Oh, surely he is fallen! fallen greatly from his high estate, since he is such a monster of ingratitude, as to hate his best friend and benefactor, even the God who gave him those very faculties of body and soul, and who continues the use of them, although he makes them the instruments and weapons of rebellion, and with them opposes God's lawful sovereignty over him.

But

But perhaps some will ask, What! are all men haters of God? Yes, in their natural state every one of them hates him, and this may be demonstrated from their love of what God hates. All have sinned, and what can tempt them all to sin, but the love of it? All men love the world, and place their affections upon the things of it; how could this be, if their hearts were placed upon God, and their affections upon the things of God? If they loved the God of infinite purity, they could not at the same time love the world that lieth in wickedness; because this is setting up their will in opposition to his holy will, in which all enmity consists. " If any man love the world, " the love of the Father is not in him." These two kinds of love cannot be in the same heart; they are at irreconcileable enmity; and yet the love of the world is in the hearts of all natural men. They are turned from the love of God to the love of evil. The heart of the sons of men is fully set in them to do evil. So says our ninth article, " Fallen man is of his own nature in-" clined to evil," his inclinations are turned from the love of God to the love of evil; yea, so entirely turned, that the imaginations

tions of the thoughts of his heart are not set upon God, but are set upon evil, and that continually. And this love of evil is deeply rooted in the very nature and frame of man, and has gotten such entire poffeffion of him, that it has made him hate God. This hatred chiefly fhews itfelf by its oppofition to the will of God, which is in fact, oppofition to and hatred of the perfon of God; according to what is written by the prophet, " ye that love the Lord, hate " evil." *Pfalm* xcvii. 10. To which agree the words of our Lord, " If ye love me, " keep my commandments," fhew your love to me by your love and obedience to my will. Does any natural man fhew his love in this way? No. His heart is in another intereft. He hates the commandments of God, therefore he hates God. There appears a fettled fixed hatred in him to the divine ordinances. How little does he read or know of the word of God? many large volumes he has perufed, many novels and play-books he has treafured up in his memory, but the facred volume, in which God has revealed all the treafures of wifdom and knowledge, is neglected. How many are there of us who never read the

Bible

Bible through in our lives? Whereas, if we loved God, we should certainly read the sweet volume of his grace and love with care and diligence, and should be meditating in it day and night. No reading would be so pleasant, as none would be more improving. But the devil's book is far more perused than God's. We hear of very few parties that meet together to read the scriptures: thank God there are some; but thousands meet together in this city every evening to study the devil's book. How can these persons love the Lord God with all their hearts, since they hate his revealed will, and can spend three or four, or more hours every day at a most stupid diversion, and at which God is not in all their thoughts? And as the natural man hates the word, so he hates prayer. It is a vast burden to him. If you propose to him to be of a party, who are going to spend an hour this evening in prayer, you will soon see he has no relish to the duty. He will try to get himself excused, if he can, and if he cannot, it will be to him a most miserable long, dull hour, and he will be very glad, when it is over. The reason is; he has no communion with God, and therefore does not

love

love to converse with him. The things of time and sense please him more than the things of God; yea so much more as to render tedious and hateful all the exercises and ordinances of religion. The very table of the Lord is not pleasant to him. God has been pleased to prepare a rich feast for his people, but the natural man has no appetite for it. He has no faith to live upon Christ's broken body, and blood shed; and therefore perhaps never was at the Lord's table in his life, unless for some prudential reasons, to please some relations, or to qualify for some good place. And as to the Lord's house, he never goes there, but out of form and custom. If he is to see some favourite new play or entertainment, he goes with very exalted spirits to the devil's house, but coming to church is a burden; and when he is there, the service is quite tiresome. He wishes it was over, and the dull sermon was ended. The Lord's day has nothing pleasing to engage his heart. It breaks in upon his business and pleasures, and is the most stupid day in the whole week. If he be a polite man, and of a plentiful fortune, he will shew how wearied he is with the divine appointment of this portion of time, by his manner of spending

spending it. The day being got over as well as he can in visiting and company, he thinks the evening may be spent at an innocent game of cards, or at a concert of music. Can these people love God, who thus demonstrate their enmity to his will and to his ordinances? And if any one reprove them, they will soon express their enmity against him, and will make him feel it too, if they have it in their power. How dwelleth the love of God in such persons? Can love beget hatred? If you love any person, will you do every thing which you know he hates? Certainly this is the way in which hatred shews itself; and therefore, since all men love sin, which God hateth, and love the world and the pleasures and enjoyments of it, and neglect and hate the divine ordinances, it is evident that the love of God is not in them.

This may be the case of the baser sort of men, may some say, but not of the more civilized and polite. Yes, it is the case of all alike. Human learning does not bring men to the knowledge of God, nor politeness to the love of him. What people were more learned and polite than the *Romans?*

S and

and yet they were " haters of God." *Rom.* i. 30. They had attained to the higheſt refinement of claſſical learning, and neverthelefs they continued to hate the true God. They were very polite and civilized in their manners to one another, but in their religion no nation was ever more rude and barbarous. Their city was full of idols, and yet they were without God in the world, for his perſon they rejected by their idolatry, and his moſt adorable attributes and perfections they hated.

But ſome may aſk, Is there no difference between us, who are born in a Chriſtian country, and others, who have no knowledge of Chriſt? No, none but what is made by grace. You have many outward privileges in a Chriſtian country; but you do not therefore partake of the love of God, becauſe you partake of theſe privileges. Is not this matter of fact? Is there not as much love of the world, of riches, pleaſures, and honours among nominal *Chriſtians*, as among *Jews* or *Heathens*? For in what does a nominal *Chriſtian* differ from a *Heathen*, but in name? He has, indeed, ſome outward privileges, but theſe cannot of themſelves change

change the inward frame and temper of his mind; becaufe they operate, not mechanically or phyfically, but by the divine influence upon them, and where this is not prefent, although *Paul* fhould plant, and *Apollos* fhould water, yet there would be no increafe either of the knowledge or of the love of God.

Does this ftate of the cafe offend you, my brethren, becaufe it gives you fuch mean ideas of human nature? Nay, be not offended at what fcripture plainly teaches, and experience demonftrates. Rather fearch your own hearts, and fee whether there be not in you a fettled hatred of God. If you examine yourfelves by the rule laid down in the text, and if confcience does its duty, you will own yourfelves to be guilty of the breach of the firft and great commandment. But whether you own it or not, it is an infallible truth. As certainly as God hates fin, fo certainly does the unpardoned finner hate God: for he that loves fin cannot love God. While he hates the mind and will of God, how can he poffibly love the perfon of God? And fuch haters of God have we all been. We have all loved fin, which is

direct

direct enmity against his sovereign will. We have all committed sin, which is open rebellion against his government. Could we have acted in this manner, if the love of God had been perfected in us? No, surely. The love of God would never have led us to break his holy laws, to insult his authority, and to provoke his justice: for hereby the wrath of God abideth upon us, and did we indeed love him, how could we bear to be under his wrath, or how could we think of its abiding upon us for ever and ever? These are undoubted proofs of our having failed in our love to God. We have all broken the first and great commandment, and are thereby become transgressors of the law. We are all subject to the pains and penalties threatened to transgression, and are unable to do any thing to deliver ourselves. This is our guilty and helpless state. My brethren, are you convinced of it? This conviction is absolutely necessary: for you can never be brought to love God, until you have been made thoroughly sensible, that by nature you were haters of God. When the Holy Spirit begins to turn your hearts from sin to righteousness, the first step he takes is to convince you

you of your former hatred to God and to his will. Under a sense of this he humbles you, and makes you pray to God for the discovery of his love. Finding yourselves miserable without it, you will earnestly ask it of him who has it to give. But these points come now in order to be considered under my

Third head, under which I purposed to explain in what way the gospel directs us to attain the love of God. One great design of Christianity was to reform our love, by bringing it back to its proper object, and by fixing it there. By sin we had withdrawn our hearts from God, and placed them upon the things of time and sense; whereby we had not only fallen into a state of guilt, but if we had continued in it, we could not have been happy, no, not in heaven. Because we cannot be happy in what we hate. Our hatred would turn heaven itself into a place of torment. Christianity was the gracious contrivance of God, by which we might be brought to love what would make us really and eternally happy; and this it does by raising our affections from the love of the creature to the love of God. It begins this work by by convincing us, that we have failed in all the duties of the first table, and have broken the great commandment of love, which includes them all. He that is never convinced of this, will never see his want of divine love, and therefore will never ask it. Have you then been convinced, my brethren, from what has been said, that in your natural state you neither do love God, nor can love him by any means in your own power? If you are not convinced what I am going to offer will be of no service to you: because it is in vain to shew you how to attain the love of God, if you see not the necessity of attaining it. May the God of love himself convince you of this necessity, and help you to follow me with profit in the consideration of the several steps, by which the gospel directs sinners to the love of God, and these are three. The

First, Is a lively sense and conviction of their want of the love of God.

Secondly, A clear discovery of what Christ did to manifest the love of the Father, and to reconcile sinners to him; and,

Thirdly,

Thirdly, The work of the Holy Spirit in bringing them to the knowledge and experience of the love of God.

The firſt ſtep towards the attainment of divine love, is a lively ſenſe of the want of it. The Holy Spirit convinces the ſinner of his guilt for having withdrawn his love and obedience from the Lord God, and for having thereby robbed him of his due honour and ſervice. The ſinner upon this feels what it is to have provoked an Almighty God, and in his guilty conſcience he has fearful apprehenſions of God's anger, and of abiding under his wrath. He finds he ſhould have grovelled on in the ſinful love of the creature, if the Holy Spirit had not thus convinced him of his guilt, and made him feel his miſery. He now ſees he has broken all the firſt table, and is become a tranſgreſſor of the law, and therefore is ſtirred up in earneſt to ſeek for the ſenſe of God's pardoning love.

This is the Lord's way, in which he brings him to know himſelf, and to experience the emptineſs of all creature love; and thus he puts him upon ſeeking happineſs in God.

God. My brethren, have you been made sensible of your want of it; and are you seeking it in him? If you are, you have great reason to be thankful; for you have already some tokens of his love. He has put it into your hearts to seek his favour; may he draw you by the cords of his love, until you have a clear discovery of what Christ did to manifest the love of the Father, and to reconcile sinners to him; which is the second step towards the attainment of divine love.

We could never have attained it by any means in our own power, and no mere creature could have attained it for us: because before the Father would manifest his love to us, he would have all the demands of his law and justice fully answered. While the broken law stood out against us, and justice was concerned to see its pains and penalties inflicted, we could have no peace with God. But Christ undertook the work of reconciliation, by doing all that his law required, and by suffering all that his justice demanded, and thereby making a full atonement for our sins. The law he fully satisfied by his infinitely perfect obedience; for by it he magnified the law, and made it honourable, infomuch that " by the obedience of " one, many fhall be made righteous." *Rom.* v. 19. His obedience was abfolutely neceffary to make them righteous before God, otherwife Chrift obeyed in vain. Juftice he fully fatisfied by his infinitely meritorious fufferings. It was decreed, that without fhedding of blood there fhould be no remiffion; but it was not poffible that the blood of bulls and of goats fhould obtain remiffion; wherefore, when he cometh into the world, he faith to his Father, Sacrifice and offering thou wouldeft not, but a body haft thou prepared me. In burnt offerings and facrifices for fin thou haft had no pleafure; then faid I, Lo, I come to do thy will, O God, by making myfelf an offering for fin. This was the Father's will. He accepted the fufferings of the juft for the unjuft; and when the holy lamb, through the eternal fpirit, offered himfelf without fpot to God, he was an offering and a facrifice to God for a fweet-fmelling favour. The Father is well pleafed with him, and is alfo well pleafed with them, who have redemption through his blood, even the forgivenefs

of

of sins. For the prophet, speaking of them, says (*Psalm* lxxxv. 2, 3), " Thou hast for- " given the iniquity of thy people, thou " hast covered all their sin. *Selah*. Thou " hast taken away all thy wrath, thou hast " turned thyself from the fierceness of thine " anger." This is the character of God in Christ. His wrath is turned away from his people. For what reason? Are they not sinners, even as others? Yes, but he is well pleased with them for Christ's righteousness sake, through whom he has forgiven their iniquity, and has covered all their sin.

When the sinner, convinced of his want of divine love, is thus satisfied that Christ has paid the full price to obtain it, having answered all the demands of law and justice, and that sinners may now be brought nigh to a reconciled Father, and may taste and see how gracious he is, then he waits for this blessing, which is the gift of the Holy Spirit. It is his work and office to bring convinced sinners to the knowledge and experience of the love of God, and this is the third particular I was to treat of.

The

The Holy Spirit directs the hearts of awakened and convinced sinners into the love of God in this way and method. He makes them sensible of their wants, and then shews them where they may have a supply. He gives them evidence to believe the all-sufficiency of Christ, whose obedience and sufferings were divine and infinitely meritorious, and made a full and perfect satisfaction for sin. God the Father accepted them as such; and since his justice was well pleased and satisfied with them, the sinner thinks he may be satisfied with them also: for as there is no objection against them in the court of heaven, so there ought to be none in the court of his conscience. Then the Holy Spirit enables him to put forth an act of faith, and to rely upon Christ as a tried foundation. He casts himself upon Christ's power to save, believing him to be Jehovah the Lord God Almighty; and hearing and reading the gracious promises of Christ's readiness to save all that come to him, he sees there is no reason for him to doubt either of Christ's power, or of Christ's love to fulfil his promises: upon which he is enabled thus to address the Lord Christ;

O almighty

O almighty and moſt merciful Saviour, in whom the Father is reconciled to returning ſinners, thou haſt the reſidue of the Spirit with thee, by whom they may be reconciled to God; I bleſs thee, I praiſe thee and glorify thee for the ineſtimable gift of thy good Spirit, by whom I have been enabled to reſt upon thy promiſes, and to rely upon thy faithfulneſs to fulfil them, even to me a miſerable, helpleſs ſinner. O Lord, ſtrengthen my faith by the grace of the ſame Spirit; that it may work by love, that having ſtill more clear evidence of the Father's being reconciled to me, I may love him with all my heart and with all my ſoul.

With ſuch actings of faith in prayer God is well pleaſed; for they are the breathings of his own Spirit in the believer's heart, and he will anſwer them. He ſtrengthens faith and increaſes love, according to what is written. *Rom.* v. 5. " The love of God is ſhed " abroad in our hearts by the Holy Ghoſt " which is given unto us." The Holy Spirit is given to the believer to bear witneſs with his ſpirit that he is a child of God: and when the word of God, and the Spirit of God, thus bear their joint teſtimony to his
being

being beloved of the Father for Chrift's fake, then he is rooted and grounded in love, and is difpofed, and mightily ftrengthened in the inner man to perform every work and labour of love.

Thus the gofpel reprefents the whole Trinity as concerned in directing the finner's heart into the love of God. The Father forgives all his offences through the atonement of his beloved Son, who did and fuffered all that was required by law and juftice, and the Holy Spirit difpofes the finner to be reconciled to God, and to believe in his word; and then gives him faith to apply the promifes to himfelf, and to love God, who firft loved him. Our love to him arifes from the evidence we have of his love to us: for without this evidence an awakened finner cannot love God. While he looks upon God as the juft avenger of his fins, it is impoffible that he fhould love him, and fo long as guilt remains in his confcience, he cannot but fear and dread the juftice of the Almighty, and thefe terrors will entirely fhut out all love: for it is againft nature to love pain; and how then can the awakened finner love that offended God, who is to inflict it upon him?

He cannot love him, until he has some sense of God's pardoning love, and of his interest in the covenant of grace. The text declares this truth—" Thou shalt love the Lord *thy* " God," thy covenant God, not an absolute God, such as the *Deists* worship, but a God related to thee in the covenant of grace. *Thy* God is a relative term, implying the relation which God stood in to the believer, and which is here expressed by the word *Alehim*, thy *Alehim*. The Trinity bound in covenant to redeem man are thine, and stand related to thee in all their covenant offices, the Father is thy Father, the Son is thy Saviour, the Holy Spirit is thy counsellor, guide, sanctifier, and strengthener, all the graces and blessings of the covenant are thine in time and in eternity; therefore thou shalt love Jehovah *thy Alehim*, for these inestimable mercies, with all thy heart and mind, and soul and strength.

My brethren, is this your experience?— You were once haters of God, have you been brought to love him, and do you know him to be your reconciled Father? The gospel has revealed no other way of attaining his love, but seeking it through Christ, and

and receiving it by the grace of his Spirit. Have you then fought and received it in this way? If you have, you will gladly follow me to my

Fourth general head, Which was to treat of the promises made to them, who love God. These promises are exceeding great and exceeding precious, containing every covenant blessing of grace and glory. The Lord has engaged to preserve them that love him (*Psalm* cxlv. 20); and to keep covenant and mercy with them that love him (*Deut.* vii. 9); yea, they that love the Lord shall be like the sun, when he goeth forth in his might (*Judges* v. 31); nothing shall stop their course, afflictions, sickness, temptations, all manner of trials shall help them forward: for all things shall work together for good to them that love God. (*Rom.* viii. 28.) But it is impossible to describe the great things, which God hath prepared for them that love him. If a man love me, says Christ, he will keep my words, and my Father will love him, and we will come and make our abode with him. (*John* xiv. 23.) This fellowship with the Father and the Son by the bond of the Spirit is the greatest

est happiness which can be enjoyed, next to the crown of life, which God hath promised to them who love him (*James* i. 12), and who shall be for ever happy in the enjoyment of his love. Are not these promises exceeding great and precious? And on whom, my brethren, can you place your affections, who has any such promises to make you? Can the world bid so high for your hearts? Are its pleasures worthy to be compared with the pleasures laid up at God's right hand for evermore? Are its honours and riches like the honour and riches which come from God? What can sin offer you, what can Satan propose, what can the flesh covet, that can be put in competition with the blessedness which God has promised to them who love him? If they promise more than God, they are liars, and if you trust them, you will be deceived. But God's promises are like himself, unchangeable. He is faithful and just to fulfil them. And he does fulfil them daily. His people are witnesses for him; they declare, that not one thing hath failed of all the good things which the Lord hath promised in his word to them that love him. All are come to pass unto them, and not one thing hath failed thereof. Oh that you were all.

all his witnesses and knew the happiness of his love. May he shed it abroad in all your hearts for his mercies sake, and enrich you with the blessings of his love in time and in eternity.

Having considered the nature of the first and great commandment, it behoves us to apply what has been spoken, and make it useful to ourselves. My brethren, have you found any use in it? Are your hearts placed upon the Lord God? Is he the reigning object of your affections? How were you brought to love him? Did you ever find yourselves miserable because you were at enmity with him? And did you seek the Father's love through Christ, as the effect of his obedience and sufferings, hoping that the Father was your Father for the righteousness-sake of his beloved Son? And did you continue in this way seeking, until you received the faith which worketh by love? If this be your experience, bless God for this unspeakable gift. It becometh you well to be thankful. Praise him with your lips. Praise him with your lives, and give him every testimony of your love, which he requires; especially give him your hearts, and let him reign in them. There let Chriſt ſet up his kingdom, and by his ſovereign power ſubdue your enemies and his: for, when Chriſt dwells in your hearts by faith, ye ſhall then be rooted and grounded in love, and ſhall be ſtrengthened with might in the inner man to do his will, and to ſuffer it. Then your conſtant language will be, What ſhall ſeparate us from the love of Chriſt? Shall any trouble, becauſe painful? ſhall any temptation, becauſe ſtrong? ſhall any duty, becauſe hard? Nay, in all theſe things we are more than conquerors through him that loved us.

Are there any of you, my brethren, who are not thus rejoicing in the love of God, but are wiſhing and deſiring to be in this happy ſtate? From whence ariſe your deſires? Do they come from the conviction of your ſin and miſery? Do you feel the enmity of your wills, and the rebellion of your hearts againſt God? And do you therefore wiſh, that although you are now enemies, yet you may be reconciled to God by the death of his Son? Have not you been trying to do ſomething in part to make a reconciliation with God? and what was the event? Have not all your attempts failed, and

and have not you been brought to see the insufficiency of your works to make your peace with God? And did the sense of this send you, as helpless sinners, to the throne of grace, intreating the Lord Christ to be your peace, and to make both one? Is this your experience? If it be, thus far you have been directed aright unto the love of God. But who brought you thus far? Is it not he who is to carry you on, and to give you the blessing for which you wait. It is the Holy Spirit who has convinced you of your guilt and misery in turning your hearts from God, and who has disposed you to seek his love, and who is also to shed it abroad in your hearts. And this he will do by giving you the faith which worketh by love. He will enable you to trust God's faithful word, which cannot be broken, and to rely upon his unchangeable promises, which cannot possibly fail of being fulfilled to every one, who comes and sues for mercy and favour through the righteousness of the Lord Christ. Thus he will give you power to put forth, and to act faith, and to apply the promises to yourselves, whereby he will bring you to see that Christ loved you, and gave himself for you, which will produce love in your hearts, and the fruits of love in your lives. Wait then upon him for this blessing. Wait under the word, hoping and praying that he would make it the means of working faith in your hearts; and when it is given unto you to believe in the name of the only begotten Son of God, then he will fulfil the work of faith with power, he will support the patience of hope, and he will carry on the labour of love even unto the end.

Perhaps there may be some persons here, who have no desire to love God. They have given up their hearts to other objects, and are pleased with their choice. O ye sons of men, how long will ye thus idolize the sinful creature, and rebel against the almighty Creator? How long will ye love vanity, and seek after happiness in the ways of sin? Can these things make you happier than God can? Nay, know ye not, that at the end of your fancied pleasures there is real misery for evermore? And are you making a good bargain? Is it worth your while to give up all hopes of heaven and glory for the sake of some present joys? And what are they? are they solid and lasting, and do they make you happy through life? Have you no uneasy sensations when you are sometimes

times alone, or when you are visited with sickness? Does not a troublesome thought then intrude, "What will become of me, "if I should die? If I was to be in heaven, "I could not be happy; because I love no- "thing that is there. I have no love for "God, nor for his will, nor for his people; "I find no pleasure in praising God here, "how then could I rejoice in singing his "praises hereafter?" If ever your mind has been led to such reflections, how did you get rid of them? Did you try to drive them away by company or diversions? And you succeeded; the melancholy fit wore off, and you thought it a great blessing you was easy again. This single instance is sufficient to demonstrate that you are not happy; and indeed it is impossible that you should be so. While your heart is turned from God, it is set upon sin, and sin has no happiness to give. Its promises are all lies, and its enjoyments are all delusions: for it undertakes to make you happy in that, to which the Almighty has threatened eternal misery, and the practice of which will bring this misery upon you. Men and brethren, are not these things so? And why then will ye set your love upon sin? Can it make you perfectly happy?

happy? Deal fairly with yourselves. Are you as happy as you would wish to be? You know you are not. I appeal to your own hearts. But if any of you are so desperately deluded as to wish for no other happiness, than what the pleasures of sin can give you, yet did you ever consider what would be the end of this delusion? Oh think upon that, and may the sense of it open your eyes: for surely you are acting a most unnatural and wicked part, to choose eternal misery rather than part with some sinful pleasure. May the God of all grace convince you of your want of his love, and bring you to know and experience the happiness of it, and oh that he may now put it into your hearts to pray for it. May he, the Lord and giver of every good gift, bless what has been now spoken, and render it the means of increasing his love in the hearts of all this congregation. May he pardon our imperfect manner of thinking and speaking of his divine and infinite love, and may he shed it abroad abundantly in all our hearts. Oh that he would send us away inflamed with his love, and would give us grace to walk in love, continually evidencing our unfeigned love to him by our love to his commandments.

Grant

Grant us thefe our requefts, moft holy Father, for the fake of Jefus Chrift, our Lord, to whom with thee and the eternal Spirit, three co-equal and co-eternal perfons in one Jehovah, we afcribe the kingdom, and the power, and the glory, now and for ever. Amen.

UPON THE RIGHT

LOVE of our NEIGHBOUR.

DISCOURSE IX.

MARK xii. 28, 29, 30, 31.

And one of the Scribes came, and having heard them reasoning together, and perceiving that he had answered them well, asked him, which is the first commandment of all. And Jesus answered him, The first of all the commandments is, Hear, O Israel, the Lord our God is one Lord; and thou shalt love the Lord thy God with all thy heart, and with all thy soul, and with all thy mind, and with all thy strength: this is the first commandment. And the second is like, namely this, Thou shalt love thy neighbour as thyself; there is none other commandment greater than these.

In these words our blessed Saviour has given us the sum and substance of all practical religion. He has reduced it to two short rules, which yet are so full and copious, that they
comprehend

comprehend all the law and the prophets. The whole scripture was to lead us to the right knowledge of the Lord God, that we might pay him the love and obedience which are his due, and might love our neighbour as ourselves.

I have already discoursed of the two parts of the first commandment, and have endeavoured to explain and to enforce the right knowledge and the right love of the Lord God, and I come now to the second commandment, which is contained in these words of the text: " And the second is like, name- " ly this, Thou shalt love thy neighbour as " thyself." The second is like unto the first, because it treats of the same subject, is enforced by the same authority, and is enacted for the same wise and gracious purposes; and the second is farther like, because it arises and branches out of the first, since if any man has the true love of God in his heart, it will evidence and prove itself to be there, by enabling him to love his neighbour as himself. The right love of our neighbour is the fruit and effect of our love of God, and can spring from no other root, especially in the perfect degree here required, Thou
shalt

shalt love thy neighbour as thyself. This is an abridgment of the whole moral law, and comprehends all the duties of the second table. As he who loves God keeps the first table, so he, who loves his neighbour as himself, keeps the second. May the Lord incline all our hearts to keep it, and may his good Spirit render useful and profitable what shall be said,

First, Concerning the inseparable connection between the two commandments, the love of God and the love of our neighbour.

Secondly, Concerning the nature and extent of the second commandment — Thou shalt love thy neighbour as thyself.

Thirdly, Concerning the scripture-method of enabling us to keep this commandment. And then,

Fourthly, I shall make some practical observations upon these particulars.

As to the first of these points, I lay this down for an evident truth; that the man can have

have no real love for his neighbour, who has not firſt the love of God in his heart, ſuch a true experimental ſenſe of God's love to him in Chriſt Jeſus, as was treated of in the laſt diſcourſe: for the love of our neighbour ſtands upon the love of God. It has no other foundation. Build it upon what you pleaſe but this, you will find nothing elſe ſtrong enough to act againſt the oppoſition of a man's own ſelfiſh heart. But as we have many pretended maſter-builders, who lay another foundation than that is laid, and as ſome of the moſt dangerous miſtakes in religion ariſe from building upon theſe men's foundation, I will therefore bring ſome arguments to prove the inſeparable connection between the two commandments, the love of God and the love of our neighbour. And

Firſt, A man cannot love his neighbour aright, until he be endued with the love of God; becauſe he has no principle of love in his heart. Man, in his natural ſtate, or as our church expreſſes it, man, before he receives the grace of Chriſt and the inſpiration of his Spirit, has no holy pure love of any kind. All his affections are placed upon wrong

wrong objects and directed to wrong ends. They are turned from God, and placed upon thofe objects, the love of which he has forbidden, and they are directed to the pleafing of felf, and not to the glory of God. This is the fcripture-character of fallen man. He has no brotherly love; and how fhould he have any? for he has no natural affection. He acts contrary to thofe very inftincts by which the brutes act invariably. With all his boafted reafon, and dignified faculties, he is in focial life lower than a brute: for are there not parents who have no love for their children, and children who have no love for their parents? Is it not a common thing to find a family divided againft itfelf, and Cain perfecuting Abel unto death? And what principle of love can he have in his heart, who is thus without natural affection? Natural affection ties men together with the ftrongeft bonds of love, but all thefe he breaks afunder; and therefore it is juft as poffible that any brotherly love fhould be in him, as that a fountain fhould fend forth at the fame time fweet water and bitter. But

Secondly, The natural man is not only without

without a principle of love, but is also described by that God who created his heart, and knows it intimately to be actuated by a principle of hatred. Until he has some of the love of God shed abroad in his heart, he cannot have any true love for his neighbour: Because he is absolutely under the influence of vicious self-love, and while this reigns in the heart, brotherly love can have no place; nay, it will be absolutely shut out, as the Apostle shews, Titus iii. 3, " We ourselves " also (as well as others) sometimes lived in " malice and envy, hateful and hating one " another." When did he, as others, live in this malicious, envious, hateful state? He was, he says, a slave to these base tempers, until the kindness and love of God our Saviour was manifested to him; and therefore until this be manifested to any man, he must be a slave to the same tempers. He cannot be delivered from them by any human means. No knowledge, no power of philosophy, no system of morality, no stretch of genius, nor refinements of polite life, can make a man less hateful in himself, or less disposed to hate others. Had not the *Romans* all these advantages, and yet we have

this

this character of them drawn by an infallible pen. They were filled with all unrighteousness, covetousness, maliciousness, full of envy, murder, debate, deceit, malignity, whisperers, backbiters, haters of God, despiteful, proud, boasters, disobedient to parents, covenant-breakers, without natural affection, implacable, unmerciful. Thus were they hateful, and hating one another; and such is every man before he receives the grace of Christ. He has all these evil tempers in him, which the *Romans* had.

But some perhaps may ask, What is the cause of this universal depravity of man's affections? The corruption of his nature is the true cause: for all our evil tempers spring from the corrupt heart. The fountain is polluted, and therefore the streams run foul. Out of the heart, says our Lord, proceed evil thoughts, murders, adulteries, with the other abominable deeds of the flesh, some of which the Apostle mentions by name, *Gal.* v. 20, such as hatred, variance, emulations, wrath, strife, envyings. These are in every heart: for the imagination of the thoughts of the heart is only evil, and that continually, continually evil, because continually

tinually set against the love of God, and against that love of our neighbour, which the will of God requires us to pay him. Surely then this heart must be changed, before brotherly love can enter into it. Grace must work upon its evil tempers, and the Spirit of God must subdue them, that love and its sweet dispositions may rule in the heart. Love first takes place in us, when the Spirit of God sheds it abroad, and manifests to us the pardoning love of our God. Then a new principle of love takes possession of the heart, which strives against and conquers our selfish tempers. But until this be done by the spirit of love, there is nothing in any man but SELF. His views are all narrow and selfish. The end of all his pursuits is self-seeking, and the end of all his enjoyments is self-pleasing. This is God's own account of his fallen creature, man. And what says matter of fact? Is this man's real character? I shall endeavour to prove under my

Third argument that it is. Experience demonstrates it. Look around you, my brethren, and see what men are doing. Does love reign in every breast? Are they studying

ing how to make each other happy, and rejoicing in each others happiness? No. The contrary spirit prevails. Is there any little village free from disputes and quarrels? Where is there any large business or manufactory free from contention and envy among the various persons concerned in carrying it on? If they be all of one mind and of one heart, is it not generally a wicked combination to enrich themselves by oppressing others? Is there any trading city, whose merchants rejoice in the prosperity of others, as in their own? Is there any state free from parties? Blessed be God for the lessening of party spirit among us. It has received a great blow, but it is not dead. It is only waiting for some public misfortune to give it a specious occasion of raising fresh disturbance and confusion. And look into the present melancholy state of *Europe:* where do you find brotherly love? Oh where can it subsist amidst the horrors of war? It was not brotherly love which raised armies, ranged them in order of battle, put them upon action, and made brethren rejoice in the slaughter and death of each other. Brotherly love has not a more distressing sight, than when it surveys a field of battle, upon which there lay ten or twenty thousand unhappy

happy men slain in one day. These are awful proofs of the ascendency which hatred has in the human breast. It has got possession, has seized the throne, and has entirely banished all brotherly love. The fact is notorious: for men are every where complaining of the miseries which they meet with in social life; and they do not complain without reason. The time is come when this character is fulfilled. "Men shall " be lovers of themselves, covetous, proud, " boasters, blasphemers, disobedient to pa- " rents, unthankful, unholy, without natural " affection, truce-breakers, false accusers, in- " continent, fierce, despisers of those that " are good, traitors, heady, high-minded." Is not this a real picture of mankind? Do we not find these unsociable tempers prevailing among them at this day, and do not these demonstrate, that man is incapable of having any true love for his neighbour, until he has the love of God in his heart.

But supposing that man, in his natural state, could do some seeming acts of love to his neighbour, yet they would avail nothing without the love of God, which is my *fourth argument*.

argument. Since fallen man has not the love of God in his heart by nature, nor is capable of attaining it by any means in his own power, the great bufinefs of religion is to bring him to love God, and to keep the firſt and great commandment; which the gofpel alone can enable him to do. Moral philofophers have been trying, but they have always failed. They make religion confiſt in the duties of the fecond table, omitting the firſt, which is the fame thing as if they laid the foundation in the air, and built the houfe downwards. Morality has no foundation without the love of God. All moral obligations to brotherly love fail in their motives, and in their end. Their motives are like fo many ropes of fand. They have no force to bind and to oblige the confcience. We have many men who write and fpeak learnedly about moral duties, but here they fail; they can offer no obligation ſtrong enough to over-balance the propenſity in the finner's heart againſt thofe duties. His heart pleads more ſtrongly againſt them than they can plead for them. They may talk eloquently to him of the beauty of virtue, and may argue with him clofely upon the fitnefs of things, and may try to perfuade him

him by a fine chain of reasoning to act agreeably to the nature of things and to the moral sense, and they may recommend the whole from the charms of universal benevolence. All this looks very pretty in theory, and may make a fine system of the religion of nature delineated, but bring it to practice. Offer these motives when self-love has some favourite passion to gratify, or self-interest has some great prospect of advantage, and what is the consequence? The man is deaf to all your moral arguments. They cannot reach his heart, nor open and enlarge it to receive brotherly love, but leave it still under the power of its selfish tempers. These have too deep a root in nature to be driven out by the mere dint of moral reasoning. Grace alone can subdue them; and when grace places the love of God in the heart, then it delivers the affections from vicious self-love, and makes them act by a constant uniform principle of love to the brethren.

And as morality fails in its motives, so does it also in its end. It proposes a wrong end. The glory of God should be the end of all our actions, but moral men seek their own

own glory by their works: for they suppose that their works are meritorious, and can procure them the love and favour of God by way of desert. Thus they set aside faith, without which no moral works can be acceptable. Faith alone directs us to a right end, and proposes the right means to attain it, and every act and exercise of faith towards the attaining of it is well-pleasing unto God. But morality without faith cannot please God: for it is an adjudged case in scripture, " that without faith it is impossible to please him," and it has been determined by our church in her thirteenth article, that works done before the grace of Christ and the inspiration of his Spirit are not pleasant to God, forasmuch as they spring not of faith in Jesus Christ. It is faith working by love, which renders those works pleasant to God, that done upon any other motive would be highly displeasing to him.

Let these arguments suffice for the proof of the first point. It appears from their evidence, that the love of our neighbour arises from the love of God. There is no other foundation for it. You must keep the duties of the first table before you can keep those of the second. The connection between them is inseparable. Unless a man first has the love of God in his heart, he cannot have any true love for his neighbour. He cannot love him at all, and much less in the perfect manner here required — Thou shalt love thy neighbour *as thyself*. And this leads me to speak of the nature and extent of the second commandment under my *second general head*.

The text requires a very exalted and refined degree of brotherly love. It commands us to love our neighbour as ourselves, with the same strength, with the same ...cy of affection: for no man ever yet ... his own flesh, but nourisheth it, and cherisheth it; so should he nourish and cherish his neighbour in all good things. Whatever good he wisheth to himself, the same should he wish to his neighbour; and whatever evil he would have kept off from himself, the same should he endeavour to keep off from his neighbour; and he should, in both these respects, exert himself for his neighbour, as much as for himself. But who are required thus

thus to love their neighbour? The law reaches to all men and to all cases. The same authority which enjoins the perfect love of God, enjoins also the perfect love of our neighbour; and can any fallen man keep these commandments? No, while he is in his natural state it is impossible. We have before proved, that he can neither love God nor his neighbour, until his affections be changed, and vicious self-love be taken out of his heart. But when grace has made him a new creature, when his understanding is enlightened, his will is rightly disposed, and his heart is under the influence of divine love, then the text speaks to this man, and says, Thou shalt love thy neighbour as thyself. The same grace, which led thee to love thyself aright, will operate with equal force in the love of thy neighbour, and will shew itself in every work and labour of love.

It is evident then, that the duty is of great extent. The object on whom it is to be exercised is mankind in general: for every one is our neighbour who stands related to us in the common bonds of humanity. If he be a *Heathen*, a *Turk*, or a *Jew*,

he is nevertheless bone of our bone, and flesh of our flesh. Nay, if he be our enemy, yet still he is our neighbour; we are of one family, and have one father, and therefore his hatred to us should not stop the current of our love to him, as our Lord has taught us in the 10th chapter of St. *Luke*. A certain lawyer asked him, Who is my neighbour? Jesus answered him in a parable. The *Jews* and the *Samaritans* were at such great variance, that they would not even have any dealings with one another; and a certain man, in going down from *Jerusalem* to *Jericho*, fell among thieves, who stript him of his raiment, and wounded him, and departed, leaving him half dead. A priest and a *Levite* saw their countryman in this distress, but passed by without giving him any help; and afterwards a *Samaritan* came to the place where he was, and when he saw him, he had compassion on him, and gave him all the assistance in his power. Which now of these three, says Christ, was neighbour to him that fell among thieves? The lawyer answered, He that had mercy on him. Then said Jesus unto him, Go, and do thou likewise. Go and imitate this *Samaritan*. Learn of him to look upon all men, even
thine

thine enemies as thy neighbours, and love them, and do good to them, as he did. Thus it is plain, from our Lord's explanation of the word neighbour, that we ought to extend our love to all men, and alfo to all cafes. It is to reach to the inmoft defires of the heart. The love of God being fhed abroad there, will take the command of the affections; and when love is on the throne reigning in the heart, it will fweetly incline and mightily enable the other faculties to obey its dictates. Love will not dwell in the fame heart with felfifhnefs and hatred, but will oppofe and fubdue them, in order to make room for brotherly love; and when this comes and dwells in the heart, the man is thereby always difpofed to think and fpeak and act for the good of his neighbour. He has in him an abiding principle of love, which, according to what is written, "think-
"eth no evil." Love works firft upon the thoughts of the heart, from whence all the words and actions fpring. It infufes its gracious influences into the root, that the fap and juices communicated from thence may partake of its nature, and that whatever grows upon this ftem may be the fruit of love. That heart-love, which thinketh no evil,

evil, will speak none: for as out of the abundance of the heart the mouth speaketh, so love being in the heart will shew itself in the tongue, and will not speak evil of its neighbour; nor can love do him any harm. " Love " worketh no ill to his neighbour, *Rom.* xiii. " 10, therefore love is the fulfilling of the " law;" to love our neighbour as ourselves is the fulfilling of the law of the second table. Which they that have the love of God in their hearts endeavour to keep, not to merit heaven; for that was the purchase of Christ's blood; but they are kind one to another, tender-hearted, forgiving one another, even as God for Christ's sake hath forgiven them, and they walk in love as Christ hath also loved them.

This is the nature and extent of brotherly love. It springs from the love of God, and is guided and influenced by it. Whatever the love of God teaches a man to do for his own good, brotherly love will put him upon doing the same for the good of others, and not only of his particular friends and relations, but also of mankind, yea, of his very enemies; even for them brotherly love has its good wishes, and its good offices. It

would

would not entertain an injurious thought of its neighbour, nor speak a word to his prejudice, nor do any thing to his hurt. Its constant breathings are, As I have opportunity, I would do good unto all men. And is this, my brethren, the language of every one of your hearts? Have you a principle of brotherly love actuating and influencing every thought and word and work? Examine yourselves closely upon this point. It may help to shew you clearly the state of your souls: for this commandment have we from him, that he who loveth God loves his brother also. If your love to God be from a right motive, and to a right end, it will work in all the kind offices of brotherly love. If you fail in these, you certainly fail first in your love to God: for these are the streams which flow from the fountain, and they could not fail, unless the fountain ceased to supply them. There is a want of the love of God in the heart, when there is a want of any of the good offices of brotherly love in the life. Search and see if this be not your case; and if it be, look up to God and intreat him to direct your hearts into his love, that you may hear with profit what shall be said under my

Third

Third general head, Concerning the scripture method of enabling us to keep this commandment. Man has no generous principle in him by nature. Vicious self-love directs and governs all his views and actions, and therefore he must be changed and renewed in the spirit of his mind, before brotherly love can have any place in his heart. The scripture treats largely of this great change, and ascribes the whole of it to the Spirit of God. He enlightens the understanding, and convinces the sinner of his guilt and of his danger; then he attacks the stubborn self-will, and makes the sinner feel, that if he follow his own will he must unavoidably perish, and that everlastingly: and he also shews him the horrid rebellion of his heart, whose affections are all apostates from God, having set up the creature and served it in the place of the Creator. The sinner becomes deeply sensible of his guilt and of his misery, and is made earnestly to wish and to pray for deliverance: and when the Lord has thoroughly humbled him, and by various ways and means has convinced him of his own utter helplessness, then he enables him to believe to the saving of his soul. He finds himself at peace with God through

through the righteousness of the Lord Christ, on which he can rely for his acceptance and pardon; and therefore he loves God, who has first so exceedingly loved him; and he proves by his unfeigned love to the brethren, that this love of God is in his heart: for, being there, it will produce the kind dispositions, and will draw forth the good offices of brotherly love. In this way grace overcomes the selfishness of nature, and anger, wrath, malice, hatred, and the other unsociable tempers of the old man are subdued, and the new man puts on bowels of mercies, kindness, humbleness of mind, meekness, long-suffering. These are sanctified affections in him; because they are the genuine fruits of that faith which worketh by love.

This is the scripture-method of attaining brotherly love. It cannot be attained but by the grace of God: for the established rule is—" Ye are taught of God to love one an- " other." It is not from human, but from divine teaching. Brotherly love is not learnt in the schools of moral philosophy. The greatest professors of Ethics may write pretty systems, and read lectures upon them to

their

their pupils, and perhaps they may explain to them something about brotherly love; but they can place none of it in the heart. Christ alone can do that. He is the great teacher of brotherly love; and it is in his school only where men can learn it practically. He teaches his disciples first their want of it; and when he gives them his love, and sheds it abroad in their hearts, then also he gives them the love of the brethren, as it is written, 1 *John* iv. 7, " Beloved, let us " love one another: for love is of God; and " every one that loveth, is born of God, " and knoweth God;" he is a child of God, because he loveth his heavenly Father, and loveth all his Father's children: which doctrine the same Apostle maintains in these words, 1 *John* v. 1, " Whosoever believeth " that Jesus is the Christ, is born of God, " and every one that loveth him that begat, " loveth him also that is begotten of him." Here the apostle discovers the true cause from which arises our love to God and to man. It is through faith apprehending and laying hold of Christ, that we are made the children of God, and therefore we love the Father of whom we are begotten, and the brethren who are begotten of him, and
who

who have obtained like precious faith with us. Believers, who are thus born again of God, and adopted into his family, are closely connected and joined together in the bonds of love. Love flowing from the head into all the members, unites them in affection to their heavenly Father, and in affection to all his children; for, being members of the same body, they have the same care one for another; and if one member suffer, all the members suffer with it; or if one member be honoured, all the members rejoice with it.

It is certain then from these scriptures, that no man can love his neighbour as himself, unless he be taught it of God. There is something called universal benevolence, and the moral sense, and the patriot spirit, which pretend to teach brotherly love upon the principles of moral philosophy; but these are false bastard kinds of love, arising from selfish motives, and directed to selfish ends. And let them appear ever so refined and exalted, yet they are not sanctified affections, because they spring not from faith in Jesus Christ; and without faith in him it is impossible to please God. Works done before the grace of Chrift and the infpiration of his fpirit are not pleafant to God. You may do many feeming acts of love, you may be the foremoft in all charitable fubfcriptions, you may be very kind to your needy relations, and very good to the poor, nay, you may build hofpitals and leave your eftate to endow them, yet if thefe things be not done in faith, they have in them the nature of fin, and are not acts of brotherly love, but acts of your own proud felfifh fpirit. God looks at your heart. He fees upon what principle you are working, and if your principle be wrong, your actions cannot be pleafing in his fight. Make the tree good, and its fruit will be good; but a corrupt tree cannot bring forth good fruit. This is the main point with refpect to brotherly love, and this comes to be confidered in the

Fourth place, under the practical obfervations upon the doctrine of the text. The doctrine is this: Whoever keeps the firft table will keep the fecond. If the love of God be in his heart, he will give proof and evidence of it by his unfeigned love of his neighbour, and he will love him as himfelf, not with that vicious felf-love which influences

fluences the views and actions of all natural men, but with that holy sanctified affection, which springs from, and is guided by, the love of God. If this brotherly love was in every heart, it would turn the world into a paradise. If all men had true heart-love to their neighbour, earth would be heaven: for so much love as there is on earth, so much of heaven is brought down upon it. The hateful and selfish tempers of mankind make the world what it is; these are the cause of all the miseries in society, and these are in all men by nature. Their love centers in self, and seeks not another's good but its own. One great design of Christianity was to reform their love, by giving them that faith which worketh by love, by love to God for his inestimable mercies, and by love to men for the sake of God; by which means the old selfish heart becomes a loving heart, and is ever prepared to do all the good it can to the bodies and souls of men. This is the true character of a Christian. He wishes well to all men, speaks evil of no man, and is ready to every good work. In thought, word, and deed, he is influenced by unfeigned love to his neighbour, whether he be a stranger, a friend, or an enemy. Is this

your

your character, my brethren? Have you the true love of your neighbour in your hearts, and are you constantly manifesting it in your lives? How many persons have we among us, that make great professions of brotherly love, even of universal benevolence, and yet they divide the two tables, and make religion consist in keeping the duties of the second. All our moralists act upon this plan. They speak and write very prettily about moral duties, but they lay the foundation of them upon sand. They neither build them upon the love of God, nor upon faith in Christ Jesus; and other foundation can no man lay for the love of God, nor upon the grace of the Holy Spirit disposing and enabling them to love God, and then to love their neighbour. Thus these men put asunder what God hath joined together. The love of God and the love of man cannot be separated: for there can be no true brotherly love, but what springs from the love of God. Let it spring from any other cause, there will be something in it selfish, it will arise from private narrow views, and will be directed to mean ends, and be it ever so refined and patriot-spirited, yet it will be unsanctified; because whatsoever is not of faith is sin. Without faith the sinner is under guilt and under sentence of death, and is as incapable of doing a single act which is good and valid in the court of heaven, as a condemned criminal is of doing any legal act, which would be allowed to be valid in a court of justice. The law of God has attainted him of high treason, and found him guilty; upon which justice has a right to inflict the deserved punishment, and to put the sentence of the law in force against him; but if he own the sentence to be just, and sue for mercy, and seek it through Jesus Christ, relying on his grace and righteousness, then by faith he is pardoned; his attainder is reversed, and he is capable of doing acts well-pleasing unto God through Jesus Christ his Lord. The moral works done by such a person are acceptable, because his person was first accepted, and he was what they call *rectus in curia*; but without faith it was impossible that his moral works should please God: " for whatsoever is not of faith " is sin."

But I need not enlarge upon this point. Perhaps there may be none of those persons here. By our presence we declare ourselves to be professors of Christianity, and as such we are nearly concerned in what has been now said. The scripture has drawn our character before we receive the grace of Christ and the inspiration of his Spirit, and has painted in very expressive colours the inward lineaments of our hearts. It not only describes every fallen man to be without any true love of God or of his neighbour, but also represents him to be at enmity with God, and to be under the power of corrupt inclinations, which are opposite to God's will, and of selfish views, which are destructive of brotherly love. But while the scripture thus describes our malady, it offers us a remedy, which faith receives, and then works by love to God and to man; by love to God in loving him and his will, and by unfeigned love to the brethren shewing itself in every good word and work. There are great complaints in the world of the want of this brotherly love; and indeed there is very little of it to be found any where. But what is the reason? Is it not, because there is a great want of the love of God? For since brotherly love springs from this, as from its only fountain, how can there be love abundant in the streams, if it fail in the

the fountain? If love does not operate in your life, how can love be in your heart? And if it be not there, what are you? Not a Christian. What the sun would be without light, such is a Christian without love. He has none of the life and spirit of Christ, and wants the very mark and badge of Christ's disciples. "By this," says he, "shall all "men know that ye are my disciples, if ye "have love one to another." O Lord, where are thy disciples at present? Hast thou not said, Ye shall know them by their love to one another? But upon whom is this mark found? Upon all nominal Christians? No; they are distinguished by a contrary temper. But is it not among professors? What professors? We have professors of so many denominations, and of so many different parties, that it is hard to say, who has the narrowest views, or the most party spirit; but it is easy to see at first sight that brotherly love is the peculiar character of few of them. Alas! alas! they have lost their proper mark, by which they were to be known to be Christ's disciples; and thus the scripture is fulfilled, which saith, "In the latter days the love of many "shall wax cold." It is cold, indeed, with many; thank God, not with all. There are some

some (although but few), perhaps of every denomination, who still have unfeigned love for the brethren. May the God of love increase their number.

Since there is so little brotherly love in the world, let each of you, my brethren, examine yourselves, and see, whether you be Christ's disciples more than in name and profession. Are you known to belong to the household of faith by your love to one another? Do you love your neighbour as yourself, with a well-regulated, holy love, arising from a right motive, and directed to a right end? If you think you have this love, how did you attain it? Was you taught it of God? Have you been humbled before him under a sense of your guilt, and have you felt the misery of being enslaved to your own wicked and selfish tempers? And did you apply to Christ for deliverance? Did he take guilt out of your conscience, and give you that faith which worketh by love to your reconciled father, and by love to your brethren for his sake? If you have been thus taught of God, you will also be enabled of God to love one another. And this I pray, that your love may abound yet more and more.

But

But if this be not your experience, then you cannot have the true brotherly love, and without it what are you? You are not a Chriſtian; for this commandment have we from Chriſt, that he who loveth God, love his brother alſo. Your want of love to your brother demonſtrates your want of love to God; and conſider what ſtate you are in, while you are not reconciled to God, nor at peace with him. You are under the guilt of all your ſins, and liable to ſuffer the deſerved puniſhment of them. That God, whom you daily provoke, daily ſpares you. He might get himſelf glory in puniſhing ſuch a rebel; but his long-ſuffering bears with you; and what return do you make him for keeping you out of hell? Do you love him, and ſerve him with grateful obedience? No, you attack him with open avowed rebellion, as if you had an arm like God, and was not afraid of the fire of his wrath: and you carry on your war againſt him by declared war againſt your neighbours, indulging the malicious envious tempers, and gratifying the unjuſt deſires of your own ſelfiſh heart. Suppoſe God ſhould call you to his bar while you are in this ſtate; as you have no love for him, you could have no happiness in beholding or enjoying him; and as you have no love for his family, you could not be happy in their company. You hated them upon earth, and they are so much unlike yourself, you would hate them in heaven. What then could you meet with at his bar, but what you are prepared to receive, even an eternal separation from the presence of the Lord, and from the glory of his power? And can you think of this without concern? Have you no fear, lest the wrath of God should abide upon you for ever and ever? What! have you not one wish to flee from the wrath to come. Oh dreadful state of hardened sinners! May the Lord take pity on you, and subdue your rebellious hearts by his almighty grace, that you may be brought to the right love of God, and of your neighbour.

Perhaps some of you may say, I thank God, I am not in this state. I have been made to see and to feel my enmity against God and against man; and I heartily desire to love both. You have reason, indeed to be thankful; for this desire is a sign and token of God's love to you. Wait upon

on him, that you may know and experience his love. He has encouraged you to afk this grace of him, and has promifed to give it, upon your afking. It is his gift; for God is love, and he is more willing to give than you are to afk. It is one of his choice gifts, which he delights to beftow upon the children of men, and with the right ufe of which he is well pleafed. " If ye fulfil the royal " law according to the fcripture, thou fhalt " love thy neighbour as thyfelf, ye do well." *James* ii. 8. Ye do well in prefenting this odour of a fweet fmell, a facrifice acceptable, well pleafing unto God. Oh! wait then upon him, and be found in the ways of his appointment, not to merit his love, it is a free gift, and it is ineftimable, the price of it is above all the riches of earth and heaven, but wait humbly for the time of his love; and when out of his fovereign grace he fheds it abroad in your heart, then he will enable you to love your neighbour as yourfelf. Surely thefe bleffings are worth your waiting for; efpecially fince you are encouraged by thofe comfortable words, the truth of which many thoufands now alive have found true by happy experience; " They fhall not be afhamed
" that

"that wait for me, faith the Lord." *Isai.* xlix. 23.

Thanks be to his rich and free love, which has fulfilled this scripture to so many in our days. You, my brethren, who know the love of God, should remember, that as you love him who begat, so you ought to love them who are begotten of him. The soundness of your love to God should be made evident from your acts of love to your fellow-creatures; for that faith which brings you to the knowledge of God's love to your soul, should work by love to them; and this work of love proves it, does not make it, but proves it to be a living faith. While it lives it loves. Love is the very breath of faith, and while love breathes in the believer, it disposes him to do all the good he can to the bodies and to the souls of his neighbours; for his is heart-love. He cannot see any one sick, poor, in prison, naked, or wounded, but love hastens to his relief. It does not say—Be ye well, be ye relieved, &c. but it freely gives them such things as they have need of. My Christian brethren, you know that these are the proper offices of brotherly love. Oh! be careful

careful then in the practice of them. If you would have your evidences kept clear for heaven, and your peace and comfort abiding, let your faith be continually working. Exercife it upon Chrift's diftreffed members. Go about doing them good. Refufe no labour of love; for he has commanded, and he has encouraged you to embrace every opportunity. This is the commandment of God, that you fhould believe on the name of his only begotten Son Jefus Chrift, and love one another, as he gave you commandment; and the day is approaching, when you will hear him fay—" Inafmuch as ye have done " it unto one of the leaft of thefe my bre- " thren, ye have done it unto me." Keep your faith then working by love; for they cannot be feparated. Faith is the root, and love is the fruit; if the root be alive, it will bear fruit, even the abundant fruits of love and charity, to God's glory, and to man's profit.

And as the believer is kindly affectioned with brotherly love to relieve the bodily wants of his neighbour, fo is he influenced towards his fpiritual wants with more affection, becaufe the foul is more precious than the

the body; at leaſt, if he be not, he ought however to be thus influenced. There is in men a ſtrange remiſſneſs and backwardneſs to the performance of the offices of love, relating to the ſouls of their neighbours: but grace makes them willing and able. It ſweetly inclines and mightily enaables them to the ſpiritual acts of brotherly love; but one cannot help lamenting how little grace is exerciſed this way. While worldly people are erecting magnificent hoſpitals, and doing princely acts of charity, oh! how ſhort of them do profeſſors come in their works of charity? You are a profeſſor, you call yourſelf a Chriſtian, and do you not know one of your neighbours who lives in open ſin, and yet you never ſpeak to him of it? You thought, indeed, ſometimes of reproving him; but then fear, or ſhame, or indolence prevented you. Theſe paſſions were ſtronger in you than brotherly love. And does not this convince you how unlike you are to your bleſſed maſter? Did he ever decline doing good for fear of ſome little inconvenience which might attend it? No, he went about doing good, although at the hazard of his life; and yet your love to Chriſt and to precious ſouls is ſo very cold, that you can suffer your neighbour to live in sin, yea perhaps to die in it, without one kind reproof. And hast thou not then, boasting professor, great reason to examine thyself, whether thou be in the faith? For how canst thou prove it to be true and alive, since it does not work by love? May this humble thee, and put thee upon seeking more of the spirit and power of Jesus Christ. Perhaps you are the master of a family, how do you shew your love to your servants? You see they do your work, and you take care to pay them their wages, and what more do you than publicans and sinners? But do you watch over their souls, instructing and admonishing them with all gentleness and diligence? Have you any family worship? Do you pray constantly with them, and for them? so that the Lord may justly say of you, as he did of the father of the faithful, " I know *Abraham*, that he " will command his children, and his house- " hold after him, and they shall keep the " way of the Lord, to do justice and judg- " ment." God knows, there are few heads of families, who take any care at all of the souls of their servants; and few indeed do their duty by them in brotherly love. The Lord pardon what is past, and reform us for

the

the future in this respect. Perhaps you may be a parent, and you take pains enough to provide for the temporal welfare of your children. You rise up early, and late take rest, and eat the bread of carefulness, that you may get a great fortune for them. And what more do you for them than for your beasts? You provide for your children's well-being in the world, and do you not the same for your cattle? Christian love would put you upon another work, and would stir you up to catechise them, to teach them to know themselves, to become early acquainted with their corrupt and sinful nature, and to see the necessity of their salvation by Jesus Christ. This is your bounden duty as a parent. The blessing upon the discharge of it is in God's hand; but he requires you to use the means; and if love be alive and active in your heart, you will strive more to have your children rich in grace, than rich in those things which perish in the using. In whatever other station of life God has placed you, do you perform the offices of brotherly love in it? Do you love your neighbour as yourself? Search diligently, and watch your heart narrowly. If you have any true love, pray for more of it, and may the Lord God Almighty help you

you to subdue self, and all your selfish tempers, that love may increase and abound in your soul. May you grow up unto him in all things, who is the head, even Christ; from whom the whole body fitly joined together, and compacted by that which every joint supplieth,' according to the effectual working in the measure of every part maketh increase of the body unto the edifying of itself in love. Hear us, thou God of love, and answer; and grant that all men may know us to be thy disciples by our edifying one another in love. May no selfish temper, no bigotry, or party spirit, hinder us from relieving the spiritual or bodily wants of any of our distressed brethren, but unite all thy members closely among themselves. Make us, Lord, of one mind and of one heart, and may all that love thee in sincerity, think and speak the same things. O give us that love which never faileth. We ask it for thy mercy's sake, to the honour of the holy, blessed, and glorious Trinity, three persons in one Jehovah, whose is the kingdom, and the power, and the glory, for ever and ever. Amen.

UPON THE

CLEANSING VIRTUE

OF

CHRIST'S BLOOD.

DISCOURSE X.

Zechariah xiii. 1.

In that day there shall be a fountain opened to the house of David, *and to the inhabitants of* Jerusalem, *for sin and for uncleanness.*

They that be whole need not a physician, but the sick stand in need of his advice and help. The persons, who feel no malady of sin, see not their want of a Saviour. They are not in pain, and therefore they desire no remedy;

remedy; but it is otherwise with the convinced sinner. He feels the misery of sin. He suffers the torment of it in his guilty conscience, and earnestly seeks for relief. No person in exquisite pain ever cried out for help with greater fervency than he does. He has heard of the almighty physician, and of his great readiness to heal all distressed objects, who come unto him, and therefore he earnestly implores his assistance. How comfortable to his afflicted soul is such a scripture as this, when explained and applied to him by the Spirit of God—" In that day "there shall be a fountain opened to the "house of *David*, and to the inhabitants of "*Jerusalem*, for sin and for uncleanness." He hears the words with joy, and blesses God for having opened a fountain for such polluted sinners, as he is, to wash in and be clean. He believes the record that God gave of his Son, namely, that his blood cleanseth from all sin, and through faith he finds great joy and peace in receiving redemption through the blood of Jesus, even the forgiveness of sins. But the case is quite different with those, who have never been in any concern about their souls. They may give a kind of simple assent to such scriptures

scriptures as this. Perhaps they may be convinced, that they shall want to be cleansed from sin some time or other, but at present they see no absolute necessity for it. They have no painful sense of the malady of sin, nor any apprehension of their danger; and therefore they give themselves no uneasiness about the great physician of souls. But the less they are concerned for themselves, the more ought we, who are sensible of their danger, to be concerned for them. We ought to preach the law to them, by which is the knowledge of sin, and to set before them their pollution and their guilt, and the misery and punishment to which they are subject; and we ought to look up to God for his blessing, that he would set home and apply by his grace to their consciences, what we speak to the outward ear. And when he has convinced them of the dangerous state in which they live, before they are washed in the fountain of Christ's blood, and they earnestly desire and pray to be washed in it, then we may safely preach to them the comforts of the gospel, and the infinite riches of a Saviour's love. Then we may exhort them to wash and be clean; though their sins be as scarlet, they shall be as white as snow, when washed in the fountain of the Redeemer's blood; though they be red like crimson, they shall be as wool. May the Lord God, who opened this fountain, be with us this day to apply its cleansing healing virtue. May his good Spirit awaken the careless and profane sinner to see his pollution and guilt; may he increase the desires and strengthen the longings of those who are waiting for the blood of sprinkling, and may he edify and comfort his own people by means of what shall be said in order to determine

First, What the fountain is, which is mentioned in the text.

Secondly, The time when it was opened, here said to be a particular day.

Thirdly, The wonderful property of this fountain—it could cleanse and do away the pollution of sins of the deepest dye; and then

Fourthly, By what means and in what way sinners receive and partake of its cleansing property.

It

It will not require many words to determine what the fountain is. There is a circumstance mentioned in the text, which will easily settle this point. It is said to be opened for sin and for uncleanness: Now what fountain could it be, which had the wonderful property of cleansing from sin? The scripture has laid down this infallible rule; without shedding of blood there is no remission; and the shedding of what blood ever obtained remission? Did the blood of the sacrifices under the law? No. " To what " purpose is the multitude of your sacrifices " unto me, saith the Lord? I delight not " in the blood of bullocks, or of lambs, or " of he-goats, *Isaiah* i. 11. For I desired " mercy and not sacrifice, and the knowledge " of God more than burnt-offerings." *Hos.* vi. 6. He commanded sacrifice, but not in preference to mercy. Men were not to rest in the sacrifice, as if its blood could atone, but to look with faith at the great sacrifice which the mercy of God had provided, and which was to make a full atonement for sin, and to bring in everlasting righteousness. This was the sacrifice of the lamb of God. No blood, but his, ever did or could atone. If all the cattle upon a thousand hills had been offered up, up, they could not have taken away the least sin. If a man had given the fruit of his body for the sin of his soul, still his sin would have remained. If he had repented, his repentance without faith in the blood of Christ could not have obtained remission. There would be occasion to repent of his repentance. If he was to shed rivers of tears, yea, tears of blood, these very tears would want washing. Nothing can cleanse and do away sin, but some divine and infinitely precious blood; and in whom is there any such? Not in a mere creature. A creature has blood, but none that has any virtue to cleanse a sinner from the pollution and guilt of sin. This is the property of the Lamb of God, who, being both God and man in the person of one Christ, did thereby give a divine and infinite virtue to the blood which he shed, so that it can cleanse from all sin. Here then is the fountain. It is the most precious blood of Christ, which is always sending out its virtue, as a fountain is always sending out water. Its cleansing streams have never stopped, since there was sin to cleanse; and they can never be exhausted. Whoever washes therein shall be made clean, let him have been ever so defiled or polluted.

The

The pool of *Bethesda* was a lively image of this fountain. After the angel went down and troubled the water, then whosoever first stept in was made whole of whatsoever disease he had. As this cured every bodily, so does the blood of Christ cure every spiritual, disease: for it takes away sin, which is the cause of all diseases and obtains eternal redemption.

Are any of you, my brethren, thoroughly sensible of the defiling nature of sin, and do you find how offensive it makes you in the eyes of an holy God? Has the angel of the covenant come down and troubled your consciences, and are you convinced that nothing can cleanse you but the blood of *Jesus Christ?* then believe his word and rely upon his promise, that if your polluted souls be washed in this fountain, how filthy and defiled soever they be, they shall be made clean: for it can cleanse from all sin. Are your pollutions numerous, of a long continuance, and of the deepest die? The blood of Christ can infallibly cleanse them and make them as white as snow: because it partakes of the infinite and divine nature of the Godman *Christ Jesus.* He who opened this fountain for sin, was God and man united in one Christ, whereby the actions of the one nature may properly be ascribed to and predicated of the other. The man *Jesus* had blood to shed, but he who shed it was God as well as man; and therefore it is called by St. *Paul* " the blood of God :" for as the reasonable soul and flesh is one man, so God and man is one Christ. The manhood suffered and bled, the Godhead merited infinitely by those sufferings, and by that blood-shedding, and so the one Christ who suffered and bled, merited infinitely, according to what the Apostle *John* says, " That God laid " down his life for us;" and the ends and purposes for which God laid it down, could not possibly be defeated. Hear this, ye poor guilty sinners! whose consciences are troubled with a sense of your many and great pollutions. The Lord God has opened a fountain for such as you are, to wash in and be clean, and he has given to it a divine and almighty virtue to cleanse all manner of sins. His power is present to make it an all-perfect cleanser. Oh that God may enable you to make use of it. Is it not your hearts' desire, that you may be made clean? And here are the means. The fountain stands open.

What

What hinders you then from washing in it, and having your consciences purged from dead works? You cannot doubt of its virtue. Has it not cleansed sinners, who were once as black as hell, a *Manasseh*, a *Mary Magdalen*, a *Saul*? Put it then to the trial. Believe the record which God has given of it. Apply it for the cleansing of your souls, and it will infallibly take effect. All the sinners from *Adam* to Christ, who have been admitted into the presence and kingdom of God, were cleansed from every spot and stain of sin in this fountain; and all the sinners from Christ to the end of the world must wash their robes in the same fountain, if they appear in spotless purity before God. But although this fountain has had its all-cleansing virtue ever since the fall, yet there was a fixed time in the council of God, called in the text *in that day*, when the immaculate Lamb of God should come into the world, and shed his blood, and put away sin by the sacrifice of himself; and this brings me to my

Second head,—Under which I purposed to consider the time when this fountain was opened, here said to be a particular day. And

And this was certainly the day when the Redeemer suffered and bled upon the cross, which being fixed and unalterable in the decrees of the most high God, they, who lived before Christ gave himself an offering for sin, were saved by faith in him, as we are since he was offered: for the merits of his sacrifice looked backward as well as forward, and like as the sun sends out light in every direction, so did the efficacy of our Lord's sacrifice. It communicated its cleansing qualities, as well to those who lived before, as to those who lived since Christ made his soul an offering for sin. But nevertheless there was a day, a precise determinate time, for his offering. Christ was the lamb slain from the foundation of the world, slain typically in every sacrifice, but in the fulness of time he came, and was really slain, and the day of his sufferings was the day when the fountain for sin and for uncleanness was opened, which is clearly determined by the context: for in the foregoing chapter the prophet is speaking of an extraordinary mourning in the land of *Israel*, and he introduces his description with these words: " And I " will pour upon the house of *David*, and " upon the inhabitants of *Jerusalem* the " Spirit

"Spirit of grace and of supplications, and they shall look upon me, whom they have pierced." These words are applied by an infallible expositor to our Lord's being pierced upon the cross: for St. *John* says, "When the soldiers came to Jesus, and saw that he was dead already, they brake not his legs, but one of them, with a spear, pierced his side, and forthwith came out blood and water: for these things were done, that the scripture should be fulfilled, "A bone of him shall not be broken." And again another scripture saith, "They shall look on him, whom they have pierced." From hence it is evident, that the fountain was opened on the day of Christ's sufferings, here pointed out by this distinguishing mark; namely, the soldiers' piercing his side, from whence there flowed blood and water. When this fixed day was come, and Christ had suffered whatever the hand and counsel of God had determined before should be done to him, then his blood had an all-cleansing virtue. What he once shed was for ever meritorious. It was so absolutely perfect, that he need not shed it any more. The sacrifice of that *one day* was sufficient to satisfy all the demands

mands of law and justice; "so that Christ "need not offer himself often, as the high-"priest entered into the holy place every "year with the blood of others: for then "must he often have suffered since the "foundation of the world; but now *once* "in the end of the world hath he appeared "to put away sin by the sacrifice of him-"self." Once, the just suffered for the unjust, and the blood which he shed on that day had such an infinite cleansing virtue, as to make scarlet-crimson sins as white as snow. The ends for which he bled could not possibly be defeated: for he was God and man united in one Christ, and the one Christ merited infinitely by the shedding of his most precious blood, and it was indeed shed as abundantly as if it had flowed from a fountain. From the time that his agony and bloody sweat began in the garden until he expired upon the cross, he was a bleeding victim, wounded for our transgressions, and bruised for our iniquities. When he was buffeted and scourged; when he was crowned with thorns, and their sharp points were struck into his head by the barbarous soldiers; when the cross was laid upon him, and the weight of it opened his wounds

and

and made them bleed afresh; when the nails went through his hands and feet, and he hung for six hours bleeding upon the cross; then was the most precious blood shed, which is the only fountain to wash away sin and uncleanness. Sinners, consider the great need you have of this fountain, and the inestimable love of Christ, who opened it for such as you are. He calls upon you, he intreats you to view him, as he hung bleeding upon the cross in his bitter passion—" Is
" it nothing to you, all ye that pass by?
" behold and see, if there be any sorrow
" like unto my sorrow, which is done un-
" to me, wherewith the Lord hath afflict-
" ed me in the day of his fierce anger."
This is his earnest request to you who are passing by and minding other things. He would have you to stop, to lay aside all other concerns, and to employ your thoughts upon his unparalleled sufferings. Oh hearken then unto him! Look upon this man of sorrows. View him tormented, bleeding, dying, and then ask your heart, Why does the innocent Lamb of God thus suffer? Was it not that there might be a fountain opened for sin and for uncleanness? And how then are you affected with the shedding of that blood,

which

which can cleanse from all sin ? If grace be stirring in your hearts, you will mourn with a godly sorrow for your sins, which occasioned his bitter sufferings, as it is written in the chapter before the text—" I will pour
" upon the house of *David*, and upon the
" inhabitants of *Jerusalem*, the spirit of grace
" and supplications, and they shall look upon
" me, whom they have pierced, and they
" shall mourn for him, as one mourneth
" for his only son, and shall be in bitter-
" ness for him, as one that is in bitterness
" for his first-born." As tender parents are affected with the death of an only son and of a first-born, so shall the holy mourners in *Sion* be affected with the wounding and piercing of Christ. They shall be in bitterness not only for his death, but for the cause of it. Their sins were the betrayers and murderers of the Son of God, and it is their constant language—" My sins pierced Christ
" with a thousand sorrows in the day of his
" suffering, while he was wounded for my
" transgressions and bruised for mine iniqui-
" ties ; and yet vile, ungrateful wretch that
" I am, daily am I piercing him with my
" sins, and making his wounds bleed afresh." Whoever can speak these words feelingly will

mourn

mourn after a godly fort, and will know how to value that precious blood which has merit and efficacy to fave him from his bafe ingratitude, as well as from his other fins. He will look upon every one of our Lord's wounds as a fountain opened for the purifying of fin and of uncleannefs; for every fin is of a polluting nature, and wants cleanfing. Nothing can be fo loathfome in the eyes of a holy God, as fin. A leper, covered over with fores and ulcers, is not more offenfive in our fight, than he that is defiled with the leprofy of fin is in the fight of God. He is not only of purer eyes than to behold it, but he alfo rejects the finner for it, as filthy and abominable altogether; and he will be rejected for ever, unlefs he be convinced of the defiling nature of fin and defire to be cleanfed from its pollution. When thefe defires come from the Holy Spirit, he will ftrengthen them, until the finner, being juftified by the blood of Chrift, be made clean and righteous altogether. But this point comes more particularly to be treated of in the

Third place, Under the confideration of the wonderful property of the fountain mentioned

tioned in the text, it could cleanse, and take away the pollution of sins of the deepest dye. The fountain is the blood of *Jesus Christ*, which is able to cleanse from sin by the divine ordinance and appointment. The ever-blessed Trinity have given it an almighty power in order to its answering all the purposes of cleansing; and therefore it is called by the apostle " the blood of the everlasting " covenant," because the eternal Three entered into a covenant, and by an eternal purpose decreed to bring many sons unto glory through the obedience and blood-shedding of *Jesus Christ*. He, being a person in the Godhead co-equal and co-eternal with the Father, undertook, as their representative, to obey the law for them, and to suffer the penalties, to shed the blood, and to die the death which they deserved, and thus to satisfy all the demands which his Father's justice had upon them. The Father accepted him as their substitute, and was well-pleased with them for his sake, even before he came in the flesh; and when he did come in the fulness of time to put away sin by the infinitely perfect sacrifice of himself; and when he said upon the Cross, " it is finish- " ed," then the blood of the everlasting covenant

venant made a full and perfect atonement for their sins. Of this there can be no doubt, because he rose from the grave in a public character, as the first fruit of the dead, and because he afterwards ascended up on high to give gifts unto men, and according to his most true promise he gave his royal gifts, even to the rebellious. He sent them the Holy Ghost the comforter, whose office in the covenant it was to awaken sinners, dead asleep in sin, to convince them of their guilt and danger, and to bring them to the blood of sprinkling to be made clean. When the Holy Spirit thus graciously stirs up and disposes them to be cleansed in the fountain, which was opened for sin and for uncleanness, why should not they instantly make use of it? The fountain *can* cleanse them. It is almighty to cleanse from all sin. The holy, blessed and glorious Trinity have covenanted to give an infinitely purifying virtue to it. Although Jesus alone shed his blood, yet the Father covenanted to accept it, and the Holy Spirit covenanted to apply it and to make it effectual to the sinner's heart; so that the whole Trinity have appointed it to be an infallible cleanser. And let troubled consciences remember, that the divine virtue and almighty power of the godhead will now work with the blood of the everlasting covenant to make it effectual for every end and purpose for which it was shed; yea, even the Father's justice, from which they had most to fear, is as much bound to save those who seek to be cleansed by the blood of Christ, as his mercy: for infinite justice has been satisfied with the shedding of this blood. All its demands have been fully answered, and justice and mercy are now alike engaged to receive those sinners, who come to Jesus to be made clean. Think of this, thou afflicted soul, tossed with doubts and fears and not comforted: Why cannot that blood satisfy thy conscience, which has satisfied the infinite justice of God? The Lord deliver thee from unbelief, and help thee to rely upon the blood of the everlasting covenant, until thou find every thing that is said of it in scripture to be infallibly true by thine own experience.

The wonderful property then of this fountain comes from hence, that there is in it the most precious blood of Christ, which has a divine virtue and power to cleanse, as the

the whole scripture bears testimony. Under the ceremonial dispensation, whenever any person had broken the law, he was pronounced unclean, and was shut out of the camp, until he was cleansed by blood. He was to bring his sacrifice to the priest, who was to slay it, and then to sprinkle the blood of it upon the unclean, that he might be sanctified to the purifying of the flesh. Thus the *Mosaic* ceremonies, which were figures of good things to come, then taught the sinner, that as his sin shut him out of the congregation of the Lord's people below, so would it shut him out of the congregation above, into which nothing unclean can enter; and then they farther taught him the infinite efficacy of Christ's blood to do away sin: for if the blood of the sacrifices could cleanse outwardly, how much more shall the blood of Christ, who, through the eternal Spirit, offered himself, without spot to God, purge the conscience from dead works to serve the living God.

Thus the ceremonial law shewed, that blood could cleanse, and referred the sinner to the blood of the Lamb of God, by faith in which he might be made clean. The

New Testament refers him to the same fountain, and has given such descriptions of it, as ought to silence doubts and fears, and to enable every convinced sinner to rely upon its virtue, and to wash and be clean. All that Jesus has purchased; all that the Holy Spirit has to apply; all the graces of time, and all the blessings of eternity, are ascribed to the merit of his most precious blood-shedding. Thus the scripture sets forth its inestimable value. By it the price of our redemption was paid. The debt was so immense, for which justice had seized upon our persons and estates, that we could not be redeemed with corruptible things, such as silver and gold, but with the precious blood of Christ. The blood alone of that God-man was sufficient to pay our ransom, and he paid it to the utmost farthing, as these scriptures testify. " In whom we have re-demption thro' his blood." *Eph.* i. 7. *Col.* i. 14. And as the redeemed of the Lord could thus say by faith, " we have redemption through his blood," so we read in *Rev.* v. that the redeemed of the Lord in heaven sung a new song, when the sealed book was given to the lion of the tribe of *Judah*, the root of *David*, who alone prevailed to open the book,

book, and to loose the seals thereof, saying, "Thou art worthy to take the book, and "to open the seals thereof: for thou wast "slain, and hast redeemed us to God by "thy blood" Through his blood also we have remission and forgiveness of sins. Without shedding of blood there is no remission, and no blood could merit remission but his; as he says himself, "This is my blood of "the new testament, which is shed for ma- "ny for the remission of sins." *Matt.* xxvi. 28. And the Apostle, speaking of himself and of the *Colossians*, says, by it they had remission, "In whom we have redemption "through his blood, even the forgiveness "of sins." *Col.* i. 14. And the Apostle *John* thus praises Christ for this blessing, "Unto "him that loved us, and washed us from our "sins in his own blood, be glory and domi- "nion for ever and ever. Amen." *Rev.* i. 5, 6. And as believers have redemption and remission of sins through the most precious blood of Christ, so have they also through it another inestimable privilege, even free justification, according to what is written, *Rom.* v. 8, 9. "While we were yet enemies, Christ died "for us, much more then, being now justi- "fied by his blood, we shall be saved from "wrath

"wrath through him." And we are thus juftified and faved through faith in his blood: "For we are juftified freely by grace thro' the redemption that is in Jefus Chrift, whom God hath fet forth to be a propitiation through faith in his blood," *Rom.* iii. 24, 25. And being thus juftified by faith in his blood we have another privilege, greater than the world can give, and fuch as the world cannot take away, even peace with God: "But now in Chrift Jefus, ye who fometimes were far off, are made nigh by the blood of Chrift: for he is our peace." *Eph.* ii. 13, 14. He was conftituted and appointed by the covenant the prince of peace, who was to reconcile God and man: "For it pleafed the Father that in him fhould all fulnefs dwell, and having made peace through the blood of his crofs, by him to reconcile all things unto himfelf, by him, I fay, whether they be things in earth, or things in heaven." *Col.* i. 19, 20. And when the finner is reconciled to the Father by faith in the blood of his Son, then the fenfe of this peace will enable him to rejoice in God through Jefus Chrift his Lord, by whom he hath now received the atonement. And when he is thus

thus redeemed, and his sins are forgiven, and his person justified, and the peace of God rules in his heart, then there is another blessed privilege received by the blood of Christ, even sanctification. " The bodies of " those beasts," says the Apostle, " whose " blood is brought into the sanctuary by " the high-priest for sin, are burnt without " the camp; wherefore Jesus also, that he " might sanctify the people with his own " blood, suffered without the gate." *Heb.* xiii. 11, 12. His people are delivered from the dominion, as well as from the guilt of sin by the merit of his blood : " For he " gave himself for them, that he might re- " deem them from all iniquity, and purify " unto himself a peculiar people, zealous of " good works." *Titus* ii. 14. He gave himself to death for them, that he might redeem them from the power of iniquity, as well as from the guilt and punishment of it, as the Apostle witnesses, *Col.* i. 21, 22. " And " you that were sometimes alienated, and " enemies in your mind by wicked works, " yet now hath he reconciled in the body of " his flesh through death, to present you " holy and unblameable and unreproveable, " in his sight:" And when believers are thus through obedience and sprinkling of the blood of Jesus Christ renewed day by day in the spirit of their minds, then they have another exceeding great and precious privilege, namely, liberty of approaching God, and access with confidence unto him, as their reconciled Father. Their happiness in this respect is greater than can be expressed. They can cast all their care upon him, and thereby ease themselves of the burden, and they can lay all their wants and complaints before him, knowing that their God will supply all their wants out of the riches of his glory in Christ Jesus. And this inestimable privilege comes to them through the blood of Christ, as the Apostle has proved, *Heb.* x. 19, 20, &c. " Having therefore, " brethren, boldness to enter into the holi- " est by the blood of Jesus, by a new and " living way, which he hath consecrated " for us through the vail, that is to say, his " flesh, and having an high-priest over the " house of God, let us draw near with a " true heart in full assurance of faith."

These are some of the privileges which believers receive from the most precious blood-shedding of Jesus Christ; and are not these

these sufficient to demonstrate the infinitely cleansing virtue of the fountain of his blood? For by it they are washed from every pollution and defilement of sin, and are presented without spot or blemish before God. Did sin bring them into captivity? The blood of Christ redeems them from all their enemies, who led them captive, from sin and satan, from death and hell. Did sin bring guilt into the conscience? The sprinkling of the blood of Jesus takes it out, and speaks pardon and forgiveness. Did sin make us unrighteous, and condemn us at God's bar? There is now no condemnation to them, who are justified by the blood of Christ. Did sin provoke a holy God, and arm his justice to execute the pains and penalties of the broken law upon the transgressors? Christ has made peace by the blood of the cross, and he gives them peace in their consciences, when they are justified by faith. Are we by nature sold under sin, and under its power and dominion? The blood of Christ has merit and efficacy in it to purge our consciences from dead works to serve the living God. Did sin shut the door of mercy against us, so that God would receive none of our prayers or services? The blood of Christ

has

has opened a new and living way, and believers may with boldnefs enter into the holieft with their petitions: for whatever they afk of the Father in his Son's name, he will give it them. Thus the blood of Chrift faves from all iniquity. Whatever pollution or guilt iniquity had brought upon the foul, all is done away in the fountain of his blood. And thefe fcriptures have fo particularly defcribed its virtue, that convinced finners might have ftrong encouragement to rely upon its power to cleanfe from all fin: for the Lord God has appointed it for this purpofe, and it cannot fail of anfwering it; becaufe he is almighty to render his own appointment effectual. The blood of Chrift cleanfes by a divine virtue, which nothing can refift. God has engaged and promifed that his almighty power fhall work in the application of this blood, and that not only in the prefent life, but alfo in the next. He has given to it an infinite and eternal virtue. It can cleanfe for ever. Oh! doubt not then of any leffer virtue afcribed to it in fcripture, fince it has the greateft that poffibly can be. Surely it can cleanfe in time, fince it can cleanfe to eternity. " Chrift by his own blood enter-
" ed in once into the holy place, having ob-
" tained

"tained eternal redemption for us. *Heb.* ix. 12. For by one offering he hath perfected for ever them that are sanctified." *Heb.* x. 14. And when the beloved Apostle saw in a vision the great multitude, whom no man could number, standing before the throne and before the lamb, cloathed with white robes and palms in their hands, one of the elders asked him, "What are these which are arrayed in white robes, and whence came they? And I said unto him, Sir, thou knowest. And he said unto me, These are they who come out of great tribulation, and have washed their robes, and made them white in the blood of the lamb." *Rev.* vii. 14. These precious robes, in which they appear before God, and stand confirmed for ever and ever in bliss, were washed and made white in the blood of the lamb, and this gives them an eternal purity and an endless glory.

Has not the fountain then, which was opened for sin and for uncleanness, a divine property, since believers receive from it all the graces of time and all the blessings of eternity? The scriptures, which I have quoted, ascribe to it the wonderful power of cleanfing from all fin, and that for ever. Sins of the greateft guilt, fcarlet-crimfon fins, whofe deep dye cannot be taken out by any other means, wafhed in the blood of the lamb become as white as fnow: And the fountain, which has this infinite virtue, ftands open night and day. It cleanfes freely, without money and without price. Whofoever will, let him come and be made clean. The Spirit and the bride invite him, and fay, Come, and let him that heareth fay, Come, and let him that defires to be cleanfed, come. Come, and try its virtue, and it will infallibly fucceed. Though thoufands, and ten thoufand times ten thoufand finners have wafhed in it, and been made clean; yet it has loft none of its virtue. Still it is almighty to do away fin. Whofoever is wafhed in the blood of Chrift is made clean and pure to all eternity. My brethren, do you believe this? And do you defire to experience its cleanfing virtue? Have you been convinced of the polluting nature of fin, and how it has defiled your fouls, and rendered them in the fight of a holy God more filthy and abominable, than the moft loathfome object is in our eyes, and would you be made clean freely by the blood of of the Lamb of God? Is this the prayer of your heart? " I am convinced that God is " of purer eyes than to behold the leaſt ini- " quity, and I am nothing but iniquity. " Oh! that the Lamb of God would take " pity on me, and out of his mere love " and mercy cleanſe my polluted ſoul from " every ſpot and ſtain of ſin. I believe no- " thing elſe can cleanſe me, but his moſt " precious blood, and it cannot cleanſe, un- " leſs it be applied and received by faith: " Lord, apply it then for thy mercy's ſake, " and waſh my ſoul in the fountain which " was opened for ſin and for uncleanneſs." If theſe be your real deſires, you will fol- low me, profitably, to the conſideration of the

Fourth particular I was to treat of, name- ly, By what means and in what way ſin- ners receive and partake of its cleanſing property. Although Chriſt has ſhed his blood, and although it can cleanſe from all ſin; yet it cannot cleanſe, unleſs it be ap- plied. You can have no benefit from it, unleſs it be ſprinkled upon your conſciences. By the ſhedding of it he obtained merit to cleanſe, but the efficacy of it in cleanſing comes from the application. The law pointed

ed out this in the sprinkling of the blood of the sacrifices, and particularly in the cleansing of the leper. When the priest had examined him and found the plague of the leprosy was healed, then the leper was to bring his sacrifice, and it was offered for him, and its blood was shed, but he was not pronounced legally clean, until the blood was sprinkled upon him. The shedding of the blood did not cleanse without the application. And these figures of the law are applied to Christ in the New Testament. The Apostle *Paul* speaks of the sprinkling of the heart from an evil conscience, and the Apostle *Peter* shews what it is which is able thus to cleanse the heart, namely, the sprinkling of the blood of Jesus Christ. This speaketh better things than that of *Abel*. *Abel*'s blood cried for vengeance, but Christ's blood cries for mercy, and when it is applied, it sprinkles the heart from an evil conscience, and purges it from dead works to serve the living God.

This consideration brings us to meditate upon the office of the Holy Spirit. As Christ covenanted to shed his blood, so the Holy Spirit covenanted to apply the merits of it, and to render it effectual to the sinner's heart. This

This is his office-character: he was to take of the things of Chrift, and to fhew them unto us, to fhew us our want of them, and then to fhew us our intereft in them. And in the prefent cafe he was to convince finners that they wanted cleanfing, and that there was a fountain opened for uncleannefs, and by his grace he enables them to wafh and be clean. As there can be no outward wafhing away of any pollution, but by an outward application; fo there can be no inward cleanfing, but by his fpiritual application. If there was a bath famous for curing fome particular difeafe, you know it could not cure the difeafed perfon, unlefs he was bathed in it: fo neither can this fountain. It was opened for ufe, and whoever is cleanfed by it, muft be wafhed in it, inwardly and fpiritually, by the Holy Spirit. He applies, and faith receives the benefit of that blood, which cleanfeth from all fin: for the Apoftle, fpeaking of Chrift, fays, " Whom " God hath fet forth to be a propitiation " through faith in his blood." *Rom.* iii. 25. The fhedding of his blood had merit to cleanfe, but faith apprehends it and receives its cleanfing virtue. That faith, which is the gift of the Holy Spirit, and is wrought in

the

the heart by his operation relies upon the blood of Chrift, and puts its whole truft and confidence in its power to cleanfe, and then finds the heart fprinkled with it from an evil confcience, guilt being taken out, and peace brought in, with love and joy, and all the graces of the Spirit of God.

From what has been faid, it appears, that there is a fountain open for fin and for uncleannefs, and that the blood of Jefus Chrift can cleanfe from all fin. It had this virtue given it by the covenant of grace, when the holy, bleffed, and glorious Trinity agreed to give their power to it, and nothing can refift the power of the Godhead. He who fhed it was God and man in one perfon. As God, he was co-equal and co-eternal with the Father, and when he took our nature, that in it he might obey and fuffer for finners, nothing could be wanting to render his obedience and fufferings abfolutely complete: for all the works of God are perfect; nothing can be added to them, or taken from them. When Jefus fhed his blood upon the crofs, it was the will of the ever-bleffed Trinity, that this blood fhould be of infinite efficacy to take away fin. It cannot want power to

cleanfe,

cleanse, because the whole power of the Godhead is engaged to make it effectual. It is the blood of the everlasting covenant. The son has shed it, and the Father has received it as a full satisfaction and atonement for sin, and the application of it is now in the hand of the eternal and almighty Spirit; and when he applies it, and gives the sinner faith to rely upon it, what can then resist its power, or hinder its efficacy? My brethren, how do you find your hearts affected with these great truths? Do you see the polluting nature of sin, and do you desire to be cleansed from it in the fountain of Christ's blood? And do you therefore desire it, that you may be made holy as well as righteous? Would you have the blood of Christ to save you by its efficacy from the dominion of sin, as well as to save you by its merit from the guilt of sin? Sirs, what say your hearts to these things? Do you really wish to be cleansed from the power, as well as from the pollution of sin? If you do not wish for it, what do you think of the text? Is it true that there is a fountain opened for sin and for uncleanness, and has the blood of Christ the cleansing virtue here ascribed to it? Can it take out the guilt of sins of the

A a   deepest

deepest dye? Are scarlet-crimson sins washed in it, as white as snow? Surely they are: for it can cleanse from all sin. By the shedding of his blood, Christ obtained infinite merit to cleanse sinners; but in order to their being cleansed it must be applied, and the application is now made by the grace of the Holy Spirit. Has he then applied it to you or not? This is the main point. Have you been washed in this fountain and made clean? What are you the better for its cleansing others, if it never cleanse your souls? You can be benefited only from its application to you in particular, and by your experiencing the power of it in your own hearts. Let each of us then examine ourselves concerning this particular, and may we do it through the assistance of God with profit and improvement.

1. It is not unlikely, but there may be some persons here who are not thoroughly acquainted with the defiling nature of sin, and who never heartily desired to be cleansed from it. This is the case of all unawakened sinners. They see not the pollution of their hearts and lives, and therefore they are easy and content in their present state without

out ever defiring to be cleanfed by the blood of Chrift. Does any one's confcience fpeak to him at prefent, and fay—" This is my " cafe; I have not been cleanfed from my " fins, nor do I defire it. My fins are fo " fweet and pleafing to me, that I fhould be " very unhappy if I was to part with them." But are they more fweet and pleafant than heaven, and would you part with heaven, rather than part with them? Confider this matter a little. You muft part with one or the other: for hear what God fays of you in his word. You are the objects of his hatred. " Thou, O God! (fays the Pfalmift) " hateft all workers of iniquity." *Pfalm* v. 5. Yea, fo great is his hatred, that he cannot fuffer you to appear before him. " Thou " art of purer eyes, fays the Prophet, than " to behold evil, and canft not look upon " iniquity." *Hab.* i. 13. And if you die in your iniquity, without the blood of fprinkling, you can never enter into heaven: " For " no unclean perfon hath any inheritance " in the kingdom of Chrift and of God." *Eph.* v. 5. To which agree the words of St. *John* in his defcription of the heavenly *Jerufalem,* " there fhall in no wife enter in- " to it any thing that defileth." This awful scripture will be fulfilled in you. In no wise shall you enter into the city of the living God, unless your polluted souls be washed in the Redeemer's blood. You will be shut out of his presence and glory, and your eternal habitation will be with unclean spirits in the regions of torment and despair.

But bad though your present state be, yet the gospel sets before you perfect deliverance. You are invited to come and be made clean. The fountain is open, and if you now find it in your heart to make use of it, you may be washed in it without money and without price. All is free. Your sins shall be freely pardoned, and your pollutions freely cleansed. Free grace shall do all for you, and all in you. And this day you have an offer of all its blessings. Close in with it, and they are all yours. But if you now reject them, you cannot pretend, that you never heard of your danger: for you have now been warned of it. You cannot plead your ignorance of the merits of Christ's blood: for you have now heard what great things the scripture says of it. From it are received all the graces of time, and all the blessings of eternity; and you have been invited

vited to come, and to be cleanfed freely in the fountain, that was opened for fin, and for uncleannefs. If then you ftill refufe to be wafhed in this fountain, you are without excufe: for if you reject this wilfully, and harden your hearts againft it, there remaineth no more facrifice for fin, but a certain fearful looking for of judgment and fiery indignation, which fhall devour the adverfaries. Meditate upon this fcripture. Think ferioufly what a fearful thing it is to fall into the hands of the living God. And may the eternal Spirit fet in with this confideration, and fo effectually convince you of the pollution and guilt of your fins, that you may feek to be made clean, and may find the blood of Jefus Chrift cleanfing you from all fin.

2. Are there any of you, my brethren, who are now defiring to be made clean, and to be wafhed from all your fins? For you the fountain ftands open, and what fhould hinder you from making ufe of it? Do you doubt of its power to cleanfe you? Remember it is the blood of the everlafting covenant. It cleanfes in virtue of the covenant of the ever bleffed Trinity, and confequently

quently by the power of the Godhead. Father, Son, and Holy Spirit have agreed to make it almighty to do away fin; so that it cannot cleanse only in time, but it can also cleanse for ever and ever. This is the plain doctrine of scripture, and if you believe it, why do you not find great joy and peace in believing it?

Perhaps you think it can cleanse, but you are afraid it is not appointed for your cleansing. Nay, my brethren, reason not against your own comforts. For whom was it appointed, if not for you, who see your want of it, and who are desirous of experiencing its divine power? You have the warrant of God's word, authorising you to wash and be clean. The text says, the fountain was for the inhabitants of *Jerusalem*, for the professing members of the visible church, that whenever any of them were convinced of their uncleanness, they might make use of this fountain, and have their hearts cleansed from an evil conscience. Oh! reject not then the offered blessing. Take it upon the warrant and authority of God's word, and doubt not but the fountain is open for you.

Why

Why then are you not cleanfed in it? Are you afraid that your fins are fo many and fo great that you cannot be made clean? As to their number, it can cleanfe from *all* fin, and as to their greatnefs, it can take out the guilt of fcarlet-crimfon fins, the greateft that poffibly can be; therefore this is no objection. You may come with all your fins and be wafhed freely from all in the fountain of Chrift's blood.

Come then—But you draw back, you fear it would be prefumption in fuch a finner as you are. What! is it prefumption to believe in the word of God, which cannot be broken, and to rely upon the promifes of God, which are as unchangeable as himfelf? No. It is glorifying God, and honouring his word. Whereas you make God a liar by your falfe modefty, as if he could break his word to you, and as if you might be difappointed, when you claimed the fulfilling of his promifes. My brethren, thefe things cannot be. God's word and promifes are like himfelf, without any variablenefs or fhadow of turning, and what ever they offer you, is yours, when you rely upon him for the receiving of it from his free grace,

grace. And since you have the authority of God's word and promises to silence your doubts and fears, are you resolved in the strength of grace to rely upon them? If you be, then they shall be made good to you. Heaven and earth shall pass away, rather than one tittle of them shall fail. Your robes shall be washed in the blood of the lamb, and whatever graces and blessings Jesus has to give his people shall be yours in time and in eternity.

3. Perhaps some persons may enquire, Of what use is this fountain to believers? The uses of it are many and great. All their graces flow from it, all their duties are to be washed in it, and all their comforts are maintained by it. Surely then it is of great and infinite service to believers. Under the third head of this discourse I considered the high character given in scripture of this fountain. From it are received redemption, forgiveness of sins, justification, peace with God, sanctification, freedom of access to God as a reconciled Father, eternal redemption, and the robe of everlasting righteousness, in which the saints stand confirmed in bliss. All these graces and blessings flow

from

m the fountain of Christ's blood, and w freely. They cost us nothing. They are the free gifts of our loving Saviour, which of his abundant mercy he bestows upon his people; and this makes his blood very precious to them, that the gifts, which are inestimable, they receive from it freely; and by their repeated trials of its worth and value they grow in the knowledge and love of its preciousness: for they find it not only necessary for their sins, but also for their duties. The holiest duty, which was ever done by a mere man, wanted washing in this fountain. The ceremonial law taught this doctrine in a very clear manner: For upon the holy crown of the high priest there was a plate of pure gold, with this inscription, *Holiness to the Lord*, " And it " shall be upon *Aaron*'s forehead, that *Aa-* " *ron* may bear the iniquity of the holy " things which the children of *Israel* shall " hallow in all their holy gifts, and it shall " be always upon his forehead, that they " may be accepted before the Lord." *Exod.* xxviii. 38. Herein he represented the office of the high priest of our profession, who bears the iniquity of our holy things: for there is imperfection in every duty, in every act
of

of obedience some short coming, which requires the atoning blood of Christ, that it may be accepted before the Lord. There is no believer, who loves God in that perfect manner, which the spirituality of the law requires. This appears very evidently from their failings in the services which they pay him. When do they pray without some wandering thoughts? When do they hear the word as in the presence of God, and receive it not as the word of men, but as it is in truth the word of God? Do they not sometimes hear with great dulness, and at other times are not able to mix faith with what they hear? Are they not negligent in searching the scriptures, and negligent in praying for a blessing, when they do search them? How little do they treasure up in their memories, and how little fruit does the engrafted word bring forth in their lives? When they go to the Lord's table, how often do they complain of their want of devotion and gratitude? And therefore their services, yea, the very best of them, because of these imperfections and short comings, would not be acceptable, unless they were washed in the fountain of Christ's blood. Sensible of this they live by faith upon fresh applications of

it,

it, suing for its merit, and hoping for its efficacy in every thing they do. And as the acceptance of their duties, so their comforts are derived from the blood of Chrift. Their love, their peace, their joy flow from this fountain. This is their continual matter of rejoicing, that the blood of Chrift was freely fhed for them, and that he, who gave his blood for them, will with it give them all things. This bears them up under trials, ftrengthens them againft temptations, supports them in ficknefs, and arms them againft death. They know that all thefe things are working together under God for their good. Yea, they experience it, and that makes them happy; happy in time, and happy in eternity. What is now their crown of rejoicing below, will be much more fo above. Then their joy will be full, when they fhall join that innumerable company, whom no man can number, and with them give honour and glory, and blessing and praife to him that was flain, and hath redeemed them unto God by his blood out of every kindred, and tongue, and people and nation, and hath made them kings and priefts unto God and his Father. Then they will know how to value that blood

which

which brought them to such perfect and eternal blessedness. O Lord, help us to set a greater value upon it than we commonly do. Teach us more of our want of it, and of its worth. Supply us more abundantly with the graces and blessings purchased by its merit, and freely bestowed by its efficacy. And may the dear Lamb of God give his blessing to what has been now spoken, although it has been in much weakness, that if it be his holy will, all who hear me this day may be brought to see and to lament their spiritual uncleanness, and to apply for cleansing to the blood of Jesus. Oh! that the Lord God would direct you all to the fountain, which he has opened for sin and for uncleanness, and may he give you faith to wash in it and to be cleansed from all sin, according to what we have been asking this day in the excellent words of our church.

" Grant, we beseech thee, merciful Lord,
" to thy faithful people, pardon and peace;
" that they may be cleansed from all their
" sins, and serve thee with a quiet mind,
" through Jesus Christ our Lord. Amen."

THE
BALM of GILEAD.

DISCOURSE XI.

JEREMIAH viii. 22.

Is there no balm in Gilead? *Is there no physician there? Why then is not the health of the daughter of my people recovered?*

ALL men love health. The desire of it is founded in nature. It is one of the natural instincts which never leaves us. So long as we love pleasure and hate pain, we cannot but love health, as the chief of all outward blessings. Indeed it is to be desired beyond them all, because without it we can enjoy none of them; without

it

it we are unfit for our worldly bufinefs and employment, and unfit for the duties of religion. A good man would therefore wifh for health with a view to the concerns of a better life, as well as to thofe of the prefent life. All men defire it upon a temporal account. But alas! how few have any real defire for the health of the foul? If the body be in great pain, with what hafte do they fend for relief, and how carefully do they follow the phyfician's prefcription? But when their fouls are wounded with fin, and they may endure the fmart and anguifh of their wounds for ever: for thefe are by any human means incurable, and when a divine remedy is propofed, and they hear of a loving and an almighty phyfician, under whofe hands no patient was ever loft, yet they have not one wifh to be healed. What can be the reafon of this? Why are the very men, who with an invariable affection love bodily health, fo far from defiring the health of the foul, that when they have an offer of being healed of all their fpiritual maladies, they neglect the remedy, and defpife the phyfician? Is not this unaccountable conduct? What can make the fame men in the fame cafe reafon fo differently? If they had an infallible

fallible remedy for the recovery of bodily health, there is not one of them who would reject it; but there is a sovereign remedy for the recovery of the health of the soul, there is balm in *Gilead,* and a most kind and able physician there to apply it, and yet spiritual maladies abound. Let us enquire into the cause of this inconsistent behaviour. It is an enquiry in which we are all nearly concerned. Our welfare depends on our being healed of the wounds of sin by this balm of *Gilead.* We can have no true peace of conscience here, nor no true happiness hereafter, unless we take this sovereign medicine. May the Lord God dispose us all to take it by means of what shall be said in opening and explaining the text, in which there is,

First, Some sickness referred to.

Secondly, A sovereign medicine—there is balm in *Gilead* to heal it.

Thirdly, A great physician to apply it; and all the means of healing being thus ready at hand, the question naturally follows, in the

Fourth

Fourth place, Why then is not the health of the daughter of my people recovered?

If we look back to the context, we find an account of the first evil in the text. The people were bit with serpents and cockatrices, and of the venomous and fiery sort, whose poison infused into the blood, acts like the most raging fire, consuming and drying up the fluids of the body, and in a short time bringing on certain death. "For behold I will send "serpents, cockatrices among you, which "will not be charmed, and they shall bite "you, saith the Lord." This is a just picture of that more deadly poison, which the old serpent the devil infused into both body and soul, the effects of which all the human race have felt: for he drew us all into sin, and the dreadful consequences of sin appear in that variety of diseases which bring down our bodies to the grave of death, and in that variety of corrupt and depraved appetites, which proves the soul to be alienated from the life of God, and to be incapable, unless it be entirely changed, of enjoying God. It was sin which thus poisoned our nature: for before sin entered into the world, all things

were

were good. There was no evil to afflict either body or soul. But when sin entered, then the sanction of the law took place, "In the day that thou eatest of the forbid- den fruit, dying thou shalt die." *Gen.* ii. 17. In that day thy body shall become mortal, and liable to those pains and diseases which in a course of years shall destroy its animal life, and thy soul shall be separated from the fountain of its spiritual life, and cut off from all communion with God in this world, and in the next it shall be separated from him for ever, which is the second death. Oh sin! what hast thou done! Thou art the author of all the evils which mankind are capable of suffering in earth and hell. Thou broughtest them all upon us, thou enemy of God and man. And wilt thou afterwards pretend to be our friend? Wilt thou come to court us with promises of happiness, that by deceiving us, thou mayest more effectually poison and destroy our bodies and souls? Look upon this base traitor, my brethren. Can he be a friend to your nature, who has subjected it to all the miseries of mortality? If you have any true love for yourselves, how can you love and cherish sin, which has made you liable to suffer the first and the second death? What! is this a friend to be taken into your bosom, one that will murder your body, and bring both body and soul into hell? Accustom yourselves to view sin in this light, and it will help you to see the horrible destructive nature of it. When you behold a dead corpse, think what a murderer sin is: for that body would never have died, if sin had not poisoned it. And then turn your eyes inwards, and let each man say to himself—This beloved body of mine, upon which I spend so much time and care, was made mortal by sin, and all the pains and diseases, which I can suffer, came from the same cursed cause; yea, from it came all the miseries which I deserve to suffer with devils and condemned spirits in the fire that never is to be quenched, and shall I love and delight to serve such an enemy? Shall I give up the members of my body as instruments of unrighteousness unto sin, and so work out mine own everlasting destruction? God forbid. As sin is the author of all the evil, which I do or can endure, I will therefore fight against it, and may the Lord God save me from the guilt, and deliver me from the dominion of it.

This

This is the language of every heart, which is made sensible of the poisonous qualities of sin. When the awakened sinner feels the malignant venom working in his constitution, he will be led to abhor and to detest it, and the more so, when the scripture discovers to him the execrable foe, who poisoned him with sin, and that was the old serpent. What these serpents are said in the 17th verse to have done to the body in poisoning it, the same did he both to body and soul; and as he did it at first in the serpent, he has therefore been known and distinguished by this name from the time that he deceived our first parents in the subtle serpent. The apostle has given us a very alarming description of him, *Rev.* xii. 9. where he is treating of the war which was in heaven between *Michael* and his angels, and the dragon and his angels. " And the great " dragon, he says, was cast out, the old " serpent, called the devil and satan, who " deceiveth the whole world." Here he is called the serpent, alluding to his crafty wiliness, and the old serpent, to denote his having employed all his wiles to deceive and ruin mankind. As soon as they were created he plotted their destruction, and he became satan, their sworn adversary, and the devil, their accuser, who sought to destroy their precious lives with the rage of a dragon; yea, with more rage than common dragons have, even with the burning fury of the great dragon. And alas! he was successful: for he deceiveth the whole world. He poisoned the whole human race. He corrupted all flesh, and we are now groaning under the dreadful effects of our total corruption. The cursed venom of sin, which he infused into our bodies, still works in them; but its more cursed venom still works, though less perceptibly, in our souls. The poison keeps working in the body, until it bring on sickness and death, and reduce us to the dust, from whence we were taken; and it keeps working in the soul, in every hateful and unholy temper, which tends to stir up the wrath and indignation of God, and to separate the soul for ever and ever from him the fountain of life and glory.

This is the great and universal malady referred to in the text, the malady of sin, with which the old serpent, the devil, has poisoned the whole world. When he deceived our first parents, he then poisoned the

foun-

fountain, and all the streams which have been ever since flowing from it partake of the direful infection: for the word of truth declares, "That as by one man sin entered into the world, and death by sin, so death passed upon all men, in whom all have sinned." Here the entrance of sin is said to be the cause of the entrance of death, and we all die in *Adam*, therefore we all sinned in him: for the wages of sin is death. Now God being infinitely just and righteous would not pay the wages, unless there were some sin to deserve them, but infants receive the wages of sin, and consequently they are sinners; they die in *Adam*, because in him they sinned. "For by the offence of one judgment came upon all men to condemnation." Thus was our whole nature, both body and soul, corrupted by the fall, and there is not a sound part or faculty in either of them. They are corrupt and abominable altogether, and in nothing does this total corruption more evidently discover itself, than in their entire blindness and insensibility of their dangerous condition. They are poisoned, and yet they know it not; nay, they are so unwilling to know it, that when we inform them of it, they are highly offended,

fended. They cannot bear to be told of it, no, not by the ministers of the gospel, whose office and duty it is. We are sure to stir up their rage and hatred, if we discover to them the workings of this poison in their hearts, and if we appeal to the effects of it in their lives, and refer them to the plentiful streams of iniquity, which are continually flowing from the corrupt fountain of the heart, then they cannot bear us; they are like the deaf adder, that stoppeth her ear; which will not hearken to the voice of charmers, charming ever so wisely. They are resolved not to be disturbed about their sins, and therefore they will not hear of their sickness or of their danger. They had rather die of their malady, than be made uneasy about it. Let sin do its worst in the next life, in the present they will enjoy it; and in sweet security too, if they can. Is not this an astonishing degree of infatuation? Is it not one of the strongest delusions of the devil, that he should make those very men insensible of their spiritual maladies, who are exquisitely sensible of the least bodily malady, whose fears are all alarmed at the thoughts of their dying to this world, but who have not the least concern about their

their dying from God and glory? Are any of you, my brethren, in this case? Are you easy about the state of your souls, having never been in any distress about original and actual sin? Did you never feel yourselves so sick of both, that you were afraid you should perish everlastingly? If not, consider what it is, which keeps you in this fatal security. Are not you sinners? For all have sinned. And has not sin poisoned both body and soul? And is not this one of the sad, stupifying effects of its poison, that while there is but a step between you and death, yet you have no concern about your being healed? Are these things so? If they be, may the almighty God awaken you to a sense of your danger. Oh! that he may set home and fix such a conviction of sin upon your consciences, that, feeling your malady, you may earnestly seek the great physician's help, and may happily find that there is balm in *Gilead*; which is the

Second particular I was to consider. Glory be to God, who hath not left us without remedy. Our disease is dangerous, but there is balm in *Gilead*, which can heal perfectly and eternally. The country of *Gilead* was famous for a precious balm which grew there. "Go up to Gilead, and take balm," says the prophet *Jeremiah*, xlvi. 11. Its healing virtue is described by him, chap. li. 8. where speaking of the downfal of *Babylon*, he says, "Take balm for her pain, if "so be she may be healed." This sovereign medicine, which then grew in *Gilead*, could assuage the pain of wounds and heal them, and thereby was a type of the gracious remedy, which God had provided for the healing of the wounds of sin; namely, the most precious blood of the lamb of God, applied and made effectual by the holy Spirit: for as this cleanses away all the pollutions, so it heals all the diseases of sin. The scripture has treated largely of its healing virtue, but it is no where more forcibly recommended than in the parable of the good *Samaritan*. Our Lord says, "A certain man "went down from *Jerusalem* to *Jericho*, "and fell among thieves, who stripped "him of his raiment, and wounded him, and "departed, leaving him half dead." This certain man was *Adam*, whose possession was in a paradise of peace and rest, and there he was innocent, safe and happy: But he left this blissful state of his own accord, contrary

trary to God's express commandment, and he fell among thieves, satan and his angels, who drew him into sin, and stripped him of his raiment, robbed him of his righteousness, in which his soul had hitherto appeared in immaculate purity before God. This spotless robe they took away, and left poor fallen man naked and wounded. They wounded his body with those pains and diseases, which bring it down to the dust, from whence it was taken; and they wounded his soul in all its faculties, his understanding with darkness, his will with a vicious choice, and his affections with worldlymindedness, so that he placed his love upon the creature instead of the Creator; they wounded his conscience with guilt, and with fear of death and of hell. "And they departed " leaving him half dead:" for his soul, the better part, was separated from God, and already dead in trespasses and sins, and the body was dying. When man was fallen into this helpless state, the patriarchal dispensation took place from *Adam* to *Moses*, under which the first-born was priest, and had a right to offer up the appointed sacrifices; but these could not give life to the sinner, and therefore the priest came and

looked

looked upon him, and paſſed by on the one ſide, being unable to raiſe him up from the death of ſin. Next ſucceeded the levitical diſpenſation from *Moſes* to Chriſt: The *Levite* came and looked upon him, and paſſed by on the other ſide, being unable, by any of the legal rites and ceremonies, to raiſe fallen man to his former righteouſneſs and perfection. " But a certain *Samaritan*, as he jour" neyed, came where he was." *Samaritan* ſignifies a *keeper*, and it here ſtands for the keeper of *Iſrael*, whoſe compaſſions fail not: " for when he ſaw him, he had compaſſion " on him." His love diſpoſed him to uſe his power for the ſinner's recovery. He was almighty, and he reſolved to uſe his almighty power to heal him. He went up to him, and applied the balm of *Gilead*—" he bound " up his wounds, pouring in oil and wine," wine, the eſtabliſhed type of the moſt precious blood of the lamb of God; and oil, the known emblem of the ſalutary influence of the holy Spirit: Pour theſe into the deepeſt and moſt dangerous wounds of ſin, and they will infallibly work a perfect cure: for the blood has a divine virtue to heal, being appointed and ordained of God for that very purpoſe. It cleanſeth us, ſays one, who had experienced

experienced its virtue, and by cleanſing healeth us, from all ſin. And no wonder: becauſe it is the blood of God. He, who ſhed it, was God and man united in one Chriſt, and therefore it had infinite and divine merit. And when he ſtood in the place of ſinners, obeyed and ſuffered for them, and was obedient even unto death; his obedience and ſufferings could want nothing to render them as ſatisfactory as the law and juſtice of the Father could require: becauſe his blood had virtue as a releaſe to diſcharge believers from all the pains and penalties, to which they were ſubjected for their ſins, and as a purchaſe to put them in poſſeſſion of their forfeited eſtate. The Apoſtle deſcribes its operating, as a releaſe, when he ſays of it, " that we have redemption through his blood, " even the forgiveneſs of ſins," and as a purchaſe, when he ſays, " that Chriſt, having " waſhed us from our ſins in his own blood, " hath made us kings and prieſts unto God " and his Father."

Now ſince the blood of Chriſt has this ſovereign healing virtue, and ſince we have through it redemption, even eternal redemption from all the pains and miſeries of ſin,
ſurely

surely then, it is an essential ingredient in that precious balm of *Gilead*, which has virtue to heal every sinner who takes it, let his case be ever so dangerous? But then it must be taken. A sick man may have a very good remedy at hand; but if he never take it, it can never cure him. In like manner, it is not enough that the blood of Christ can heal, but in order to heal, it must be applied. The application makes it effectual, and therefore we read of the blood of sprinkling both in the Old Testament, and in the New. The blood must be sprinkled upon the conscience in order to heal the wounds of sin, and this is the office of the holy Spirit. He applies the blood of Christ: He brings this healing balm to the wounded soul. And as oil was the emblem of his salutary influence, therefore in the good *Samaritan*'s prescription we find the medicine was made up of oil and wine, of the blood of Christ, and of the grace of his Spirit, which two, sweetly joined and tempered together, make up the healing balm of *Gilead*. There is not a wound of sin so deep, a disease of sin so desperate, but the blood of Christ applied by the holy Spirit can heal them: for God hereby healeth the broken in heart, and giveth this medicine

dicine to heal their sickness. Although they be half dead, yet it can recover them; because it operates by a divine and almighty power. The blood of Christ can raise the deadest soul to justification of life, and through sanctification of the Spirit this life is renewed and strengthened day by day, until every spiritual malady of sin be removed, and sorrow and sighing be done away for ever. Hear this, ye mourners in *Sion*, and lift up your drooping heads. Looking into yourselves you may have reason to grieve. Your sins are many and great. They have wounded your consciences. You feel the smart, and your distress is exquisite. But despair not. Lo, there is balm in *Gilead*. The blood of Jesus is an infallible remedy. The holy Spirit is almighty to apply it, and he has already shewed you your want of it. Oh! that he may give you grace to wait until he supply your wants, and you feel its sovereign virtue healing your wounded consciences. And to encourage you to seek and wait until you find, remember that there is not only balm in *Gilead*, but also that there is a physician there; as I am, in the

Third

Third place to confider, under whofe hands you cannot fail of a perfect recovery; and he is no lefs a perfon than the great phyfician of fouls, who is alfo God over all, bleffed for ever. He who created all things, vifible and invifible, and who fupports them by the word of his power, vouchfafes to heal his people of their fins; fo there can be no doubt of his power, becaufe he is almighty to heal. And can there be any doubt of his love? Did not his love bring him down from heaven to the loweft humiliation, even to veil his divine glory under a covering of flefh, and did not his love then lead him to put forth his divine power to heal every one who applied to him for a bodily cure? Whereby he demonftrated to us his readinefs to exert the fame power to heal the fpiritual infirmities of thofe who come to him for his affiftance. The eternal God, whom angels and arch-angels worfhip and adore, was pleafed to be manifefted in the flefh, fo that God and man were one Chrift, and the one Chrift, the God-man, ftood up in the place of finners, as their reprefentative; for them he obeyed the law, and fuffered the pains and penalties due to the breach of it, that by his ftripes they might be healed:

He

He was obedient, even unto death, and then rising from the dead, as their representative, he wrought out an all-perfect righteousness for them, which being imputed unto them by faith, they thereby receive justification to life, and all the deadly wounds of sin are healed. Thus the great physician of souls has demonstrated his love. You may read it in every action of his life, and in every suffering unto death. You may read it engraven in every wound of his crucified body. What were the marks and scars which the crown of thorns made in his head, and the whips and scourges made on his back, but visible signs and seals of his love? The love which led him to his agony and bloody sweat, to his bitter cross and passion, was greater than that of the strongest instinct and natural affection in the human breast: " For can a woman forget her sucking child, " that she should not have compassion upon " the son of her womb? Yea, they may " forget, yet will not I forget thee, faith " the Lord: for I have graven thee upon " the palms of my hands." While he looks upon them, he cannot forget his people: because on the palms of his hands are the prints of the nails by which he was fastened to the cross, and these prints are the precious engravings of his wonderful love. Look upon the crucified Jesus, my christian brethren, as wounded for your transgressions and bruised for your iniquities, and see if ever there was love like his. Every wound speaks forth his love, every bruise loudly proclaims the greatness of it. His death demonstrates his love to have been stronger than death, and his pierced side shewed that he had set his people as a seal upon his heart; for from thence there flowed blood and water, water to cleanse the pollution, and blood to heal the wounds of their sins. Surely then, he who shed his heart's blood for them cannot want love? Let this encourage poor dejected souls to wait upon him. Why are ye so troubled, as if God had not provided a medicine to heal the broken-hearted? Is there not balm in *Gilead?* Is there not a physician there? Oh! wait upon him then for his kind assistance, and you will certainly find that the fountain of his love is not dried up. He is now indeed on the throne of glory, king of kings, and lord of lords, but he has the same tender heart, which once bled to death upon the cross. Apply to him for relief, and he will not cast you out.

You

You can have no diftemper, but what he has power to heal: for he is an almighty phyfician. And no diftemper but what he has love to heal; for God is love, and the Saviour the Lord Chrift is God. How great foever the wounds of fin may be, yet if you fall low at his footftool, crying for mercy, he will not reject your fuit. What! was it ever known that he caft out the prayer of the poor deftitute? No. There never was, and there never will be fuch an inftance. When he was upon earth he never refufed to heal any one who afked his help. He never fent one fingle perfon away unrelieved, whatever his difeafe might be, or however unworthy he was to be healed of it. He cured all that came to him, and he did not half cure them, but it is written, "they "were made perfectly whole." Perfectly does he heal all the wounds of fin, and eternally. He heals for ever. His medicines reftore his patients to everlafting health. He forgiveth all their fins, and healeth all their infirmities, and thus admits them into the city of the living God, the inhabitant of which fhall not fay, I am fick; for the people that dwell therein fhall be forgiven their iniquity, and fo freely and fully forgiven, that God will remember it no more. And is this indeed the character of the great physician of souls? Is his heart so full of love, that he is always disposed to use his power for the perfect recovery of convinced and afflicted sinners? Is he as willing as he is able to heal them? No doubt he is. Let such persons then seek his help, and look up unto him for medicine to heal their wounded consciences. He hath wounded you out of love, and he will heal. He hath convinced you of your wants, in order that you might wait upon him to have them supplied. Wait then, and he will give you abundant reason to admire and to praise the wonders, which he will do for you and for your salvation. He will pardon you freely, and will heal all the wounds which sin has made, and then he will enable you to declare upon your own happy experience, that there is balm in *Gilead*, and a physician there.

Now since this is the case, why do men labour under the maladies of sin? Since the blood of Christ is the sovereign balm, and Christ is the physician, whose power and love are able and willing to heal the most desperate disease, and the holy Spirit is almighty

mighty to apply the healing balm; may we not then reasonably enquire, Why is not the health of the daughter of my people recovered? And this is the

Fourth and last particular to be considered. Why are any men sick, when they have an offer of health? Do they choose, do they love sickness? Yes. The same men, whose every pulse beats after bodily health, choose and love spiritual sickness. They are alarmed at the least disorder which attacks the body, and yet they have no concern about the soul, although it be wounded with sin, and sick unto death, yea just ready to perish. How absurd is this conduct? Thus to prefer the health of the meaner and baser part of their constitution to the more noble and exalted part, is a flagrant absurdity. Nay, not to desire the health of the soul, when it is offered them, is acting unnaturally against their own interest. To reject it, when the great physician himself offers it in his word, is treating him with vile ingratitude; and not to receive this inestimable remedy at his hands, when he sends out his ministers to invite sinners to take it, to spurn it from them, as if it was a thing which they did not value or did not want, this is the height of sin and wickedness; for whosoever thus accounteth the blood of the covenant an unholy thing, and thereby doth despite unto the spirit of grace, for him there remaineth no more sacrifice for sin, but a certain fearful looking for of judgment and fiery indignation.

This being the case, the question returns, What can be the reason, that the health of the daughter of my people is not recovered. Here is the all-healing balm of *Gilead*, here is an all-wise, and an almighty physician, and why then, my brethren, will you not for his sake, for your own sakes, receive the sovereign medicine at his hands? What other cause can be assigned, but that you love your disease more than health. Sin, with all its infirmities, is dearer to you than the full enjoyment of the pleasures of a perfect recovery. Sin, although you die of it, is more precious, than to receive life from the hands of our redeeming God. Sin, although it send you to hell, is more desirable than health in heaven. Sin, although it bring on you never-ending torments with devils and condemned spirits, is sweeter to you
than

than these eternal joys which are at God's right hand for evermore. Oh! what a wonderful delusion is there in sin, that it should thus make men love it more than health and happiness? How strong is the delusion, since the same men reason in the things belonging to the body, directly contrary to what they do in things belonging to the soul! Propose immediate relief to any of them lying in a severe fit of the gout or stone, they embrace the proposal with eager joy. Propose immediate relief from the pains and miseries of sin, they will not hear of, much less take the remedy. There is balm in *Gilead*, a physician is there, even the Lord Jesus, the sovereign physician of souls, and yet they will not apply to him. Sick as they are, and ready to expire with the infirmities of sin, yet they had rather perish than be beholden to him for a cure. All his attributes, his power, his wisdom, his goodness, cannot win them. All his graces, his pardoning, justifying, sanctifying grace, have no influence. He may be a God almighty to save, but the charms of sin, though but for a season, seem to them preferable to the blessings of his present and eternal salvation.

But whence is it that sin should be capable of deluding men so far as to make them prefer sickness to health? The true cause is this. Sin blinds their eyes, and hardens their hearts. It stupifies and deadens the senses, so that they feel not their spiritual in the same manner as they do their bodily diseases. The understanding is in darkness, they know not that it is diseased. When they know it, the memory is short and soon forgets it. When they remember it, yet conscience is fast asleep; it neither checks the will in the choice, nor the affections in the love and enjoyment of sin. Thus has sin impaired all their faculties, and they have no desire to be healed, because they are insensible of their malady. When we endeavour to convince them of it, they will not believe us: And because they do not feel the immediate smart of their sins, they will not therefore give credit to us, when we declare, from the word of God, that they will smart for them, and to eternity, unless they come to the physician of souls to be healed. And this will be the case, so long as they are intent upon their present pursuits, and live entirely to sense and to its enjoyments. All this time their own hearts deceive them: for it is one of the greatest delusions of sin, to keep men ignorant of the true state of their souls. It flatters them with peace, while the Almighty is at war with them; and it promises them happiness in the enjoyment of those things, which will bring on them eternal torments. And while it keeps them in this state of carnal security, nothing can appear to them more absurd than to hear that they are sick, when they fancy themselves to be in perfect health.

1. My brethren, are any of you in this state? Do you feel no pain, and do you apprehend no danger from your sins? Are you entirely secure, although your sins be unpardoned, and God might glorify his justice by immediately inflicting the deserved punishment? Nay, do you not find part of sin's punishment already inflicted, and why then should you hope to escape the remaining part? For have you not suffered some of those pains and sicknesses, which in a course of years will infallibly bring down your bodies to the grave, and inflict the sentence on them, "Dust thou art, and unto dust "shalt thou return." The body was not

at first liable to this sentence, until sin poured its cursed poison into it, and infected it with those painful maladies, which no art of physic can heal, and which wear it down to the grave of death. Every pain which it feels, every sickness which it labours under, all the outward and inward dangers which threaten its mortal life, are owing to sin; for the wages of sin is death. All the harbingers of death, which afflict and weaken men's bodies, and thereby prepare the way for his seizing on them, and carrying them prisoners to the dark and cold regions of the grave, all these derive their power over us from sin; for, as by one man, sin entered into the world, and death by sin, so death passed upon all men; for that all have sinned. Sin has most undoubtedly wounded your bodies with pains and sicknesses, with mortality and death; and what a madness then and infatuation is it to think, that sin has not wounded your souls as well as your bodies? For what says the scripture? "The "soul that sinneth it shall die." Is not that a desperate wound? " It shall die." How! Can the soul die? Yes. It may be dead in trespasses and sin. Its death consists in being separated from God, the fountain of life, and in having no communion with him either in this world or in the next. And is not this a greater punishment than the death of the body, and is it not infinitely more painful too, thus to die from God and glory, and to be tormented with the worm that never dieth, and in the fire that never shall be quenched? What! is not that a wound indeed which thus alienated you from the life of God? yea, a most dreadful wound, the torment and anguish of which you may suffer for ever and ever? Men and brethren, are these things so? Examine the evidence and determine. Is not sin the great murderer, who has wounded your bodies with pains and diseases, and mortality, and has separated your souls from God, the fountain of life, and made you subject to the first and second death? Is not the proof of these truths as complete and full as the case will admit of? Does it not amount even to a demonstration? And do you not then stand in need of some sovereign balm to heal you, and do you not want a physician? You certainly do, as much as ever dying men did. And why then do you neglect the remedy, and slight the physician?

But

But perhaps some person may say, How can these things be? Am not I in perfect health, and how then can I labour under those diseases which you are mentioning? Yes, my brother, you may be in health, your body may be perfectly well, but you have a miserable, sinful soul within you, which is infected with the plague and foul leprosy of original sin, and which has been wounded with thousands of actual crimes. This is your case, and it is most deplorable. All the powers in nature can give you no relief. There is no remedy in heaven or earth, but the blood of Jesus Christ applied by the grace of his good Spirit, and yet sin has such power over you as to persuade you to neglect that precious medicine, without which you must perish everlastingly.

What! say you, Can I be in this desperate condition, and not know and feel it? Yes, you may. It is an undoubted matter of fact, that sin brought as many diseases upon the soul, as it did upon the body. Indeed it left the soul entirely sick, and without any soundness in it, as we daily confess in the words of our church, " there is no health " in us." And if there be no health in you, surely

surely then you are sick in every part? And you have no sense of your malady, because sin has so impaired all your faculties, that you have no spiritual discernment. You do not discern your case to be dangerous, which is one of the worst symptoms you could have. It proves you to be far gone in a spiritual lethargy, so that the less sense you have, the greater is your danger. And is not this a dangerous disease which makes the patient insensible? For how can he avoid perishing of it, while conscience, which ought to give the alarm, is seared with a hot iron, and the other faculties of the soul are past feeling? This is the scripture account of your condition, and if it has not convinced you, may the Lord God Almighty make you sensible of your malady, that you may apply to the great physician of souls for the balm of *Gilead* along with those convinced sinners, who are now waiting upon him for the sovereign remedy.

2. When sinners are first brought to a sense of their guilt and of their danger, and conscience begins to do its duty, they are apt to write bitter things against themselves, and through unbelief to reject the offered

mercies

mercies of the gospel. They feel the wounds of sin more sharp and painful, than ever its pleasures had been sweet and delightful. The law stirs up guilt, terrifies their consciences with its threatenings, sets God before their eyes as armed with almighty justice to inflict the threatened punishment, and they see no way open to escape. Speak to persons in this distress of the balm of *Gilead*, the remedy appointed of God for their disease, they cannot believe it as able to heal them, or if they are brought to believe this, yet they reject the comforts of the blessed medicine, for want of faith to apply it to themselves.

Let us consider this case a little. My brethren, sin has wounded your bodies and souls, and you are become sensible of the malady. You feel the anguish of it, and you desire to be healed. What objection have you to the remedy which the Lord God had appointed for your recovery? Has it not virtue to heal your wounded consciences? You know what the remedy is: It is the balm of *Gilead*, the most precious blood of the lamb of God, applied by the eternal Spirit, and it heals not by any natural

tural or physical qualities, but by a divine and spiritual efficacy. The power of God is always present with it to heal. You cannot therefore object against the medicine; because God has provided it, and he, with his own arm, renders it effectual for the cure of wounded consciences.

True, say you, I believe the remedy is infallible, but how do I know that God will apply it to my soul? You are wounded, and it is balm for wounded consciences, therefore for yours. God has awakened you, he has brought you to the knowledge of your disease, and you feel the pain of it. For what reason has God done this? but that the sense of your misery might send you to the physician for his advice and assistance. When the enemy of souls sees you thus escaping out of his hands, he would try to persuade you, that the remedy is not for you; whereas you are the very persons to whom the gospel offers it. Christ says, he came not to call the righteous, but sinners, to repentance; and you are sinners, you feel the misery of sin, and therefore Christ came to call you. Since you are sick, he calls you as much as if he had called you by name in the gospel, to receive of him the balm of *Gilead* to heal all your spiritual infirmities.

You think you should be happy, if you could believe this, but you find so many and such desperate wounds, so many soul-murdering sins, that you dare not believe the remedy is for such as you. But why not? Is not the medicine for sin-sick souls? And the more sick you are, the more you want the medicine, and be your case the worst that ever was, yet the virtue of the medicine is almighty. If from the sole of the foot, even to the crown of the head, there was no soundness in you, but in every part wounds and bruises, and putrifying sores, yet the balm of *Gilead* can make a perfect cure; yea, if you have ten thousand more wounds than you have, it could heal them all. Consider then how greatly you disparage and vilify the love and power of our divine physician, by supposing your sins more able to kill than he is to heal. Is not he the Lord God Almighty, and are not all things possible with him? Oh! be not faithless then, but believing.

But

But perhaps guilt suggests to you, My case is singular, I have sinned against light and conviction; often did I resolve to leave my sins, but I as often broke my resolutions, and therefore I fear that I have sinned away my day of grace, and that there is no mercy for me. Your case is bad, but not desperate. Looking back on your past life, you should be humbled, but not despair; for are you not convinced of your want of the balm of *Gilead*, and does not it, by a divine virtue, heal all manner of sins? Sins against light, against many solemn resolutions, and against many warnings of conscience, as well as other sins? The medicine certainly can heal them all; because it is appointed of God for that purpose, and by his almighty power he renders it effectual, and therefore whatever keeps you from relying upon its power to heal you, is an enemy to your soul. Oh! pray against unbelief, for that is at the bottom of all your objections against this sovereign medicine, and may the Lord give you faith to be healed.

What! can it heal me, says some poor dejected broken-hearted sinner, who sees

nothing

nothing but sin in his heart and life? Yes, it is appointed for you by name. "He healeth the broken in heart, and bindeth up their wounds." *Psalm* cxlvii. 3. The great physician has an especial regard for your case. He says, he was sent to heal the broken-hearted. But not such as I am, says one, my heart is worse than broken, it is dead to God, and to the things of God. Be it so. Our physician is famous for raising the dead. It is his office and his glory. In the parable of the good *Samaritan*, he healed the man who was half dead. His soul was as dead to God as yours is. But the precious balm, which was applied to him, made him alive to God. The same remedy can quicken you, although you have been dead in trespasses and sins; and as you are so far quickened as to see your want of this remedy, may you soon experience its sovereign virtue, and receive from it saving health.

After many doubts and fears have been silenced, new ones still arise. Unbelief may perhaps have been suggesting to some of your hearts; the medicine certainly can heal all cases, but I have nothing to recommend me to the physician. Have you nothing? Then

Then this is your best recommendation. He always relieves poor distressed dying objects, who have nothing to bring him, but their sins and their miseries. He is therefore a physician, that he may relieve such; for by healing those, whom none else can heal, he gets all the glory; and by healing them freely, he exalts his sovereign grace. Thus he acted in the parable of the good *Samaritan*. What had the wounded traveller to recommend him? was it not, that he was miserable and helpless? This moved the Lord's compassion, and he shewed him mercy. "Go, and do thou likewise." Apply to the great physician, because thou art sick, and canst not heal thyself, and then he will exalt his rich grace and love, by freely forgiving thee all thy sins, and by pouring the balm of *Gilead* into thy wounded conscience to heal all thine infirmities.

When this objection, which arises from pride and unbelief, is removed, and we would persuade the convinced sinner to rely upon the promises of health and salvation, which God has made in his word, he has still difficulties to get over. He is afraid it would be presumption in him to rely upon the pro-

D d   mises,

mifes, and to take comfort from believing, that he fhall have his fhare and intereft in them. Whereas he is the very perfon to whom the promifes are made. His particular cafe is defcribed in *Luke* iv. 18. Our Saviour fays, The fpirit of the Lord is upon me, becaufe he hath anointed and commiffioned me with full powers to relieve every diftreffed object, that fhall apply to me for help. Are you a poor afflicted finner? He has good news for you: He was ordained to preach the gofpel to the poor. Have you a broken contrite heart? He is fent to heal the broken-hearted. Are you in bondage to fin and fatan? He is fent to preach and to give deliverance to the captives. Is your underftanding blind and ignorant of fpiritual things? He is fent to preach and to give recovering of fight to the blind. Are you faft bound with the chains of fin, and has the iron entered into your foul? He is fent to fet at liberty them that are bruifed. Here is your character: you are poor broken-hearted captives, blind and miferable. Here is your promife; Chrift is appointed of God, and has a divine commiffion to fupply all your wants. Is it prefumption then in you to apply this promife

to

to yourselves? What! after God has graciously made it for the comfort of your afflicted consciences will you say, It would be presumption in us to take comfort from it? My brethren, the promise cannot be broken. By relying upon it, it is yours. Your dependance upon it calls upon God's faithfulness to fulfil it to you. And it is no presumption, it is a high act of faith, not to stagger at the promise through unbelief, but to give glory to God, by relying upon it. May he enable you thus to give glory to him, and you shall find that his promise is like himself, unchangeable, and that his word cannot be broken.

Since then there is balm in *Gilead* for wounded consciences, provided purposely for you, and since your objections against receiving it are groundless, why, my brethren, will you not apply to the almighty physician, and now ask his help? Oh! that this may be the accepted time, and this the day of your salvation! Fall down at his feet, implore his assistance, and his tender heart will melt with compassion towards you. If you are discouraged in your addresses to him, it is because you have not clear ideas
of

of his power and love. He is almighty. He can heal the moſt broken heart, and the moſt wounded conſcience; and his love never failed to influence his power to heal ſuch caſes, when they came before him. Keep not then poring upon your wounds and ſores. By looking too much at them, you cheriſh your doubts and fears. Look unto Jeſus. Remember his advice, "Look unto "me, and be ye ſaved." You ſhould look into yourſelves, to ſee your want of ſalvation, and look unto him for a ſupply of your wants. And that you may be ſupplied out of his fulneſs, believe his promiſes. Rely upon his faithfulneſs to fulfil them to your ſouls, and thereby you engage his power to give you health and ſalvation.

3. Bleſſed be his holy name, for exerting his divine virtue at this day, and for healing all manner of ſpiritual ſickneſs and all manner of diſeaſe among the people. Great numbers, now alive, are witneſſes for him, that his hand is not ſhortened. Still he ſaves his people from ſin, and from all the maladies brought upon them by ſin. You, my chriſtian brethren, who have had experience of his divine power and love, ought to ſhew

forth

forth his praise. It becometh you well to be thankful. Much has been forgiven you, therefore you should love much. The sweet Psalmist of *Israel* calls upon you by his example to a grateful acknowledgment of the Lord's mercies—" Bless the Lord, O my
" soul, and all that is within me, bless his
" holy name. Bless the Lord, O my soul,
" and forget not all his benefits; who for-
" giveth all thine iniquities, who healeth all
" thine infirmities." *Psalm* ciii. 1, 2, 3. After you have received such great benefits, it will be your delight to praise him with your lips, and with your lives. The health and strength which he has freely given, you will use in his service and to his glory, until he take you to himself, and give you more happy experience of his great salvation, by delivering your soul from every infirmity and corruption; and the time will not be long before he will raise your bodies from the grave, and make them like his own glorious body. And then he will get himself honour indeed, when he shall heal both body and soul of all the wounds of sin, and shall heal them for ever and ever. That is the glory of our physician, he heals to eternity. He makes the spirits of just men per-

fect; and they stand before the throne of God without any spot or stain of corruption. And in the morning of the resurrection, this corruptible body shall put on incorruption, and this mortal shall put on immortality. Thus he bestows eternal health and salvation upon both body and soul. Where is there, nay, where can there be such a physician? There is none like unto thee, O Lord, glorious in holiness, fearful in praises, doing wonders. Still thou are displaying the wonders of thy power and love, and administering thy sovereign balm for recovering the health of the daughter of thy people. Oh! that thou wouldst display thy divine virtue among us this day. Arise, thou sun of righteousness, upon all this congregation, with healing under thy beams, and save us from every malady of sin, from the pollution, from the guilt, and from the power of it, and save us from the punishment of it with thine eternal salvation. Hear us, thou almighty Saviour, and answer us to the glory of the Father, and of the holy Spirit, three co-equal and co-eternal persons in one Jehovah, to whom we give honour and worship, and blessing and praise, now and for ever. Amen and Amen.

UPON THE

PROMISES of GOD.

DISCOURSE XII.

2 PETER i. 4.

Whereby are given unto us exceeding great and precious promises.

WHEN the Lord God firſt publiſhed his law in paradiſe, he enforced it with proper ſanctions. He promiſed to our firſt parents the continuance of his favour and immortal life, if they continued to keep the law; but if they ſhould tranſgreſs it, he threatened them with the loſs of his favour, and with the firſt and the ſecond death. Upon their tranſgreſſion, the promiſes became null and void. All
right

right and title to them was forfeited, and the sovereign law-giver was bound to inflict the threatened penalties. His truth, his justice, his holiness called upon him to put the sanctions of the law in force. Accordingly the offenders were arrested and brought to his bar; and being examined, they confessed their crime, but studied to throw part of the blame upon their tempters. The man could make no other defence, but that the woman offered him the temptation; and the woman had no plea to urge, but that the serpent beguiled her. Upon this confession they were found guilty; but the Lord God, whose mercies are over all his works, was pleased to make a discovery to them of the covenant of grace. He revealed to them his mind and will concerning the pardon of their transgression, and promised them a Saviour, who should bruise the serpent's head, and thereby destroy his power. The serpent's poison lies in his head, and when this is bruised, he can do no more mischief. The promised seed was to undertake this work, and for this purpose was the Son of God to be manifested, that he might destroy the works of the devil. This first promise, and all the following promises of grace

and

and mercy centre in Jesus Christ: for all the promises of God in him are Yea, and in him Amen unto the glory of God. In him they are Yea; he undertook to ratify and to make them good: and in him they are Amen; they are confirmed and fulfilled to believers. Every promise made in Christ is an act of God's free grace, and which being made, his perfections bind him to fulfil; for he has engaged, in the promise, to give the grace and blessing therein mentioned, to those who believe in Jesus Christ; so that the believer's happiness consists in living by faith upon the promises. Faith apprehends and receives Christ as held forth in the promise, and thereby gets possession of the promised blessing. While faith is kept thus in act and exercise, the believer walks safely and comfortably: although he has many enemies, and is in the midst of many dangers, yet he has a promise of God's help to support him in every estate and circumstance of life, and to carry him through all trials and troubles. If he rely upon this promised help, he cannot be disappointed; for the promise cannot possibly fail. All the perfections of God stand engaged to see it fulfilled, and when faith calls upon God, and

and relies on him for the fulfilling of it, he cannot deny himself, or break the word that is gone out of his mouth. Faith brings down his almighty power to make a way for the fulfilling of the promise, and thus the believer receives a support under all dangers, safety against all enemies, and a cordial against all troubles. This is his happiness. He staggers not at the promise of God through unbelief, but is strong in faith, giving glory to God, and God gives grace to him and makes his faith stronger, by which he finds more of the sweetness and riches of the promises. My brethren, I wish you were all in possession of this happiness, and it is my present design to direct and to encourage you to seek it. The scripture which I have chosen for this purpose affords us some very powerful motives: May the Lord God render our present consideration of them useful and profitable to all our souls, that we may know clearly,

First, The nature of the promises of God.

Secondly, The character of those to whom the promises belong; and

Thirdly,

Thirdly, Their exceeding greatness and preciousness. And while we are considering those particulars, may we have the Lord's presence with us. We have a promise of it, " Wherever two or three, says he, are met " together in my name, there am I in the " midst of them." Oh! that he may be present with us at this time. May he send the holy Spirit of promise into all our hearts to teach us,

First, The nature of the promises of God. I define a promise to be an act of God's free grace, whereby he has engaged, in his word, to bestow upon believers all the blessings, which come to them through the obedience and sufferings of Jesus Christ. The promise can spring from no other cause than from free grace. God had no motive to induce him, but what arose from his own abundant and unmerited love, and there was no power to compel him to make any promise to fallen man. He had broken the law, and was subject to all the pains and penalties threatened to transgression, and if God had left him in this state without any promise, he would have dragged on a miserable life under the terrors of his guilty conscience,

conscience, until the executioner came to call him to God's awful bar, and being tried there, and found guilty, how could he escape the damnation of hell? To fallen man, thus subject to the present and eternal punishment of sin, God was pleased to make a revelation of mercy. He took compassion on him, and provided for his salvation, by the covenant of grace, which is a covenant of promises. Such is the exalted grace of God, that he has made a free promise of deliverance from all the miseries of sin, and that convinced sinners might be enabled to rely upon the promise, and to find comfort in it, God revealed it in his word, which cannot be broken. There it is written and entered upon record; and what he has there engaged to bestow upon believers, shall be made good to them for ever and ever. To them he will freely give without money and without price, both in time and in eternity, all the blessings which are the fruit of the obedience and sufferings of Jesus Christ. To them he gives freely what cost him an infinite sum. The merit of all that he did and suffered is made theirs by faith, and faith is one of the blessings which he obtained among the rest; for it is one of his precious gifts which he

bestows

bestows upon his people by the operation of his good Spirit, who works with, and animates the incorruptible seed of the word, rendering it the means of forming faith in their hearts. The word of promise begets faith in them, by the holy Spirit's enabling them first to rely upon it, and afterwards to experience its sweetness and richness, and then they know the truth of the fore-mentioned definition, namely, that a promise is an act of God's free grace, whereby he has engaged, in his word, to bestow upon believers, all the blessings which come to them through the obedience and sufferings of Jesus Christ.

Now since this is the nature of the promises, there is but one point to be cleared up, and it is this—What security has God given for the fulfilling of the promises? The Lord knew what power unbelief had over careless sinners, and how hard it was to bring convinced sinners to believe, and how believers would be tempted by their remaining corruptions to entertain doubts and fears, and therefore he provided the most full and perfect evidence, that the case will admit of.

First,

First, Every promise stands confirmed in his revealed word, which word is the mind and will of God made known to his creatures, and which is therefore as perfect and unchangeable as God himself is. His word cannot be broken. It is impossible to break it. What weapons would you use? Force of arms? What force can you use against the almighty God? His mind cannot alter or change, and thereby suffer his word to be broken: for with God there is no variableness or shadow of turning. And since nothing from without, and nothing from within can cause any variableness in him, his word therefore will stand fast for ever and ever. God is not a man, that he should lye, neither the son of man, that he should repent: hath he said, and shall he not do it? Or hath he spoken, and shall he not make it good? What should hinder him? Is not his hand almighty to fulfil what he hath spoken with his mouth? Here then is safe ground for faith to stand upon. You can rely upon one another's word. When a man has a fair character, and is known to be of good principles, you can trust him, and you have a saying among yourselves, That an honest man's word is as good as his bond.

And may you not give better credit to God's word? For what suspicion can you entertain of its ever being broken? He, who is truth itself, has said, " Heaven and earth shall pass away, but my words shall not pass away;" they shall not pass away, because my almighty power shall establish them in time and in eternity. And is there not then sufficient reason to rely upon those words which God declares shall not pass away? And is there not abundant evidence to encourage the convinced sinner to trust to that word of promise, which can never fail, but shall stand fast, when heaven and earth shall pass away, and the place of them shall no more be found. Even then, when all things else fail, the promises will be receiving their full completion. Surely then the word of God, which cannot be broken, is a good security for our relying upon the promises.

But *secondly*, God, who knoweth our hearts, out of tender compassion to our infirmities, has been graciously pleased to confirm his promises, not only by his word, but also by his oath. The oath was the obligation which the persons of the ever-blessed Trinity

nity entered into to fulfil their distinct parts and offices in the covenant of grace, and they entered into this obligation for the sake of those who should flee to Christ for refuge, that they might see the immutability of God's counsel to save them: because he had confirmed it by an oath, and had thereby given them two immutable things to rely upon. The Apostle has reasoned thus upon the subject. "When God made promise to *Abraham*, because he could swear by no greater, he sware by himself; for men verily swear by the greater; and an oath, for confirmation, is to them an end of all strife. Wherein God willing more abundantly to shew unto the heirs of promise the immutability of his counsel confirmed it by an oath, that, by two immutable things, in which it was impossible for God to lye, we might have a strong consolation, who have fled for refuge to lay hold of the hope set before us." In which words we have a clear account of the nature of the oath, "God sware by himself," and of the persons for whose sakes he sware, namely, the heirs of promise, and the design of his swearing, namely, to put an end to all strife in their consciences concerning his faithful-

ness

ness to fulfil his promises to them. And the Apostle's argument stands thus: when there is any dispute or strife among men, and the matter comes to be tried in a court of justice, the cause is finally determined, by examining the parties and their witnesses upon oath. And there being a strife between God and sinners, on his part he proclaims his grace, promising them full pardon, if they seek it through Christ, binds himself to give it, by his word, and confirms his word by his oath. And ought not this oath for confirmation of the word of promise to put an end to all strife in the sinner's conscience? For how can God's oath be broken? Here are two immutable things, which cannot possibly fail, the counsel of God to save the heirs of promise, and the oath of God to carry his counsel into execution. His counsel is what he decreed in the covenant of grace, when all his attributes determined to bring many sons unto glory by Jesus Christ. This divine counsel revealed to his creatures in his word was sufficient evidence, and ought to induce them to believe; but he was " willing " more abundantly," more than was needful, if they had not been very faithless and unbelieving, to convince them, and there-

fore confirmed his counsel by an oath; so that here are two immutable things in which it is impossible for God to lye, and which consequently ought to make the faith of the heirs of promise immutable. The foundation upon which faith stands can never fail. It relies upon the unchangeable word of promise, and the promise is confirmed by the counsel of God, of which he says himself, "My counsel shall stand, and I will do all "my pleasure. *Isaiah* xlvi. 10. Yea, the "counsel of the Lord standeth for ever, "and the thoughts of his heart to all gene-"rations." *Psal.* xxxiii. 11. and the promise is also confirmed by the oath of God, which is immutable and cannot be broken. "The "Lord hath sworn, and will not repent." He will not repent of his oath, unless he could cease to be wise, or could be perjured, which to suppose possible would be the highest blasphemy. Oh! what full security then has a gracious God given to the heirs of promise? He would not have them to doubt of his love, or of his power to save them, and therefore he condescends to give them two immutable things for the support of their faith: but knowing whereof they were made, and how slow of heart they were to believe,
he

he has been pleased to exalt his free and sovereign grace by giving them a

Third immutable thing to enable them to rely still more stedfastly upon his promises, and that is the unchangeable covenant. The ever-blessed Trinity, moved by mere love and rich mercy, contrived the gracious plan of the sinner's redemption, and each person was to get himself glory by sustaining a distinct office in the œconomy of the covenant. The Father was to glorify the truth, justice, and holiness of the Godhead, by demanding full satisfaction for sin. The Son covenanted to pay it, and to glorify the wisdom and love of the Godhead by satisfying all the demands of law and justice. And the holy Spirit was to glorify the power and grace of the Godhead by raising the dead in sin to life, and quickening them together with Christ, and then enabling them to walk against all opposition in his steps and after his example, until they attain eternal life. This is the covenant of promise. And what could induce the holy Trinity to make it? What, but the divine love and mercy? And what can hinder the fulfilling of this covenant? Can any thing resist and defeat

defeat the will of the Almighty? No. His power will carry his will into execution. But may not the will of God change? That is impossible. The covenant is everlasting, and how then can it change? Though it be but a man's covenant, yet if it be confirmed, no man disannulleth or addeth thereto; and since a human covenant is not liable to change, certainly the everlasting covenant is alike ordered in all things and sure? For he that cannot lye, hath said, "My covenant will I not break, nor alter the thing that is gone out of my mouth." *Psalm* lxxxix. 34. It cannot be broken, it cannot alter, and how then can one tittle of it ever change or fail? All things else shall pass away. "The mountains shall depart, and the hills be removed, but my kindness shall not depart from thee, neither shall the covenant of my peace be removed, saith the Lord, that hath mercy on thee." *Isaiah* liv. 10.

This is the security which God hath vouchsafed to give for the fulfilling of his promises, and it is the most full and complete evidence, that any promise can have; and what then can the heirs of promise desire more?

more? Has not God been willing more abundantly to shew them the immutability of his counsel? For he has given them his word to rely upon, which cannot be broken, his oath, of which he will not repent, and his covenant, which he will not break or alter. It is impossible any of these securities should fail, and why then should unbelieving doubts arise in their minds, and tempt them to think they could fail? My brethren, if you give way to those doubts, they will soon rob you of your peace and comfort: for although you be heirs to a great estate, yet it is chiefly in reversion. You have very little in possession at present, but the promises. You are heirs of promise, and if you lose your reliance upon the promises, you lose sight of the evidence of your estate, and the comfortable hope of your inheriting it. Oh! remember then how dishonourable this is to God, after he has provided such immutable things for faith and hope to rest upon, and how hurtful this is to your own interest, and therefore whenever doubts and fears begin to tempt you, ask yourself, " What am I going to do? Shall I fancy, " that God can lye, or be perjured, or be a " covenant-breaker? Would not this be
" blaf-

"blaspheming his word, and his oath, and "his covenant? O Lord, keep thy servant "from this great wickedness, and strengthen "my faith, that it fail not." And if you thus go to the throne of grace for help, you shall find it in time of need. God will enable you not to stagger at his promises through unbelief, but will make you strong in faith, relying stedfastly upon his fulfilling them all to your souls.

Some persons perhaps may be thinking, "God has provided full and complete evi"dence for the certainty of his fulfilling his "promises, and I think I could rest upon this "security, if I did but know that I was an "heir of promise." Rely upon the promise, and it is yours. Live upon it, and you are undoubtedly an heir of promise. But this point comes to be more particularly considered under the scripture character of the persons to whom the promises belong, which is the

Second general head of discourse. When our Lord gave his apostles a commission to preach, it was in these words, "Go ye into "all the world, and preach the gospel to "every creature." The gospel brings the
glad

glad tidings of the covenant of promise made in Christ, and full security for all the promised blessings of the covenant. You have the gracious call this day. In my master's name I stand up, and invite every unpardoned sinner to come and receive of him free mercy and forgiveness. "And the Spirit and the bride say, "Come, and let him that heareth say, Come; "and let him that is athirst, Come." Ho! every one that thirsteth for redemption in the blood of Christ, even the forgiveness of sins, come to the blood of sprinkling, that you may be made clean from all your sins. And if you find it in your hearts to accept of this free invitation, let not the sense of your unworthiness keep you back. Jesus is able to save you, be ye ever so unworthy; for he can save to the uttermost. All is finished on his part. He is able; he is also willing; and he engages to use his almighty power for you, if you ask it. He freely calls you, without money and without price, to take pardon, righteousness, holiness, glory. He promises them in his word, binds it by oath, and confirms it by covenant. All he has of blessedness and glory to give his people shall be yours, if you will accept his call, and rely upon his promise.

But you are thinking still with yourselves, the promises are indeed freely offered to all, but they belong to none, except to the heirs of promise. That is very true; and therefore it concerns you to be assured, that you are an heir of promise. Do you desire to be so? Would you willingly be an heir to the unsearchable riches of grace and glory? Oh! say you, from my heart I desire it: What would not I give to know that the exceeding great and precious promises in scripture belong to me. But how came this desire into your heart? Was it from any uneasiness in your mind about your sins? Have you been awakened to see that all the threatenings of the law belong to you, and that you have an interest in none of the promises of the gospel, and was it from hence that you waited upon God for mercy, desiring to experience his promised grace and salvation? And are you now waiting, deeply humbled under a sense of your sinfulness and helplessness? If this be your case, thus far you are right: for this is the first work of God's Spirit upon all the heirs of promise. He begins with convincing them of sin. They are lying in the same mass of corruption with other men, under the law, under guilt for

breaking

breaking it, subject to death and hell. The holy Spirit makes them sensible of their being in this state, and apprehensive of their danger, and puts them upon seeking deliverance. They seek, but cannot find, for want of faith. They hear and read in scripture of the love and power of Christ to save such sinners as they are, but they have no faith to rely upon the promises. This is not a comfortable state, but it is the way to get comfort: for none will ever ask faith of God, whose gift it is, until they know the want of it, and therefore the holy Spirit convinces all the heirs of promise, that they have no faith, and they find, that without faith they cannot take comfort in any of the precious promises: upon which they look up to him, who, by his mighty operation, is alone able to work faith in the heart. And let every one of you, who are thus waiting upon God, seek and you shall find. He that put the desire into your heart will give you possession of the blessing desired. The Spirit of God will enable you to rely upon the word of promise, and to apply it to your own soul, and thereby he will speak peace and comfort to your conscience. And by acting faith thus upon the word, you will be
brought

brought to the knowledge of your union with Chrift. United to him by the bond of the Spirit on his part, and by faith on yours, you will be a member of his myftical body, and will derive influence and nourifhment from him for the growth of your fpiritual life. And being thus one with Chrift, and Chrift with you, you will have an intereft in all that he has. His grace fhall be yours, his Spirit yours, and all his promifes fhall be yours; for all things fhall be yours, whether the world, or life, or death, or things prefent, or things to come, all fhall be yours; becaufe ye are Chrift's.

This is the experience of every heir of promife. The Spirit of God has convinced him of his finfulnefs and of his mifery. He has been brought to fee his loft and helplefs ftate; and in his guilty confcience he was felf-condemned, finding himfelf to be a child of wrath, and an inheritor of everlafting torments. After the holy Spirit had thus humbled him, he difcovered to him the excellency of the Lord Chrift, the infinite dignity of his perfon, and the infinite perfection of his righteoufnefs; and then by the grace of the fame good Spirit, he was led to
rely

rely upon Chrift for falvation; and to truft the word of promife, which engages to give free and full and eternal falvation to every one who believeth in the name of the only-begotton Son of God. And after the holy Spirit has enabled the foul to believe, and to rely upon the word of God, he carries on his work, until faith be grown exceedingly, even up to full affurance. This the fcripture calls the feal of the Spirit, which he fets upon all the heirs of promife. Sealing comes from believing, and is a frefh evidence in confirmation of it. " After that " ye believed, fays the Apoftle, ye were " fealed with the Spirit of promife." Firft, he enables the foul to reft upon the promife and to apply it in this manner—He that believeth fhall be faved: I believe, therefore I fhall be faved; and then he confirms this with his own teftimony, and feals it to the heart: fo that the fealing is for the believer's affurance, and not for God's. The Lord knoweth them that are his. Their names are written in his book. He knoweth their weaknefs, and how to ftrengthen them with might in the inner man. And when temptations are ftrong, and trials great, then the holy Spirit commonly ftrengthens faith with

his

his inward witness. He honours faith with his own seal, bearing testimony with the believer's Spirit, that he is a child of God. Every child of God has this seal set upon him some time or other. When it is most for his advantage, and most for God's glory, then the Spirit gives him this earnest of his inheritance, until the redemption of the purchased possession.

But perhaps some person may enquire, How shall I know that I am sealed by the Spirit of God? You may know it by these scripture marks. First, have you been deeply convinced of sin, and of Christ's power to save you from sin? Have you been convinced of your damnable estate without faith, and have you been asking faith of God? And has he enabled you to rely upon the word of promise, which offers you free and full salvation, and are you verily persuaded that God cannot break his word to you, who are relying upon it? And have you been waiting for the seal of the Spirit, hoping he would give you the inward witness of your adoption? All this is right. This is the work of the holy Spirit, by which he puts his seal upon the heir of promise; and if

this

this be your experience, you need not doubt but the witness is from heaven, when the Spirit of God beareth testimony with your spirits, that ye are the children of God: For, secondly, in the act of bearing witness with your spirits he will give sufficient evidence, that it is his testimony, both for his own glory, and for the assurance of your faith. He comes to bear witness to a matter of fact, that there may be no more doubt concerning it in the court of the believer's conscience. The fact is this—" Thou art now a child " of God through faith in Christ Jesus." He seals this testimony upon the heart with his own seal, that it may be authentick and lasting, and then doubts and fears vanish, conscience is assured that all enmity is now slain, and that God is a loving reconciled Father, upon which the soul is led out into acts of praise and thankfulness, and with a holy triumph can say, " My beloved is mine, " and I am his."

But some may think it is an easy matter to be deluded in this case. No, there will be no room for delusion, if your experience by the testimony of the Spirit was such as I have been mentioning, and if you attend, thirdly,

thirdly, to what follows after it. Does the witness abide? Is conscience at peace? Is your heart grateful? Is your faith lively and active? Not perhaps in so high a degree, as when the Spirit did bear his testimony, but still in some good degree. In this case there can be no delusion; because that which has thus drawn your heart up to God, did certainly come from God. If the seal had not been from the holy Spirit, how could this fruit of the Spirit have been produced? The impression, which is left, demonstrates that it was made by a divine hand; for when the holy Spirit seals the soul, he not only seals it for Christ's property, but he also stamps the image and likeness of Christ upon it, which appears outwardly by its love to Christ, and by the acts of love. The soul is in love with the person, and with the offices and excellencies of Christ, and evidences this love by its love to his life and to his example, following and pressing close after them, and by its love to his graces, desiring strength from God so to walk even as Christ walked. This constant love to Christ, proves the soul to be sealed by his Spirit, and the person thus sealed to be an heir of promise: for now he lives by faith upon Christ, and

believes

believes that all the promises made in Christ shall be made good to him. He has the earnest of their completion in his heart, and he has some of them fulfilled to him every day for a daily pledge of the perfect completion of the rest.

This is the character of the heirs of promise: and if any of you are thinking with yourselves, some part of this character is agreeable to our experience, but not the whole of it, and therefore we doubt, whether we are heirs of promise or not; you should remember, that the heirs of promise grow up to this character by several steps and degrees, and if any part of it be yours, you ought to press on to the attainment of the other parts. The fathers in Christ were once babes in Christ. The Spirit begins his work with conviction of sin, which is necessary to put the sinner upon seeking the promised mercies of the gospel. If you are seeking, that is another step towards your reliance upon God's word, and believing him faithful to fulfil his promises to your soul. And if you can rely upon his word, you have advanced one step farther towards the assurance of faith and the seal of the Spirit. So

So that if any part of this character be yours; doubt not but the rest will be yours also, only press you on to the attainment of what is yet before. Let what has been done in you, encourage you to proceed. You have some evidences of your inheritance, endeavour to get more, looking up to him who has begun, and praying him to carry on his own work, and fear not but you shall be brought to know, that Christ is yours, and that all the promises made through him are yours also. And may this consideration stir you up to press forward, that what you are seeking is of inestimable value, and the happy possession of it will be eternal. When you are once heirs of promise, you will be heirs of God, and joint heirs with Christ, born to inherit the riches of grace, and the riches of glory. All the blessedness which God has promised to give his children in time and in eternity is yours. You are heirs to the exceeding great and precious promises, and this brings me to the

Third general head of discourse, under which I was to treat of their exceeding greatness and preciousness. They are great in quantity, containing the greatest blessings

ings, which God has to give; yea, exceeding great beyond all description, and they are as good as great, they are exceeding precious, containing every thing truly valuable in earth or heaven. The greatness of the promises might be proved from many considerations. I shall mention, at present, but three or four. And the

First, is the state from which the promises offer to save man. He is fallen into a most miserable and helpless bondage, and to the worst of enemies, and none but an almighty arm can deliver him. Before the promise is brought to him, he is a transgressor of the law, under the curses of it, liable to be cut off every moment, and to suffer them in everlasting torments. And when justice comes to inflict the curses of the law upon him, what satisfaction can he make? What has he to plead, why sentence should not be immediately executed? He is silent. His mouth is stopped. He is self-condemned, and owns the sentence to be just, which assigns him over to the tormentors to suffer with them the vengeance of eternal fire. This is the desert of every son and daughter of fallen *Adam*. Sin has made them subject to all this misery, and has left them totally helpless; they can no more save themselves from the second death, than they can from the first. While the long-suffering of God bears with them in this mortal life he sends them his promises; in which he offers to save them from guilt and misery, to cleanse them from the pollutions, and to heal them of the wounds of sin. And are not these great promises, which engage to see such an almighty work performed? Surely they are exceeding great, since it requires the arm of the Lord God omnipotent to fulfil them by saving poor, guilty, helpless man from sin and satan, from death and hell. Must not that be an exceeding great promise, which engages to save man from exceeding great misery? And this greatness appears evidently in the

2. Next place from what the promises offer to bestow upon the sinner. They not only engage to save him from all evil, but also to bestow upon him all good. They offer him a free pardon, that his sins may be forgiven, and he may be justified by faith and reconciled to God, and may have the love of God shed abroad in his heart, and may walk as an adopted son of God, worthy

thy of his high calling unto all well-pleasing. And in this holy walking heavenwards, the Lord promises him every grace and blessing which shall be needful for him, yea, he has engaged to make all things, sickness, reproach, persecution, trials, and troubles of every kind, work together for his good. Are not these great promises, which engage to bestow pardon, justification, peace with God, adoption, sanctification, and grace to profit under every dispensation of providence; yea, are not these exceeding great promises, which bestow upon the sinner such exceeding great blessings? And bestow them upon him,

3. Upon the greatest motive, that possibly can be, even the free grace of God. Deliverance from the evils of sin, and the bestowing of the blessings of salvation is all of grace, proceeding wholly from the unmerited love and mercy of God. He is the sovereign Lord of heaven and earth. All creatures are his, bound to obey his holy will, and in case of disobedience, bound to suffer the threatened punishment; and when man had disobeyed, he had a right to nothing but punishment, and if it was remitted, yea, but for a day, this was an act of grace; but how much

much greater an act was it to pardon the sinner, to put honour upon him, and to restore him to a better state than he was in before he fell. If a friend bestow upon you a free gift, you acknowledge yourselves to be under a greater obligation, than if he was to pay you the same sum for a just debt. How much then are you indebted to God? For he had no motive, but mere love, to induce him to make you any promise. Consider this motive, consider the promises, consider from what a state of misery, to what a state of happiness God offers to raise you, and then admire and praise the greatness of that love, which led God to make you such great promises. Well might the apostle call upon us to behold what manner of love it is: for it passeth knowledge, it is so exceeding great. The blessings which his free grace has promised, surpass all understanding. Even the souls of just men made perfect, who are now inheriting the promises, cannot adequately set forth the greatness of them: for they are eternal. And this is another

4. Consideration, which exalts the greatness of the promises. They are of everlasting duration, and can never fail. When
nature

nature itself shall be diffolved, and heaven and earth shall pafs away, then the promifes shall be eftablifhed. Not a tittle of them shall fuffer in the univerfal conflagration; but they shall be then in their full extent moft glorioufly fulfilled. Many of them are referved for the wonders of that great day. The raifing of the body, free from corruption and mortality, admitting it to the vifion of God, putting upon it and the foul never-fading glory, a crown of righteoufnefs, and palms of victory; and then bringing them to drink of thofe rivers of pleafure which are at God's right hand for evermore, thefe are fome of the exceeding great promifes, which are to be completed at the Lord's coming to judgment. In that day the redeemed of the Lord will find that his divine power will fulfil the greateft of his promifes. When the captain of their falvation has brought them to the heavenly *Canaan*, the promifed land of everlafting reft, then he will put them into the actual poffeffion of all the promifes. Like as *Jofhua*, when he had brought the people into the promifed land, called upon them to be witneffes for God, that every promife had been fulfilled to them, so may our almighty *Joshua* say to his redeemed people in the same words, "Ye know in all your hearts, and in all your souls, that not one thing hath failed of all the good things, which the Lord your God spake concerning you; all are come to pass unto you, and not one thing hath failed thereof." *Joshua* xxiii. 14.

Let these considerations suffice to set forth the greatness of the promises. They are exceeding great in offering to deliver us from all evil, and to bestow upon us all good; the motive for doing this is the infinite love and sovereign grace of God, which advances the greatness of the promise by the freeness of it, and still further advances it by what grace has promised to do for us in glory, even to give us the actual possession and eternal enjoyment of all the promises.

And are these things so? If they be, who then would not wish to be an heir of promise? Are the promises thus exceeding great? Why then do they not appear so to every one of us? What is the reason that the generality of men had rather be heirs to any other estate, eftate, than to the promifes? The text tells us the true caufe: They know not the precioufnefs of them. They are exceeding great in themfelves, but they are not apprehended to be fo without faith. As the Apoftle fays of Chrift, "to them that believe, he is "precious," fo we may fay of the promifes, to them that believe they are precious, and therefore their greatnefs does not ftrike any man, until he by faith taftes fomething of their precioufnefs. Chrift is the fum and fubftance of all the promifes. Chrift himfelf is the firft promife, and all the reft are branches from that radical promife. They are all made in Chrift, and in him they are all completed. God has no good to give to finners, but in relation to Chrift, and all the promifes of good are made in him, in confequence of his meritorious life and death, his refurrection and afcenfion, yea, the fpirit of promife is given as the bleffed fruit of Chrift's interceffion. Now no man fees any thing precious in Chrift without faith; fo neither without it does he fee any thing precious in the promifes. Chrift has no form or comelinefs, that he fhould defire him, and the promifes have no fuch charms as to perfuade him to live upon them. But faith gives

gives a substance, a substantial presence to the things hoped for in the promises, and gives evidence of the believer's interest in the things not seen by the bodily eyes, and thus it enables the soul to experience the reality, and to find something of the value of the good things contained in the promises.

Perhaps you may be convinced of the necessity of faith to discover the preciousness of the promises, but you do not clearly understand, how faith acts upon them when it first discovers and afterwards lives upon their preciousness. The word of promise is the established means in the hand of the Spirit of begetting faith, and of strengthening it: for a sinner can expect no good from God, unless he vouchsafe to give him a free promise. The scripture is a revelation of God's will, in which he engages, for Christ's sake, to bestow graces and blessings upon his children; but the unawakened sinner sees no want of those graces and blessings, until the holy Spirit convince him of sin, stir up guilt in his conscience, and make him sensible of his danger. Then he is glad to hear of a promise, and is asking, Who will shew me any good? The Lord God sends him

the

the gospel with a free title to all good, and out of his infinite grace to enrich him with the unsearchable riches of Christ. The holy Spirit enables him to receive the gospel, and to rely and to act faith upon the word of promise. Faith looks at the word, sees what God has promised therein, rests and stays upon him for the fulfilling of it, and by this dependence and reliance upon the word of promise, the believer calls upon and engages the divine power to fulfil it. And the fulfilling of it gives it a peculiar sweetness and preciousness to the believer's soul. Every fresh proof of God's faithfulness to fulfil it strengthens the believer's reliance and dependence upon it, and thereby it grows more precious to all the faculties of his soul. The understanding sees and acknowledges the promises to be important realities, the will chooses them for its inheritance, and the affections love them and live upon them. Thus they become more and more precious. Tried promises are precious promises. Every time the believer goes boldly to the throne of grace, and asks, through Christ, the fulfilling of any promise, and receives it, then his faith grows, and as

his

his faith grows exceedingly, so the promises grow exceedingly precious.

But all our experience here, is only an earnest and foretaste of their future preciousness. The chief part of them is to be fulfilled beyond the grave, and many of them at the last day, and even then there will be no adequate description of their preciousness. The saints in glory will be able only to set forth half their praise, the promises being still completing through the endless ages of eternity, so that it will require an eternity to shew forth all their praise. May it be your happiness, my brethren, now to experience, by faith, the greatness and preciousness of the promises, and to have reason daily to praise him, in whom they are made, and by whom they will be all made good for ever and ever. Such are the promises. They are exceeding great and precious. They are certainly so in themselves, but do they, my brethren, appear so to you at present? If they do not, consider a little what your state is before you are interested in the promises. You are transgressors of that law, which has decreed—" The soul that sinneth it shall "die."

"die." Under this sentence you live, subject to whatever is meant by the soul's dying from God. You are liable to the wrath and justice of the Almighty, and to those eternal torments, which he has threatened to inflict upon sinners; and was it not for his long suffering, which of you would have been spared to this hour? And while the long-suffering of God is waiting, he sends his ministers with the glad tidings of the gospel to call you to a free pardon. They invite you in Christ's name, and in Christ's words. They assure you of his readiness to receive you into his favour, and to forgive, and to forget all your offences. For your encouragement they relate unto you his promises, which cannot be broken. They earnestly press you to accept of them, and to be happy in the enjoyment of them. But in vain. Their message is ineffectual. You had rather have the realities of sin, than the earnests of the promises. And what is this but absolute infidelity? For if you knew what sin is, and believed the divine promises to be so great and precious as they are, you would certainly prefer them to the delights of sin. Whereas you neither believe the word, nor the oath, nor the covenant of God; which is really

practical

practical *Atheism*: for you are without Christ, you are strangers from the covenant of promise, you have no hope, and you are without God, *Atheists* in the world. You may not perhaps deny the being of God, but you live without Christ, and without God in the world; and therefore you are practical *Atheists*. While you are in this state you cannot possibly have any true happiness, not in time, because your sins are unpardoned, not in eternity, because then you will receive the punishment of unpardoned sin. And is this a true description of your guilt and of your danger? You know it is. The word of God will not suffer you to doubt of it, unless you deny its authority. And how then do you determine to act? What! will you still seek your happiness in the ways of sin? God forbid. Turn ye, turn ye unto the Lord; certainly he bids higher for your hearts, than satan can. His promises are greater than sin or the world can make. You know they are. And still his promises follow **you,** although you have often turned a deaf ear to them. Once more I call and invite you in his name; oh that he would speak to your hearts, and call effectually. My brethren, ye are sinners, God offers you pardon.

don. You are guilty, he offers you free justification. He promises you his Son to be your Saviour, his Spirit to be your sanctifier, his grace to be your strength, his glory to be your eternal inheritance. He opens his treasury, and invites you to come, and to receive freely of him unsearchable and inestimable riches. Come then at the invitation of this gracious God, and hearken no longer to the lying promises of sin. If the Lord has now put it into your hearts to seek the fulfilling of the great things, which he has engaged to give his people; may he enable you to seek, until you find him faithful and just to fulfil all his promises.

2. There are many of you seeking and waiting for the fulfilling of them. You are convinced of the sinfulness of your hearts and lives, and are humbled under a sense of your vileness and helplessness, and you find the necessity of being saved from your sins, but you cannot rely with such confidence upon the word of God, as to believe that you shall be heirs of promise. But why not? To whom are the promises made? Are they not made to sinners? And are they not discoveries of God's gracious intentions towards
them

them in the Son of his love. And since you are sinners, convinced of sin, and waiting for mercy, surely the promises are made to you, and by relying on them they are yours.

But you are afraid to rely upon them. What! are you afraid God will break his promise? Consider what has been before said of the security, which God has vouchsafed to give you, in order to silence your doubts and fears, and to put an end to all strife in your consciences. He has given you his word, and his oath, and his covenant. These are immutable things; and why then should you fear to rely upon those things, which cannot possibly change or fail?

Perhaps you believe, that the promises are immutable, and yet you are afraid to rely upon them, because of the greatness of your sins. The greatness of your sins should humble you, but not drive you to despair: for are there not great promises for great sinners, yea exceeding great promises for exceeding great sinners? Is it not written, " Come now, and let us reason together, saith " the Lord, though your sins be as scarlet,
" they

" they shall be as white as snow; though
" they be red like crimson, they shall be as
" wool?"

But still you are afraid to rely upon the promises, because you have got such a wicked heart: You think there is not any person in the world, whose heart is so wholly set in them to do evil, as yours is. Be it desperately wicked, yet can you desire God to create in you a clean heart, and to renew a right spirit within you? If you can, then hear what he has promised, " A new heart " also will I give you, and a new spirit will " I put within you."

Why then do you stagger at the promises of God through unbelief? Are you complaining of your corruptions, and are they so many and strong, that they tempt you to think there is no mercy for you? Bring them to the blood of sprinkling, and when you are cleansed from the guilt of sin, the Lord has promised that his grace shall be sufficient for you, and that sin shall not have dominion over you. Your corruptions, be they ever so many, or ever so strong, shall be subdued by his almighty grace.

What

What then still hinders you from relying on God's promises? Can they ever fail? No. On God's part all is fixed and immutable, and whatever it be on your part which makes you stagger at the promises, has itself a promise, that you shall be delivered from it, which renders your unbelief more inexcusable. Whatever sin it be, or guilt, or corruption, or misery, the Lord has promised you salvation from it. He will redeem you from all evil; from all the evil of sin, and from all the evil of punishment. He has given his word, and his word cannot be broken. And why then cannot you rely upon it, especially since God has promised to deliver you from that very thing which hinders your reliance upon his word? Is this indeed the case? And are you convinced of it? Why then do you make God a lyar, by not believing the record which he hath given of his Son? Oh! beg of him to enable you to give glory to his word of promise, by relying upon it, and by setting to your seal, that God is true, and then God will set to his seal, and the Spirit of promise will seal you to the day of redemption.

3. Blessed

3. Blessed be his rich grace and love, who is daily fulfilling his promises. Many of you have had happy experience of his faithfulness to fulfil them. You ought always to remember, my christian friends and brethren, that whatever you enjoy of grace, or hope for in glory, is freely promised and freely given you in Jesus Christ; and let your gratitude bear some proportion to his mercies. He has opened the treasury of his promises, and has put you in possession of his unsearchable riches. Oh what manner of love is this! that he should raise you from the lowest beggary to such an exceeding great and precious inheritance. Every promise made to you in this life is a banknote of heaven, and when you go to the throne of grace to demand the payment of it, he cannot send you away with a denial. If you plead the promise, and desire the fulfilling of it in the name of your Lord and Saviour Jesus Christ, he cannot deny the word that is gone out of his mouth. His divine power will give you all things that pertain to life and godliness. For when he gave you Christ, with him he gave you all things. In Christ there is all that you can want treasured up for you: for it pleased

the Father that in him should all fulness dwell. There is a fulness of wisdom to teach you the true nature of the promises, and a fulness of salvation to deliver you from every thing that hindered your relying upon them, and a fulness of power to put you into the eternal possession of them all. Having then these promises, dearly beloved, let us live upon them, and we shall thereby live to his glory, in whom they are all made. Let us beg of him to act as our prophet, for the enlightening of our understandings, that we may see the great promises made through him, and as our priest to pardon and to forgive us our sins, that we may have by faith the earnest of our inheriting the promises, and as our king to rule in us and over us, until he bring us safe to the promised inheritance. In these three offices Christ has engaged to act for his people here below. He was to be their wisdom, their righteousness, and their sanctification, and they find him faithful to fulfil his offices, and to perform his promises. And this experience keeps their minds stayed upon him for the performance of what remains as yet unaccomplished. They have no reason to doubt of his love: for they continually find his

power

power exerted in their behalf. Happy men, who have the Lord for their God, a faithful promise-keeping God, who will be their God for ever and ever. His covenant mercies shall never fail. They shall be receiving their perfect accomplishment hereafter, when time shall be no more. May he, in whom they are all made, and in whom they are all established, now get himself glory by enabling every one of us to rely upon his promises, and may we at this time find the promise, which he has made to us while we are here gathered together, fulfilled to us all. He has said, "Wherever two or three "are met together in my name, there am "I in the midst of you." Oh that we may all find his spiritual presence. If there be any poor deluded worldlings here, who had rather have the possession of this world's goods, than the riches of the promises, may the Lord convince them this day of their guilt and of their danger, and put them upon seeking the promised mercies of the gospel. And may he be graciously pleased to vouchsafe his presence to those who are seeking him, that they may no more by their unbelief dishonour his word, and his oath, and his covenant. Put an end, blessed Lord, to all strife in their consciences, that they may no longer stagger at thy promises. Enable them to believe to the saving of their souls, that the promise by faith of Jesus Christ may be given to them that believe. And accept of thanks and praises from thy redeemed people. Oh! make us more thankful for thy great and precious promises, and for faith to apply them, and to live upon them. May they grow more precious to us every day. Fulfil, Lord Jesus, what remains, that we may be receiving continually out of thy fulness, strength of faith, increase of grace, power over sin, and may at last be more than conquerors, through him that loved us. Hear us, for we ask those things according to thy promise, and grant us them for thy great name's sake, to the honour of the Father and of the eternal Spirit, the holy, blessed and glorious Trinity in one Jehovah, to whom be equal honour and glory, and blessing and praise, in earth and heaven, in time and in eternity. Amen and amen.

F I N I S.